+RC488.5 .J347 1988

AUDREY COHEN COLLEGE
50664000163529
Jacob, Theodore/Family assessment : rati
RC488.5 .J347 1988 C.1 STACKS 1988

Y0-DMB-347

RC
488.5
J347
1988

Jacob, Theodore.
Family assessment

DATE DUE

FAMILY ASSESSMENT
Rationale, Methods, and
Future Directions

APPLIED CLINICAL PSYCHOLOGY

Series Editors:
Alan S. Bellack, *Medical College of Pennsylvania at EPPI, Philadelphia, Pennsylvania,* and Michel Hersen, *University of Pittsburgh, Pittsburgh, Pennsylvania*

Current Volumes in this Series

CHILDHOOD AGGRESSION AND VIOLENCE
Sources of Influence, Prevention, and Control
   Edited by David H. Crowell, Ian M. Evans, and Clifford R. O'Donnell

FAMILY ASSESSMENT
Rationale, Methods, and Future Directions
   Theodore Jacob and Daniel L. Tennenbaum

FAMILY INTERACTION AND PSYCHOPATHOLOGY
Theories, Methods, and Findings
   Edited by Theodore Jacob

HANDBOOK OF ASSESSMENT IN CHILDHOOD PSYCHOPATHOLOGY
Applied Issues in Differential Diagnosis and Treatment Evaluation
   Edited by Cynthia L. Frame and Johnny L. Matson

HANDBOOK OF TREATMENT APPROACHES IN CHILDHOOD PSYCHOPATHOLOGY
   Edited by Johnny L. Matson

A PRIMER OF HUMAN BEHAVIORAL PHARMACOLOGY
   Alan Poling

THE PRIVATE PRACTICE OF BEHAVIOR THERAPY
   Sheldon J. Kaplan

SEVERE BEHAVIOR DISORDERS IN THE MENTALLY RETARDED
Nondrug Approaches to Treatment
   Edited by Rowland P. Barrett

TREATING ADDICTIVE BEHAVIORS
Processes of Change
   Edited by William R. Miller and Nick Heather

A Continuation Order Plan is available for this series. A continuation order will bring delivery of each new volume immediately upon publication. Volumes are billed only upon actual shipment. For further information please contact the publisher.

FAMILY ASSESSMENT
Rationale, Methods, and
Future Directions

Theodore Jacob
University of Arizona
Tucson, Arizona

and

Daniel L. Tennenbaum
Kent State University
Kent, Ohio

PLENUM PRESS • NEW YORK AND LONDON

Library of Congress Cataloging in Publication Data

Jacob, Theodore.
　Family assessment: rationale, methods, and future directions / Theodore Jacob and Daniel L. Tennenbaum.
　　p.　　cm.—(Applied clinical psychology)
　Bibliography: p.
　Includes index.
　ISBN 0-306-42755-9
　1. Family psychotherapy. I. Tennenbaum, Daniel L. II. Title. III. Series. [DNLM: 1. Family. 2. Interpersonal Relations. 3. Psychopathology—methods. WM 100 J153f]
RC488.5.J347　1988
616.89′156—dc19　　　　　　　　　　　　　　　　　　　　　　　　　　　88-2319
　　　　　　　　　　　　　　　　　　　　　　　　　　　　　　　　　　　　　CIP

© 1988 Plenum Press, New York
A Division of Plenum Publishing Corporation
233 Spring Street, New York, N.Y. 10013

All rights reserved

No part of this book may be reproduced, stored in a retrieval system, or transmitted in any form or by any means, electronic, mechanical, photocopying, microfilming, recording, or otherwise, without written permission from the Publisher

Printed in the United States of America

PREFACE

The purpose of this book is to review existing and developing family assessment methods relevant to the study of psychopathology. It is our intention not only to inform clinical researchers of the many valuable family assessment methods that are available, but also to encourage the incorporation of such procedures into future research efforts. In so doing, we believe that our understanding of the etiology, course, treatment, and prevention of adult and childhood disorders will be greatly enriched.

The book begins with an overview of the larger social and intellectual forces which have led to the current interest in studying family influences on psycopathology in children and adolescence. For each "stream of influence," we attempt to highlight theoretical and methodological contributions relevant to the family's role in the etiology, exacerbation, and treatment of childhood disorders. Next, a framework for classifying family measurement procedures is introduced in which three major dimensions are emphasized: unit of analysis, source of data, and construct assessed. The third and most important chapter provides detailed reviews of a selected number of methods within each of the major groupings that have been delimited, references and brief descriptions of other measures that cannot be reviewed in detail, and a discussion of the promising and developing techniques that are known to the authors. Finally a concluding chapter attempts to identify major gaps in this literature, elaborates on several developing techniques referred to in the previous chapter, indicates critical issues of methodology (strengths and limitations) that characterize the various types of family measures, and suggests theoretical and methodological studies that future research efforts could profitably address.

Our efforts in preparing this volume were aided by many people. The initial impetus for this undertaking was an invitation by Hussain Tuma to contribute a chapter on family assessment to his edited book, *Assessment and Diagnosis of Child and Adolescent Psychopathology*. In the early formative period, David Reiss exerted an important influence on the organization and direction of our thinking. We would also like to thank Cynthia Bost, Sheri Johnson, Deborah Bremer, Richard Finklestein, and especially Kay Bargiel for their contributions to this project. Additionally, we are very grateful for the support we received from various individuals and agencies: for T. J., the University of Arizona Department of Family Studies, and NIAAA Grants R01 AA03037 and K02 AA00027; and for D.T., the Kent State University Department of Psychology, and an NIAAA Postdoctoral Fellowship in Alcohol Epidemiology at the University of Pittsburgh under the direction of Nancy Day.

Finally, our own families have been a continuing source of inspiration throughout this process: on Ted's side—Miriam, Charlotte, Jules, Brian, and Julie; and on Dan's side—Iris, Stella, Elie, Vallery, and Marc. To them, we dedicate this book.

Theodore Jacob
Daniel L. Tennenbaum

Tucson and Kent

CONTENTS

1. *Family Research: Streams of Influence* 1
   - I. Family Sociology 1
   - II. Systems/Communications Theory 4
   - III. Child and Developmental Psychology 6
   - IV. Social Learning Theory 8

2. *Classifying Family Measurement Procedures* 13
   - I. Data Source 13
   - II. Unit of Assessment 15
   - III. Constructs Assessed 16
     - A. Affect 18
     - B. Control 18
     - C. Communication 19
     - D. Systems Properties 20

3. *Detailed Review of Methods* 23
   - I. Introduction 23
   - II. Individual Assessments 25
     - A. Communication Deviance 26
   - III. Relationship Assessments: Questionnaires Regarding Marital Relationships 30
     - A. Marital Adjustment Test (MAT) 31
     - B. Dyadic Adjustment Scale (DA) 33
     - C. Areas of Change Questionnaire (ACQ) .. 36

		D. Marital Satisfaction Inventory (MSI)	39
		E. Primary Communication Inventory (PCI)	41
		F. The Sexual Interaction Inventory (SII)	43
		G. Relationship Belief Inventory (RBI)	46
		H. Conflict Tactic Scales (CT)	49
		I. Other Marital Scales	51
	IV.	Relationship Assessments: Questionnaires Regarding Parent–Child Relationships	52
		A. Structural Analysis of Social Behavior (SASB)	53
		B. Child Report of Parental Behavior Inventory (CRPBI)	57
		C. Parent–Adolescent Communication Scale (PAC)	60
		D. Parent–Child Areas of Change Questionnaire (PC–ACQ)	63
	V.	Relationship Assessments: Questionnaires Regarding Sibling Relationships	66
		A. The Sibling Relationship Questionnaire	67
	VI.	Relationship Assessments: Questionnaires Regarding Whole Families	70
		A. Family Environment Scale (FES)	70
		B. Family Adaptability and Cohesion Scales II (FACES II)	74
		C. Family Assessment Measures (FAM)	78
		D. Family Crisis-Oriented Personal Evaluation Scales (F-COPES)	82
	VII.	Relationship Assessments: Structured Interviews	84
		A. Expressed Emotion	85
		B. Family Ritual Interview	89
	VIII.	Relationship Assessments: Quasi-Observational Procedures	92
		A. Parent Daily Report (PDR)	93
		B. Spouse Observation Checklist (SOC)	95
		C. Parent–Adolescent Observation Schedule (PCOS)	98

CONTENTS

	D.	Sibling Observation Schedule (SOS)	99
IX.		Laboratory Observational Procedures: Outcome Measures	100
	A.	Card Sort Procedure	101
	B.	Revealed Difference Technique (RDT)	106
	C.	Family Hierarchy Test	110
X.		Laboratory Observational Procedures: Coding Systems	114
	A.	Marital Interaction Coding System (MICS)	116
	B.	Specific Affect Coding System (SPAFF)	121
	C.	Relational Communication Coding System (RELCOM)	126
	D.	Constraining and Enabling Coding System (CECS)	130
	E.	Other Laboratory Coding Systems	133
	F.	Coding of Family Interactions with Younger Children	136
XI.		Laboratory Observational Procedures: Rating Scales	138
	A.	The Marital Communication Rating Scale (MCRaS)	139
	B.	The Communication Rapid Assessment Scale (CRAS)	141
XII.		Naturalistic Observational Procedures	144
	A.	Family Interaction Coding System (FICS)	145
	B.	Home Observation Assessment Method (HOAM)	149
	C.	Home Interaction Scoring System (HISS)	153

4. *Conclusions and Future Directions* *159*

I.	General Limitations of Report and Observational Methods	159
II.	Within-Method Assessments	161
III.	Correspondence between Methods	165
IV.	Underdeveloped Assessment Targets and Concepts	167

V. The Need for Additional Assessment Methods 170
VI. The Interplay between Theory and Instrument Development 173

References 177

Index 201

FAMILY ASSESSMENT

1

FAMILY RESEARCH: STREAMS OF INFLUENCE

In order to appreciate the potential value of family variables in studies of psychopathology, it is important to understand the development of family research as a major and formal area of study and the contributions that this field has made to studies of disordered behavior. In this chapter, four major influences will be identified— family sociology, systems/communications theory, child and developmental psychology, and social learning theory. Although these areas of study will be described sequentially, implying that the contributions of each tradition have been made independent of knowledge development in other areas, this is certainly not the case. In many instances, cross-fertilization between domains has been clear, whereby concepts originating in one field have been translated into models and language systems associated with another area of inquiry. In other cases, a larger social or intellectual *Zeitgeist* can be seen to have provided a common background and motivation for similar theoretical developments occurring in seemingly distinct disciplines. The format we have selected, then, is an aide to expository clarity and not necessarily a reflection of actual independence among the various sources of influence.

I. Family Sociology

For many, the field of family studies was launched by the publication of Ernest Burgess's (1926) seminal paper, "The Family as a Unity of Interacting Personalities." As noted by Handel (1965), this position paper—published nearly 60 years ago—anticipated many concepts and perspectives that are now critical ones in the current literature on family theory and research. Three examples can be noted. First, Burgess conceived of the family as a group of interacting personalities that "has its existence in the interaction of its members" (p. 5). Within this framework, Burgess emphasized the process versus content of interaction and the family group as the unit of study—emphases which can be seen as important forerunners to later views of the family from systems and small group perspectives. Second, Burgess raised central research problems for family investigation when he encouraged efforts (a) to conceptualize the family as the unit of study, (b) to study the personalities of several members and the interrelationships among them, and (c) to analyze family life in terms of family patterns and roles. In many ways, family research is still struggling with three basic issues; specifically, how to conceptualize the family group and what to assess. Finally, Burgess's early writings can even be read as forerunners of current family theories of psychopathology and of family therapy as a treatment intervention. For example, in speaking of a case study involving a disturbed child, Burgess (1926) noted that

> any program of treating this case would lie not in assessing the proportional share of blame on the father, mother, or child, but understanding their attitudes in light of each one's conception of his role in the family. (p. 9)

During the 30-year period from 1920 to 1950, the discipline of sociology made the most significant contributions to the general field of family studies—a period of time that witnessed (a) the development of major theoretical frameworks within which family behavior was conceptualized, (b) the initiation of programmatic research efforts that became cornerstones for family theory and practice in the years ahead, and (c) the introduction of important methodologies by which family relationships could be probed. Contributing to all of these directions was the work of Talcott Parsons and Robert Bales (Bales, 1950; Parsons & Bales, 1955). Although this brief introduction does not allow for an extensive discussion of their efforts, their major contributions should be acknowledged. First, Parson's structural-functional model of group process, emphasizing the importance of role behavior and task performance, was extremely influential in subsequently developed models of direct relevance to conceptualizing and treating disordered behavior within the family context (Steinhauer, 1987; Tharp, 1965). Second, Parson's primary dimensions of group functioning, instrumental and socioemotional role functions, still represent the major dimensions of family interaction thought to be relevant in understanding the emergence and/or perpetuation of psychopathology within the family. Third, the collaboration between Parsons and Robert Bales resulted in the development of Interaction Process Analysis (IPA), an observational coding system for analyzing group process in *ad hoc* problem-solving groups. Both the methodology (i.e., direct observations of ongoing interaction) and the key variables assessed (instrumental and socioemotional communications) provided the basis for numerous coding systems developed between 1950 and 1970 and aimed at assessing the problem-solving and naturalistic interactions of disturbed individuals and their families.

From 1950 until the mid-1980s, small group theory and research on families grew rapidly. In a recent review of one segment of this literature, Klein and Hill (1979) identified four major activity centers: (a) studies of the family as the context in which social and interpersonal problems (including psychiatric disorders) develop, (b) developments in theory and research concerned with the family's response to crises, (c) attempts to conceptualize and measure change in family relationships over the family life cycle, and (d) studies of the problem-solving, decision-making characteristics of family groups. Many of these efforts are of direct relevance to family studies of psychopathology and contribute significantly to the conceptual foundations on which clinical theories of child and family disturbance are based. Most important to this presentation, various family assessment procedures that this book reviews owe a large intellectual debt to the theoretical and methodological contributions of family sociology and to the social psychology of small group behavior; for example, the Revealed Difference Technique (Strodtbeck, 1951), the Card Sort Task (Reiss, 1981), and the various observational coding systems which were strongly influenced by Bales's studies with IPA. Although not without its detractors (Burns, 1973; Walters,

1982), we would contend that the concepts, methods, and theories that are developing within family sociology have made and continue to make significant contributions to understanding the family's role in psychopathology.

II. Systems/Communications Theory

In addition to the theories and methods that have appeared within family sociology, several other forces can be identified that have greatly fostered and shaped the present character of family research on psychopathology. The most significant of these influences was the emergence of the family theories of schizophrenia during the 1950s—in particular, the work of Jackson, Bateson, Haley, and Weakland; Lidz; Wynne; and Bowen (for reviews of these frameworks, see Mishler & Waxler, 1965). Common to all of these efforts was the primary emphasis on family communications and their distortions as the cause of psychopathology—that is, the etiological role of family interaction in understanding the genesis of severe psychiatric disorder and its emergence during adolescence. Distorted role structures and communications were certainly highlighted by all of these clinical theories, although the major theoretical/conceptual underpinnings for the various positions were quite different. On one hand, in the case of Lidz's writings on marital schizm and skew, the intellectual debt to Parson's theory of role structure and differentiation was clearly acknowledged as was the link to traditional psychodynamic formulations of children's psychosexual development. Wynne's notions of "transactional thought disorder and pseudomutuality" on the other hand, were embedded within a conceptual framework characterized by a mix of psychodynamic, existential, and role theories (Wynne, Ryckoff, Day, & Hirsch, 1958).

The Palo Alto group (Jackson, Bateson, Haley, and Weakland) introduced the most radical framework, emphasizing systems and communications concepts such as positive and negative feedback processes, homeostasis, subsystem interaction, and boundaries. Briefly, this systems/communications perspective offered a new model within which to view disordered behavior—a model that first and foremost emphasized the primacy of the *interactional* context in attempts to understand any behavior, disordered or not. The "strong" variant of this model suggested that it is not even meaningful to discuss psychopathology from an individual perspective because behavior is inextricably intertwined within a interpersonal context and only has meaning when viewed within this context. If this position is accepted, one would conclude that the smallest appropriate unit of analysis is not an individual's behavior, but an interactional sequence involving a pattern of exchange that occurs between individuals— in a word, the unit of importance is the *system* of members in mutual and interdependent relationships with one another, not individual behavior in isolation of this context.

Since the mid-1950s, this interactional framework has had a significant impact on both clinical developments and research efforts concerned with linking family interaction and psychopathology (Steinglass, 1978, 1987). Regarding the former, beginning interests and curiosities with family treatment approaches in psychiatry grew into a major treatment modality, and to some extent became an intellectual and personal movement. First, various schools of family therapy were spawned during the 1960s and 1970s, each with a group of dedicated adherents and associated with clinicians of great charisma and influence. Second, the general model stimulated a considerable amount of empirical research on family interaction and psychopathology from 1960 to 1980, although most of these efforts were not initiated by the original theorists/clinicians themselves but arose within the larger clinical research community, (Jacob, 1975). Third, the system's model was not only accepted as a primary rationale for intervention and prevention efforts focused on the family, but was incorporated into other theories of family dysfunction and clinical models of treatment (Vincent, 1980). Finally, the perspective, more than any of the others, underscored the complexity of relationships that can exist between family relationships and psychopathology. In the present context, the major implication of this perspective is that investigators must attempt to develop assessment procedures which go beyond single variables aimed at only one level of the family matrix. At the very least, the attempt should be made to develop a multilevel assessment package, containing instruments focused on different levels of family behavior.

III. Child and Developmental Psychology

A third stream of influence that provided a critical cornerstone for family studies of psychopathology involved the contributions from child and developmental psychology. As noted by Achenbach (1982), the study of childhood and its disorders achieved only formal status during the twentieth century. Various intellectual and social forces contributed to this evolution, the most important including the development of intelligence tests among school children, the growth of the child study movement stimulated by the pioneering efforts of G. Stanley Hall and Lightner Witner, the formulation and dissemination of psychoanalysis, and the growth of child guidance clinics and the child guidance movement. Throughout the second quarter of the twentieth century, psychoanalysis, in pure or revised form, dominated conceptualizations and treatments of childhood disorders in which therapy was "aimed at assisting the child in modifying basic underlying personality structure" (Ollendick & Hersen, 1983, p. 9). Although early parent–child relationships were assumed to be important contributors to development gone astray, it was the work of researchers in developmental psychology and learning theory, rather than the child clinicians who would eventually give elaboration and full meaning to the role of these parent–child relationships.

From the seminal writings of Symonds (1939) to the elaborated, circumplex models of Becker (1964), Schaefer (1959), and Seigelman (1965a,b), a great deal of theoretical and empirical effort was directed toward explicating parental behaviors related to children's cognitive and socio-emotional development. Since the mid-1940s, these efforts have identified, replicated, and elaborated three primary dimensions of parental behavior—*affect, control,* and *consistency*—that are linked to a wide range of child outcomes related to personality, social-interpersonal, and cognitive variables (Rollins & Thomas, 1979).

In reviewing this period of research, Hartup (1977) characterized the emergent parent–child conceptualizations as "social mold theories" in which influences were assumed to be unidirectional—the parent acted and the child responded. Several other areas of investigation, however, that soon gained greater recognition, began to characterize the child as an active organism who contributed significantly to the nature and course of the evolving parent–child relationship. Piaget's (1970) descriptions of organismically based schemas and White's (1959) competency-based view of motivation sensitized researchers to the child's "choosing, action-producing" nature (Rollins & Thomas, 1979), whereas studies of child temperament invigorated theoretical and empirical interests in biologically rooted child variables and their impact on patterns of parent–child relationships (Thomas & Chess, 1977). The linking of parent behaviors to variations in child temperament was impressively forged by Bell in his classic 1968 paper entitled, "A Reinterpretation of the Direction of Effects in Studies of Socialization." After Bell, it became obvious that the next generation of models would be truly interactional in which a process of mutual influence would compete with simpler, unidirectional conceptualizations of parent–child relationships (Maccoby & Martin, 1983; Parke, 1984).

The contributions of developmental perspectives in family studies of psychopathology are obviously critical, alerting us to age and stage-related changes in individual, dyadic and system behavior. The consistency of change is assured by inevitable developmental changes that occur in the psychosocial, cognitive, and social characteristics of both children and parents and in the patterns of relationships that link members to one another over time. From the varieties of literature that contribute to the developmental model, we are told that a child's behavior—and our evaluation of its so-called deviance—must be evaluated within a temporal context. Without this context, ideally derived from both theory and normative data, it is extremely difficult to anticipate whether the behavior is likely to change, over what period of time, to what degree, and in what direction. When speaking of behaviors that have clinical or psychiatric significance, such knowledge can be of critical importance to issues of course, outcome, and treatment alternatives. Finally, knowledge of developmental parameters can be of great value in evaluating family theories of child psychopathology. One example will suffice. In a recent review of the literature on inconsistent communication and family disturbance, Jacob and Lessin (1982) found only mixed support for the contention that incongruities in verbal and nonverbal communications are reliably associated with childhood disorders. In considering this issue in greater detail, it was suggested that the child's level of cognitive and linguistic development was a potentially key variable that was given only scant attention in this literature. In essence, verbal content is much more influential in message interpretation made by younger children than are voice tone and nonverbal cues. Only as children approach preadolescence do the paralinguistic and facial cues take on marked importance in the decoding of incongruent messages. The major implication of such data is that the perception of a message as incongruent is importantly related to the child's developmental stage, and that incongruent messages disturb, that is, have an impact, only if the child is old enough to recognize and appreciate the channel discrepancy.

Regarding the assessment of psychopathology within the family, the developmental tradition underscores the importance of the key parenting dimensions of acceptance, control, and consistency—dimensions that are clearly represented in various measurement procedures that are discussed in Chapter 3 (Rollins & Thomas, 1979). In addition, child and developmental psychology contribute importantly to the development of observational procedures used in both laboratory (Hughes & Haynes, 1978) and naturalistic settings as well as various report procedures concerning children's perception of parents (e.g., Margolies & Weintraub, 1977). Finally, theory and research within the developmental tradition were integrated into other models, and in so doing, resulted in more compelling theories and methodologies than existed previously.

IV. Social Learning Theory

A final influence on family studies of psychopathology is behavioral psychology in general and social learning theory (SLT) in particular. SLT is certainly not independent of the other influences nor is it a homogeneous, tightly defined set of concepts drawn from and evaluated within a single discipline. This approach is characterized by certain features, however, which give it a strong identity in the literature.

The roots of this tradition can be traced back to the early years of the twentieth century—a brief period of time (1900 to 1920) which witnessed the emergence of the first scientific studies of learning processes. During the second quarter of this century, the full impact of these seminal works was to be realized in the elegant and highly influential theories of Hull, Spence, and Skinner along with several competing models stressing cognitive variables (e.g., Tolman) (Hilgard & Bowers, 1966). It was not until the late 1950s and early 1960s, however, that principles derived from classical and operant conditioning models were applied to the analysis and treatment of major clinical disorders; in particular, Wolpe's (1958) reciprocal inhibition in the treatment of anxiety-based disorders and application of operant conditioning techniques to the treatment of a wide range of disorders (Ayllon & Azrin, 1968; Hersen, Kazdin, & Bellack, 1983).

By that time, the so-called pure strains of learning theory—the Hull–Spence and the Skinnerian paradigms—were being challenged by rapid developments in cognitive theory and research, and the competing paradigm proposed by Albert Bandura. Briefly, Bandura sought to broaden earlier learning models through greater emphasis on the social aspects of learning and the mutual, interactive effects of behavior, person, and environment (Bandura, 1977; Bandura & Walters, 1963). The focus on the interplay among these several sources of influence emphasized the importance of cognitive variables; in particular, the contention that learning through observing complex behaviors and then modeling such patterns is the source by which the most important learning of the social world takes place. Consistent with this emphasis, Bandura's theoretical framework became known as social learning theory (SLT).

During the past two decades, SLT has been revised, elaborated and integrated with other frameworks and models within the social sciences. Although still referred to as SLT, the approach is now a diverse and rich one, containing several subapproaches which vary in the relative emphasis given to key concepts and methodologies. As noted by Vincent (1980), "Social learning theory is not a unified, original statement of propositions; instead, the theory is an assemblage of several models" (p. 3). The most prominent components in the framework are operant learning and social exchange theory plus a more recent integration with concepts from general systems theory and attribution theory. Notwithstanding this diversity, the general model can be characterized by several distinguishing features, the most important of which include (a) a focus on systems, whereby interest is directed toward reciprocal, bidirectional interactions among members; (b) a continuing emphasis on variations in behavior as a function of changes in the environment, including the continued incorporation of cognitive variables into the model; (c) a preference for the naturalistic study of families; (d) a commitment to clinical application and development; and (e) an overriding investment in the study and treatment of disordered behavior through scientific, methodologically rigorous procedures.

The contributions that SLT made to the study of psychopathology within the family context were significant. Conceptually, the sustained efforts of various family researchers resulted in further delineation and elaboration of two key constructs in developing models of family interaction and psychopathology—*coercion* and *reciprocity*. Given the dynamic interplay between conceptualization, empirical assessment, and model revision that characterizes the SLT model, these key concepts have been refined significantly since the mid-1960s. As noted earlier, the model is presently characterized by greater appreciation of cognitive, individual, and extrafamilial infuences that impact on the more molecular and momentary patterns of behavioral interaction.

Another major contribution made by the behavioral approach involves the development and validation of a number of observational coding systems for use in both laboratory and naturalistic settings—procedures that allow for the rigorous and rich description of interaction relevant to theory development and treatment evaluation in the area of psychopathology (e.g., Reid, 1978). In addition, various statistical methods for analyzing complex patterns of interaction are offered by researchers in this area, the most notable involving the application of sequential and time-series analyses aimed at clarifying the contingent and temporal nature of complex patterns of family interaction (Gottman, 1979, 1982).

A final contribution made by behavioral family researchers

involves the development and evaluation of family-based treatment programs for child, marital and family disturbance (Jacobson & Margolin, 1979; Patterson, 1982). The early parent-training, child-management models of Patterson, Wahler, and Bernal (although modified and elaborated significantly since the mid-1970s) still represent major clinical strategies in the treatment of childhood conduct disorders. Similarly, behavioral marital therapy approaches were subjected to a tremendous amount of evaluation and revision during this period, incorporating concepts from cognitive theory and techniques from other schools of family therapy in search of maximally effective interventions for marital discord (Hahlweg & Jacobson, 1984). Given the commitment to both scientific rigor and clinical relevance, we anticipate that the behavioral approach offers significant theoretical insights and clinical intervention relevant to the family context of psychopathology.

2

CLASSIFYING FAMILY MEASUREMENT PROCEDURES

In the context of describing family assessment procedures relevant to theoretical and treatment studies of psychopathology, three organizing dimensions are particularly helpful: the source from which information is obtained, the family unit that is the focus of assessment, and the major constructs that the instrument attempts to measure.

I. Data Source

The major issue of data source involves a distinction between instruments based upon the *reports* of family members and instruments based upon the direct *observation* of families during some type of actual interaction. Common to all variants of the first method, the report approach, is the requirement that the informant be asked for his or her perceptions of family events. These perceptions can relate to individuals (self-reports or reports of others), relationships, the family in general, or to links between the family and extrafamilial influences. There are many advantages to this strategy, including (a) the strong face validity that is associated with test (questionnaire) items (e.g., do you consider your family relationships to be warm and supportive?); (b) ease of administration and scoring; (c) test developments based upon large representative samples to which individual assessments can be generalized; and (d) access to family data which cannot be reasonably obtained by other procedures (e.g., the nature of sexual interactions and members' expressed satisfaction/happiness with different aspects of family life). The second method, the observational approach, provides direct access to the actual interactions of family members. Under the best of circumstances, this method provides highly detailed information regarding streams of behavior that characterize the family in operation as well as precise information regarding the family's response, solution, or performance on objective tasks and problems. Given such data, specific coding systems can be applied to these interactions, allowing for detailed descriptions of family processes and patterns of interaction.

Within each of these major approaches, one can find important subgroups of instruments. Self-report procedures, for example, include objective tests, projective tests, structured interviews, and behavioral reports (sometimes referred to as participant observation or quasi-observation procedures). Instruments included within the observation approach can be further subdivided into laboratory analogues and naturalistic observations. One type of laboratory procedure involves the use of structured tasks or games that yield some outcome measure based upon the family's performance. A second procedure involves the assessment of actual interactions among family members—interactions that are generated from discussions of problems or conflicts that the researcher presents to the family during the experimental session. These discussions, often videotaped or audiotaped in order to provide a permanent record, are then assessed by various means (a) detailed, multicomponent coding systems which preserve the ordering of behavior over time; (b) ratings of the total interaction along general/global dimensions of interest; and (c) the recording of members' psychophysiological or physical responses during ongoing interactions. In contrast with these laboratory-based procedures, naturalistic observations involve the assessment of family interaction in the home setting. These data can also be subjected to detailed coding systems or to more general ratings. In some cases, permanent records (audiotapes or videotapes) are obtained whereas at other times ratings (assessments, codings) are conducted by "live" observers who remain in the family's home during the period of observation.

The differences (advantages and liabilities) between report and observational data have been the subject of much discussion in many areas of social science, including the assessment of family behaviors (Hetherington & Martin, 1979). In the last chapter of this book, a more critical discussion of each approach is presented in which strengths, limitations, and future research needs are highlighted.

II. Unit of Assessment

In the measurement of family influences, the assessment focus involves individuals, relationships between two (dyads) or more members, the whole family, or the interface between the family and extrafamilial environment.

Individual assessments involve traditional tests of personality or psychopathology, including both objective or projective procedures—instruments that provide important data regarding the psychiatric and psychosocial status of the individual members. In addition, some individual assessment data provide the primary basis on which key family variables are operationalized—for example, the measurement of communication deviance is based upon analysis of each parent's individual Rorschach responses (Singer & Wynne, 1966).

The second level of assessment focuses on relationships, and, most importantly, includes descriptions of the marital, parent–child and child–child dyads. In contrast with the assessment of individuals, relationship assessments provide information about dyadic status and functioning whether determined from an individual's reports regarding the relationship or from an observer's coding of an ongoing interaction between the two family members. By far, the most extensive group of dyadic assessment measures concern marital relationships, whereas procedures for assessing parent–child and child–sibling relationships are fewer and more limited in scope.

The next level of assessment is that of the whole family,

whereby test scores, ratings, or performance variables are intended to characterize the family in general or as a totality. Again, assessments of this unit can be obtained through report procedures (i.e., an individual's perceptions/descriptions of his or her family), laboratory outcome procedures (i.e., the family's performance on a structured task), or process and content codings obtained from laboratory or naturalistic observation interactions among family members.

Finally, there are several assessment procedures that provide information about extrafamilial variables and their impact on family functioning. Measures of social support and social networks (Anderson, 1982) have recently begun to surface in the family assessment domain, based on the recognition that the family system varies in its permeability, and in turn, the degree to which extrafamilial systems impact the family unit.

III. Constructs Assessed

The ways one conceptualizes and examines the relationship between family influences and childhood or adult disorders vary in relation to one's theoretical model, study objective, and psychopathology under consideration. First, the family's role in psychopathology is often seen to vary as a function of the particular theoretical or clinical-theoretical model one selects. For some family researchers, global, system-wide variables (often referred to as family environmental influences) assume primary importance, whereas other investigators emphasize highly circumscribed behaviors and specific responses as the key variables in understanding the family's impact on childhood problems. Second, different study objectives dictate the selection of those family variables most germane to the investigative focus. Interests in etiology, for example, may direct attention toward one level or type of family influence which may not be as relevant to studies of course and maintenance or to efforts aimed at developing effective programs of intervention or prevention. Finally, the particular psychopathology of interest directs attention toward some family variables rather than others. Interests in the cognitive dysfunctions of schizophrenia, for example, have led Goldstein and Wynne to assessments of communication deviance—a family variable that is probably less relevant to psychopathologies in which behavioral and affective disturbances, rather than cognitive deficits, are the primary features of the disorder (Doane, Jones, Fisher, Ritzler, Singer, & Wynne, 1982; Lewis, Rodnick, & Goldstein, 1981).

In light of these considerations, together with the fluid and developing nature of family theory, research, and treatment, one conclusion seems obvious: There is no single family variable or family model which can guarantee immediate and profound insights if selected to guide the researcher's quest to unravel the mysteries of adult or childhood disorders. At the same time, theoretical and empirical efforts of the past four decades—involving the fields of family sociology, childhood development, systems/communication theory, and social learning theory, offer a rich, and in some cases, compelling matrix of family variables and models that deserve the serious consideration of psychopathologists. The careful selection and inclusion of one or more of these influences into studies of disorder can only enrich such studies. In some cases, their incorporation into rigorous and illuminating research protocols yield relationships that significantly expand on conceptualizations of childhood disorders.

Our own survey of the literature reveals several sets of constructs that are most relevant to understanding the family–psychopathology complex. This relatively small matrix of influences appears to capture most of the thought regarding the family's potential roles in childhood disorders. The four sets of constructs are here refered to as *affect, control, communication,* and *family systems properties*. Theoretically, each of these processes can be assessed in regards to the interaction of family dyads (marital, mother–child, father–child, child–sibling), triads, or the entire family. As will be seen, however, certain constructs (processes) have been discussed most extensively in regard to certain family levels with much less attention—theoretically, clinically, or psychometrically—directed toward other construct by level interfaces.

A. Affect

The primacy of the affective bond as a determinant of relationship satisfaction and individual outcome is emphasized across a broad range of disciplines and types of interpersonal relationships. From studies of infant attachment (Ainsworth, Blehar, Waters, & Wall, 1978) and group process (Parsons & Bales, 1955; Steinhauer, 1987) to investigations of marital dissatisfaction (Lewis & Spanier, 1979; Weiss, 1981) and patterns of childhood socialization (Rollins & Thomas, 1979), the importance of a supportive and nurturing affective relationship is repeatedly underscored. Clearly, the affective relationship characterizing the parent–child and marital dyads has received most emphasis by theorists and clinicians, although various researchers have suggested that this "feeling" dimension—the ties that bind—can and should be assessed in regards to the family in general (Moos & Moos, 1976; Olson, Sprenkle, & Russell, 1979). Assessment of the affective nature of the child–sibling relationships is only beginning to receive attention.

B. Control

As with the affective dimension, interpersonal influence is of major importance in conceptualizations over a wide range of relationships (Foa & Foa, 1974; Leary, 1957). In studies of adult relationships (in particular, the marital dyad) various terms have been used to describe this dimension, the most common descriptors being power, influence, and dominance (Hadley & Jacob, 1976). In studies of relationships involving members of unequal status—specifically, the parent–child dyad—the literature focuses on strategies, techniques, and styles of parenting behavior with an overriding interest in those processes by which parents attempt to control and shape the behavior of their offspring during early childhood and adolescence (Rollins & Thomas, 1979). As in the assessments of support, the measurement of influence at the family level (in particular, the control strategies that characterize family interaction in general) is encouraged by various family researchers (Moos & Moos, 1976; Olson et al., 1979), whereas the assessment of the dominance structures in child-sibling relationships receives only minimal attention.

C. Communication

The term *communication* can be defined so broadly as to almost be interchangeable with behavior. In family literature of relevance to psychopathology, however, several specific meanings can be identified, each of which is related to particular model linking patterns of family communication with offspring status.

First and foremost, there has been continued interest in relating certain types of communication distortions to the development and perpetuation of cognitive disorder in children. Most importantly, this line of theory and research began during the early 1950s with the appearance of several family theories of schizophrenia (Mishler & Waxler, 1965). These models emphasized the unique patterns of communication that characterize families and the role of communication distortion in the subsequent development of the child's cognitive disturbances. During the next 30 years, key concepts from these early efforts (in particular, the notions of double-bind transactional thought disorder and, more recently, communication deviance) guided several research programs aimed at identifying, prospectively, those patterns of family communication that predict severe psychiatric disorder as the offspring enter late adolescence and early adulthood (Lewis *et al.*, 1981).

Although originally related to schizophrenia, the meaning of double-bind communications was soon broadened and integrated into a rapidly developing literature on nonverbal communication; soon thereafter, various investigators initiated studies of family communication with disturbed (but nonpsychotic) samples (see review by Jacob & Lessin, 1982). As a result of these developments, there has been considerable interest in exploring the relationship between verbal and nonverbal communication channels. Within this area, a particular focus has involved the conditions under which channel inconsistency (i.e., nonredundant information) emerges and the impact of such inconsistent messages on receivers. A number of these efforts have been directed to issues of psychopathology, its etiology, course, and treatment (Jacob & Lessin, 1982).

Finally, various communication studies have assessed family problem-solving in dysfunctional family units and the development of treatment programs aimed at enhancing those communication skills thought to be most relevant to the effective and satisfactory resolution of conflict (Gottman, Notarius, Gonso, & Markman, 1976; Olson, Russell, & Sprenkle, 1980; Thomas, 1977). In large part, this direction of research and practice was stimulated by the efforts of family researchers most closely identified with social learning theory (Vincent, 1980).

D. Systems Properties

This set of constructs derives most directly from the application of systemic concepts to the family unit. Bateson's collaboration with Jackson, Haley, and Weakland during the early 1950s provided the major foundation and stimulus for this clinical-theoretical framework, which, in turn, generated a variety of provocative and highly influential models of family psychopathology and treatment. In contrast with the other major constructs, systemic analysis directs attention toward general properties and principles of family systems that characterize relationships within the family and interaction between the family and extrafamilial systems. As with the other constructs, these system properties can be related to the etiology, impact, and modification of various forms of psychopathology. Included in this domain of processes are such characteristics as system flexibility and adaptability, that is, the family's ability to change patterns of control and emotional expression in response to changing needs of members and situational stresses imposed on the family (Olson *et al.*, 1979). Related processes such as boundary permeability, subsystem relationships, and alliance structures (Minuchin, 1974) are also emphasized in the application of systems perspectives to the diagnosis and treatment of family dysfunction. Other theorists highlight the family's use of time and space along with the amount of interaction that occurs within different family subsystems being relevant to understanding the nature of functional versus dysfunctional family systems (Kantor & Lehr, 1975;

Steinglass, 1979). Finally, the family's response to extrafamilial systems (i.e., the impact of social networks, extended family relationships, and community agencies) is thought of as an important interaction that should be understood in order to fully appreciate the internal workings of the family system itself.

3

DETAILED REVIEW OF METHODS

I. Introduction

From the foregoing discussion of major organizing dimensions for classifying family assessment procedures, it is clear that many subgroups of instruments can be defined. Table 1 (p. 24) provides an overview of a relatively complete classification system in which instruments are first grouped into report versus observational procedures, and then within each major division, are divided into more narrowly defined subsets.

Within the general domain of report procedures are individual assessments of adults and children based upon structured or unstructured, objective or projective instruments. Given the many tests that are included in this grouping as well as various reviews that are available (Buros, 1978), the only instrument we will discuss is an individually based assessment of *communication deviance* because of the extremely important role that this variable has assumed in family studies of schizophrenia. The next grouping of instruments focuses on relationship assessments (marital, parent–child, child–sibling, whole family) as determined from questionnaires (psychological tests), structured interviews, and quasi-observation procedures.

The second major division, observation procedures, is divided into laboratory-based instruments and naturalistic observational procedures, the former including structured tasks yielding

Table 1. Classification of Family Assessment Procedures

Data source	Assessment target[a]			
Report procedures				
Individual assessments	M	F	C	S
Relationship assessments				
Questionnaires	HW	PC	CS	Family
Structured interviews	HW	PC	CS	Family
Quasi-observations	HW	PC	CS	Family
Observational procedures				
Laboratory analogues				
Outcome measures	HW	PC	CS	Family
Process measures				
Coding measures	HW	PC	CS	Family
Rating scales	HW	PC	CS	Family
Contentless measures	HW	PC	CS	Family
Physiological recordings	HW	PC	CS	Family
Naturalistic observations	HW	PC	CS	Family

[a] M = mother, F = father, C = child, S = sibling, HW = husband-wife, PC = parent-child, CS = child-sibling, Family = whole family

outcome measures, detailed process and content codings of planned discussions, global ratings of planned discussions, and physical and psychophysiological recordings of participants during planned discussions. (The latter subgroupings—physical/psychophysiological data—will not be given detailed attention in this section, but will be referred to in the last section of this book.) The final grouping includes naturalistic observation procedures involving the application of detailed process and content codings of family interaction in the home environment.

In the following review, detailed evaluations of a few procedures within each subgroup of instruments will be presented. Instruments selected for detailed review were chosen on the basis of several considerations, including psychometric strength, accumulative scientific data, frequency of use, and relevance to key family variables. Notwithstanding these criteria, there were still more "worthy" instruments than could be reviewed so that criteria involving uniqueness and "promise" were sometimes used in selection of instruments for detailed review. When appropriate and helpful, brief descriptions of instruments not given detailed reviews are included. Each instrument selected for detailed review will be described in regards to background, variables assessed, description of instrument, and psychometric properties and applications.

Before the reviews are presented, a brief comment should be made regarding the "search" process that we followed in identifying relevant family assessment procedures. We began with an examination of Straus's major compendium of family assessment procedures published between 1935 and 1974 (Straus, 1969; Straus & Brown, 1978). Then we referred to several other sources reviewing aspects of this literature (Forman & Hagan, 1984; Olson, 1976). Subsequently, we examined all articles relevant to child psychiatry and family studies appearing in 19 major journals from 1980 to 1985 in order to identify additional instruments of potential interest.* Finally, our derived "lists" of instruments within each grouping were shared with various colleagues from whom we asked for additional nominations. Given this multifaceted identification process, we hoped to identify most relevant instruments that had some "track record" of application and potential. If any worthy procedures have been missed in our efforts, we apologize to their developers and promoters.

II. Individual Assessments

The smallest unit within the family is the individual. Member characteristics relevant to understanding the etiology, course, and treatment of child psychopathology include both hereditary/biological influences and social/personality variables. Considerable literature now exists that indicates that a child is at increased risk for disturbance if one or both parents exhibits significant psychopathology, and that parental characteristics (i.e., psychopathology) influence the course and outcome of child dis-

---

*American Journal of Family Therapy, American Journal of Orthopsychiatry, American Journal of Psychiatry, Archives of General Psychiatry, Behavior Modification, British Journal of Psychiatry, Child Development, Child Psychiatry and Human Development, Family Relations, Family Process, Journal of Abnormal Child Psychology, Journal of Abnormal Psychology, Journal of American Academy of Child Psychiatry, Journal of Behavioral Assessment, Journal of Child Psychology and Psychiatry, Journal of Consulting and Clinical Psychology, Journal of Marital and Family Therapy, Journal of Marriage and the Family, and Merril Palmer Quarterly.

turbance (Campbell, 1984). Likewise, there have been suggestions that variations in child characteristics (e.g., temperament) may predispose the child to disturbed parent–child relationships and/or to psychosocial and psychiatric disturbance during adolescence and adulthood. The relative importance of such biological variables, environmental influences, and their complex interactions, remains to be specified and more completely understood. Notwithstanding this knowledge gap, the behavior, attitudes, and cognitions of individual members, as well as their perceptions of self and others, can and do influence the expression of disorders.

A review of the many individual measures of personality, psychopathology, and attitudes is beyond the scope of the current paper. The interested reader is referred to several major sources for further information (Buros, 1978; Olson, 1976; Straus & Brown, 1978). One individual assessment procedure is reviewed because of its continued importance in studies of the family's impact on schizophrenia—communication deviance (Singer & Wynne, 1966).

A. Communication Deviance

1. Background

The concept and measurement of communication deviance (CD) grew out of Singer and Wynne's (1966) early observations of family interactions of disturbed individuals, typically schizophrenics, and the belief that deficits in the so-called ego development of the psychotic patient are systematically related to difficulties in parent–child communication. In recent years, CD has been related to a severe psychopathology that encompasses schizophrenia and other disorders such as borderline personality.

Major emphasis is placed on distortions in the process by which parents and their children attain "a shared attentional focus." Although CD is measured by testing the parent individually (outside of the family), it is assumed that communication deficits extend into the family system. More recently, it has been suggested that CD is probably best tapped by more direct observation of the parents and identified patient together.

Wynne and Singer are not interested in flagrant language and communication difficulties, or in the content of the message *per se*. Rather, they pay attention to more subtle communication difficulties that predispose an individual, in interaction with other forces, towards the development of schizophrenia. They view communication difficulties subsumed under CD as long-term habits, rather than acute symptoms.

2. Variables Assessed

Singer and Wynne (1966) developed a scoring manual for rating 41 communication deficits observed in an individually administered Rorschach. These are subsumed under three main headings: closure problems, disruptive behavior, and peculiar verbalizations. Closure problems are ways in which parents of young adult schizophrenics cause a listener to be uncertain whether closure over an idea, a response, or a part of an exchange has occurred. Disruptive behaviors are more obvious difficulties that involve "interruptions and distractions and set disruptions in which the parent says something that disrupts the task set established by the tester" (Singer & Wynne, 1966, p. 274). Peculiar verbalizations include "instances in which words, syntax, and logic are used in idiosyncratic ways that would ordinarily interfere with the sharing of meaning" (p. 277).

In a later publication, Jones (1977) performed a factor analysis of Thematic Apperception Test (TAT) ratings from parents of nonschizophrenic outpatients and identified six factors. In the revised version of the individual Rorschach scoring manual, Singer has grouped the 41 items into five problem areas: commitment problems; referent problems; language anomalies; contradictory, arbitrary sequences; and disruptions.

A variety of tasks have been used to measure CD, including the Rorschach and TAT procedures as well as the less well-known object sorting task, the 20-questions task, and family therapy interactions.

3. Description of the Instrument

Various coding systems and revisions have been developed as ways of giving operational definition to subtle deficits involving "deviations in handling attention and meaning, especially in sharing foci of attention (Singer & Wynne, 1966, p. 263). Singer and Wynne (1966) describe the development of the first extensive Rorschach scoring manual and a briefer TAT scoring manual, both for individual administration. A revision of the original CD criteria for TAT records has been proposed by Sass, Sunderson, Singer, and Wynne (1984). Singer has also produced a revision of the Rorschach criteria (Singer, 1973), whereas Doane and Singer (1977) have developed criteria for scoring family Rorschach protocols. Jones (1977) developed his own revision of a scoring manual for the TAT. The original procedures developed by Singer and Wynne were applied to individual parents, but in recent years, CD has been assessed in individuals, couples, and families (Doane et al., 1982; Shapiro & Wild, 1976; Wild, Shapiro & Goldenberg, 1975).

The original instrument developed by Singer and Wynne (1966) had 41 codes for the Rorschach grouped into three categories: closure problems, disruptive behavior, and peculiar verbalization. Typically, audio recordings are made of responses, and the scoring is conducted from typed transcripts, although in earlier reports detailed written records were also used.

A protocol is typically divided into coding units each of which can be further coded. A summary score of communication deviance consists of "total deviations per protocol divided by total number of exact typed lines" (Doane et al., 1982, p. 215), thus controlling for verbal output. In more recent studies, not all TAT and Rorschach cards are used (Doane et al., 1982).

Training. In one publication using TAT material, Jones (1977) noted that training by Singer in the definition of CD categories was necessary. Other publications do not describe the training procedure in detail. In our view, the categories of CD are often subtle and, therefore, considerable training should be anticipated. Given sufficient training, however, professionally trained clinicians would not be necessary as raters.

4. Psychometric Properties and Applications

Reliability. Doane et al. (1982) reported test–retest reliability of $r = .96$, with a mean interval between testings of 25 days. In addition, Doane et al. (1982) reported interrater reliabilities of 85% (percent occurrence agreement). Kappa coefficients were acceptable for the assignment of subjects to high, medium, and low CD categories ($\kappa = .80$, $p < .001$). In a more recent study, Sass et al. (1984) report reliability coefficients for various categories of CD ranging between .84 and .90.

Validity Studies and Applications. 1. In recent years, there have been attempts to examine whether CD scores from the individual testing are related to family and spouse interaction data. Hermann and Jones (1976), for example, found a relation between severity of CD and the tendency to not acknowledge the communications of other family members during a family interaction task. On the other hand, Lieber (1977) failed to find a relationship between the level of CD and a measure of attentional focusing in a family interaction task. Lewis et al. (1981) reported a relationship between severity of CD and disturbances in family communication as well as parental role structure and affective expression. Doane et al. (1982) concluded from their results that when measured in different settings CD scores are not always correlated.

2. According to theory, parental CD should discriminate between various diagnostic groups. Over the years, the findings have generally confirmed this expectation. Wynne and Singer's most recent summary of their findings support the usefulness of CD in discriminating between schizophrenics, normals, and neurotics (Wynne, Singer, Bartko, & Toohey, 1977). Other studies also offer confirming evidence (Jones, 1977), although Hirsh and Leff (1975) failed to confirm Wynne and Singer's findings. Various sampling problems between the studies and issues involving the role of verbal output have been argued back and forth, but Liem (1980) suggests that, overall, results are supportive of parental CD as a valid discriminator of diagnostic groups.

3. Can the level of parental CD predict a psychiatric outcome for children not having any diagnosable condition at study onset?

The results of one longitudinal study suggest that severity of parental CD does predict the onset of schizophrenia or schizophrenic spectrum disorders in adolescents who, at study onset, were at high risk for future psychopathology (Goldstein, Rodnick, Jones, McPherson, & West, 1978). In addition, Doane, West, Goldstein, Rodnick, and Jones (1981) found that a combination of high affective style, (AS) that is, the negative emotional climate of family assessed from direct observations, was a better predictor of child outcome than the presence of high CD alone.

4. In a recent summary of research in this area, Goldstein (1985) reported preliminary results from the extended, 15-year follow-up of the above sample of adolescents at risk. In addition to the assessment of CD and AS, another measure, Expressed Emotion (EE), has been incorporated into their work. EE taps parental criticism expressed towards the index subject that was measured at study onset. Follow-up data indicate that all schizophrenia and schizophrenia spectrum disorder outcomes derive from families in which one or both parents was rated high on CD and in which there was high EE, and high AS (negative behavior) reflected in direct interaction with the teenager.

5. In a slightly different approach, Doane *et al.* (1982) assessed social competence of children ages 8 to 10 years, who had a parent hospitalized for diverse psychiatric conditions, and who were not symptomatic at the time of assessment. Based upon teacher ratings, parental reports, and peer ratings, high CD mothers had children who were low functioning in different settings.

III. Relationship Assessments: Questionnaires Regarding Marital Relationships

Within the family complex, the relationship that has received most attention by theorists, researchers, and clinicians has been the marital dyad. The primary questions asked about this dyad are concerned with what features characterize happy marriages and how such factors can be predicted. This extensive literature is the subject of a number of integrative reviews (Lewis & Spanier, 1979). Additionally, theoretical and empirical efforts have been directed toward understanding the link between marital interaction and both adult psychopathology (Hafner, 1986) and child psychopathology (Margolin, 1981b). More recently, the increased interest in marital therapy research has led to a concern for describing changes in marital quality across and beyond the delivery of treatment. For all of these questions, investigators have described the level of marital satisfaction or adjustment reported by spouses. Consequently, satisfaction has been the most frequently assessed dimension of marriage.

Appropriately, this section begins with reviews of four measures that assess marital satisfaction. The Marital Adjustment Test (Locke & Wallace, 1959) and the Dyadic Adjustment Scale (Spanier, 1976), described first, have probably been the most influential and frequently used instruments for assessing this variable. Subsequently, the Areas of Change Questionnaire (Weiss, Hops, & Patterson, 1973), which attempts to quantify a more behavioral perspective on marital satisfaction, and the Marital Satisfaction Inventory (Snyder, 1979), which offers a multidimensional perspective, are described. Questionnaires have also been developed to assess more specific aspects of the marital relationship. The remaining reviews in this section therefore cover several instruments designed to assess different facets of marriage including communication (Navran, 1967), sexual interaction (LoPiccolo & Steger, 1974), and the general strategies used for resolving conflicts (Straus, 1979). Additionally, the growing interest in cognitive theories and therapies has led to the development of a new scale for assessing potentially important dysfunctional beliefs that spouses may hold (Eidelson & Epstein, 1982).

A. *Marital Adjustment Test (MAT)*

1. *Background*

The study of marital adjustment or satisfaction has probably been the focus of family research longer than any other issue. According to Locke (Locke & Wallace, 1959), the first attempt at quantifying this construct was made by Hamilton (1929). Subsequently, the family sociologists, Terman (1938) and Locke (1951), developed their own questionnaires for this variable. In general, the early scales were lengthy and therefore required considerable time to complete. As a result, researchers began to investigate whether shorter questionnaires were able to assess this variable in a comparably reliable and valid manner. Because it has been used so frequently, the Marital Adjustment Test (MAT; Locke & Wallace, 1959) is an important representative of the many instruments that were developed to meet this need.

The construction of the MAT began with Locke and Wallace (1959) reviewing all previous marital adjustment scales. From these they selected 15 items "which (1) had the highest level of discrimination in the original studies, (2) did not duplicate other included items, and (3) would cover the important areas of marital adjustment" (p. 252).

2. Description of the Instrument

The MAT contains 15 items with variable response formats—6- and 7-point Likert-type scales, and multiple-choice answers. For scoring purposes, the original weighting scheme suggested by Locke and Wallace (1959), based on initial results comparing the responses of well-adjusted and maladjusted marital groups, has typically been used. Scores range from 2 to 158. The test can easily be completed in 10 minutes by a person with a ninth-grade reading level (Dentch, O'Farrell, & Cutter, 1980, p. 791).

3. Variables Assessed

Marital adjustment—defined as "accommodation of a husband and wife to each other at a given time" (Locke & Wallace, 1959, p. 251).

4. Psychometric Properties and Applications

Reliability. Split-half reliability was reported as .90 (Locke & Wallace, 1959).

Applications. The MAT has been a frequently used instrument across the broad range of studies where an index of marital satisfaction is desired. Since its publication, it has been used to discriminate distressed from nondistressed couples across an extremely wide range of studies. In their original article, Locke and Wallace (1959) reported that well-adjusted couples scored an average of 135.9 compared to 71.7 by maladjusted couples. Many subsequent reports have replicated these group differences. Among its many other uses the MAT has been used in studies of marital therapy (Jacobson, 1979) and in assessing the impact of various influences on marital adjustment such as the birth of a child (Waldron & Routh, 1981), development of problems in children (Emery & O'Leary, 1982), chronic pain (Kerns & Turk, 1984), and locus of control (Doherty, 1981).

As an effective measure with an extensive history, the MAT remains a viable choice for assessing marital adjustment/ satisfaction. However, because it was almost entirely incorporated into the dyadic adjustment scale (Spanier, 1976; see next review), its use is not as common as it once was.

B. Dyadic Adjustment Scale (DA)

1. Background

Continued interest in the assessment of marital adjustment/satisfaction has encouraged efforts to develop better measurement methods. The Dyadic Adjustment Scale (DA; Spanier, 1976) is the most recent version within this domain of instruments. It was developed, according to its author, using improved test development procedures. Additionally, the scale includes four subscales aimed at assessing what the author describes as four empirically determined components of dyadic adjustment: dyadic consensus, dyadic satisfaction, dyadic cohesion, and affectional expression. Finally, although it has primarily been used in marital research, its applicability extends to all cohabiting dyads as well.

As part of the test-development procedure, Spanier initially extracted 300 items from previously used marital adjustment scales that he could identify. Some items were eliminated based on judgments concerning their content validity and other items were added that covered new content areas the author believed had been omitted from previous scales. A preliminary, 200-item version was subsequently administered to one spouse from each of 218 married and 94 divorced couples. The subjects in the divorced sample were asked to report on their last month of married life. Items were then eliminated on the basis of low variance, high skewedness, or because they did not differentiate married from divorced couples. The remaining 40 items were then factor-analyzed and eight more items were deleted due to their lack of sufficient factor loadings. This process resulted in the present scale.

Ironically, although the original item pool was large, 11 of the 15 items contained in the MAT (Locke & Wallace, 1959; described in the previous review) were selected for inclusion in the DA scale. This outcome insured that the correlation between the two scales would be substantial. It also allowed researchers to change more easily to using the DA scale from the MAT because much of the information gathered on the MAT was still obtained.

2. Description of the Instrument

The DA scale is a 32-item questionnaire that provides an overall measure of dyadic adjustment. Additionally, each of the four subscales provides a more specific description of the major components of dyadic adjustment. Items are worded so as to be applicable to married as well as cohabiting couples. The response formats vary across the 32 items to include 5-, 6-, and 7-point Likert-type scales and two "yes–no" items. The range for the total scale is 0 to 151.

3. Variables Assessed

1. Marital adjustment—total scale score reflecting overall level of marital adjustment.
2. Dyadic consensus—for example, "Aims, goals, and things believed important," answered from "always agree" to "always disagree."
3. Dyadic satisfaction—for example, "How often do you and your partner quarrel?" answered from "all the time" to "never."

4. Dyadic cohesion—for example, "Calmly discuss something" answered from "never" to "more often (than once a day)."
5. Affectional expression—for example, "Demonstrations of affection" answered from "always agree" to "always disagree."

The latter four subscale names were chosen to best describe the four factors that emerged from the original factor analysis of the DA scale.

4. Psychometric Properties and Applications

Reliability. Item analysis suggests that the total scale is reliable. Spanier (1976) reported a coefficient alpha of $r = .96$, which he ($r = .91$; Spanier & Thompson, 1982) and others ($r = .96$; Sharpley & Cross, 1982) have replicated. Coefficient alpha's for the four subscales varied from $r = .73$ to $r = .94$ (Spanier, 1976).

Two attempts to replicate the original factor structure of the DA scale have been conducted. Spanier and Thompson (1982), found a good correspondence between the original and the replication samples, the latter composed of divorced or separated subjects who were asked to report on the quality of their marriage during the last few months they lived with their spouse. An attempt by a different group of investigators to replicate the factor structure of the DA scale was less successful. Although they found the total scale to be reliable, Sharpley and Cross (1982) identified only one underlying dimension rather than the four that had been previously reported. Although the small sample size (95 subjects for a 32-item scale) makes their results difficult to interpret, it seems most prudent to conclude that, at present, support exists for the use of the total scale score although use of the four subscales remains questionable.

Applications. Since its development, the DA scale has been frequently used in studies that have an interest in marital adjustment/satisfaction:

1. At a basic level this scale discriminates between samples

containing well-adjusted couples and distressed, separated, or divorced couples (Spanier, 1976).
2. As with other marital adjustment scales, this scale has been used in studies which evaluate theoretical questions regarding marriage. For example, it has been included in studies of marital satisfaction over the life span (Medling & McCarrey, 1981) and prediction of marital adjustment (Filsinger & Wilson, 1984).
3. The DA scale has been used to document changes that occur in marital adjustment over the course of marital treatment (Johnson & Greenberg, 1985).
4. The continuing issue of how to resolve the close relationship between marital conventionalization or social desirability and marital adjustment measures has also been addressed using the DA scale (Hansen, 1981).

C. *Areas of Change Questionnaire (ACQ)*

1. *Background*

From the perspective of social learning theory, naturalistic observation procedures involving systematic assessment of significant interactions among family members represent the most theoretically and methodologically compelling approach to assessment. At the same time, we acknowledge that such procedures are probably not suitable as a broad-based assessment strategy, given the considerable time and cost involved in collecting and coding naturalistic observations. Also, many family behaviors of great significance are of such an intimate nature that observation procedures would be inappropriate as a means of identifying and recording such events. In light of these limitations, various investigators have been stimulated to develop and refine self-report procedures that attempt to provide specific data about behaviors which characterize family relationships.

By far, the major thrust in this effort has been within the area of marital functioning (Jacob, 1976). In particular, Weiss and his colleagues have developed several self-report and quasi-observational instruments aimed at assessing various aspects of the marital relationship and providing behaviorally specific information regarding this relationship (Weiss & Wieder, 1982; Weiss et al., 1973). An important impetus for this work has been the need for developing assessment instruments which help clinicians identify relevant marital behaviors to target for change and help researchers in their efforts to conduct systematic evaluations of marital therapy. The ACQ is one of these instruments (Weiss et al., 1973).

Developed during the early 1970s, the ACQ is aimed at describing marital satisfaction in a more behaviorally precise form than standard marital satisfaction measures. Specifically, the instrument attempts to evaluate satisfaction in terms of the amount and direction of change that partners would like to see in their marriage. Each spouse is asked to indicate whether he or she wants the other spouse to change certain behaviors and, if so, in what direction and to what extent. As Weiss et al. (1973) reported "deviations from 'no change' indicate reported dissatisfaction and presumably reflect attempts at behavior change" (p. 313).

2. Description of the Instrument

The ACQ consists of 34 items selected to represent a range of potential conflict areas in marriages including issues of emotional expression, companionship, finances, sex, child management, recreation, and so on. Respondents are asked to rate items on a 7-point scale, ranging from "much less" (-3) to "no change" (0) to "much more" ($+3$), with regard to whether they want their partner to change the frequency with which he or she engages in these particular behaviors. Examples include: "I want my partner to help with housework," "I want my partner to express his or her emotions clearly," and "I want my partner to discipline children."

These 34 items are then repeated in the second part of the ACQ where respondents are asked to indicate, on the same -3 to $+3$ scale, how much change their partners would like to see in the respondents' own behavior. Examples include: "It would please my partner if I would have meals on time" and "It would please my partner if I would express my emotions clearly."

3. *Variables Assessed*

   1. Desire for change—degree to which a spouse desires change from his or her partner in regards to a range of relationship-relevant issues. This is calculated by taking the sum of the absolute values of all of the desire for change scores. A larger score, therefore, indicates a greater desire for change which is assumed to be related to a greater level of marital distress.
   2. Perceived desire for change—degree to which spouse believes his or her partner desires change in spouses' own behavior.

4. *Psychometric Properties and Applications*

Reliability. The internal consistency of the ACQ has been reported as .89 (Weiss & Margolin, 1977). A split half reliability of .83 ($p < .001$) has been reported by Margolin (1978). Finally, Stein, Girodo, and Dotzenroth (1982) reported test–retest reliability over a 5-week interval for six couples (n = 12) to be $r = .96$.

Validity and Applications. 1. Significant and strong relationships (r's varying from $-.42$ to $-.70$) between the ACQ and MAT or modified versions of the MAT have been reported (Margolin, Talovic, & Weinstein, 1983; Margolin & Wampold, 1981; Weiss et al. 1973) suggesting that the ACQ is related to the general dimension of marital satisfaction.

2. The ACQ has been successfully used to differentiate distressed from nondistressed couples by comparing the total "desire for change" score across such groups (Birchler & Webb, 1977; Margolin, 1981a; Margolin & Wampold, 1981; Margolin et al., 1983). In fact, almost all individual items discriminate between such groups as well (Margolin et al., 1983).

3. When included in marital therapy studies, the ACQ has effectively documented expected pretreatment to posttreatment changes (Baucom, 1982; Maroglin & Weiss, 1978; Weiss et al., 1973).

D. Marital Satisfaction Inventory (MSI)

1. Background

The Marital Satisfaction Inventory (MSI; Snyder, 1979; 1981) was developed to provide a psychometrically sound, multidimensional self-report measure of marital interaction. Although measures of marital satisfaction have a long, successful history, the MSI was designed to provide, in an integrated fashion, additional information concerning specific aspects of the marital relationship. For example, scales related to sexual satisfaction and satisfaction with child-rearing practices are included. In developing this instrument Snyder was strongly influenced by work in the area of personality assessment that led to the creation and validation of the Minnesota Multiphasic Personality Inventory (MMPI; Hathaway & McKinley, 1951). The MSI clearly reflects this influence both in its format and supplementary material.

Initial development of the MSI involved the construction of a 440-item pool of test items. Many of the items were original, but some were taken from previously used scales. The items were divided into 11 nonoverlapping scales and counterbalanced for scoring in the true and false directions. The 440-item scale was administered to 42 couples in the general population and 13 couples in marital therapy. Following subsequent item analysis, the final form was decided upon. Subsequently, it has been utilized in several validation studies.

2. Description of the Instrument

The Marital Satisfaction Inventory is a 280-item (239 items for couples without children) measure of marital satisfaction composed of 11 scales. The response format is true/false. Raw scores are converted to T-scores to facilitate the use of profiles for presenting the results and making clinical interpretations. Test completion takes approximately 30–45 minutes.

3. Variables Assessed

There are 11 subscales on the MSI. One scale assesses conventionality (CNV), which may influence the values of other scales; a second scale provides a global measure of distress (GDS); and nine special scales measure specific areas of marital interaction.

1. Conventionalism (CNV)—a 21-item scale that assesses whether subjects tend to describe their marriage in an excessively, socially desirable manner.
2. Global distress scale (GDS)—a 43-item measure of marital satisfaction.
3. Affective communication (AFC)—a 26-item scale that assesses satisfaction with the quality and quantity of affectional expression and understanding engaged in by a spouse.
4. Problem-solving communication (PSC)—38 items measuring a couples' ability to resolve disagreements.
5. Time together (TTO)—20 items that assess the informant's satisfaction with the couple's common interests and the time and activities they share together.
6. Disagreement about finances (FIN)—22 items measuring the importance of how financial matters are handled as a source of marital conflict.
7. Sexual dissatisfaction (SEX)—29 items that assess the quality of the sexual relationship.
8. Role orientation (ROR)—a 25-item scale that indicates whether the informant has a traditional versus nontraditional orientation toward marital and parental sex roles.
9. Family history of distress (FAM)—a 15-item scale that assesses the extent of problems in the informant's family of origin when he or she was a child.
10. Dissatisfaction with children (DSC)—22 items that measure the informant's own satisfaction with the parent-child relationship.
11. Conflict over childrearing (CCR)—19 items that assess the extent of marital conflict related to disagreements regarding childrearing practices.

4. Psychometric Properties and Applications

Internal consistency (coefficient alpha) values derived from combined samples of 650 individuals in the general population and 100 individuals in marital therapy range from .80 (DSC) to .97 (GDS) with a mean for all scales of .88. The test–retest reliability for all scales over a 6-week interval was a mean of .89 (Snyder, 1981).

Evidence for the construct validity of the MSI is being accumulated primarily through work of Snyder and his colleagues. MSI has been used to discriminate between distressed couples in marital therapy and couples from the general population. Snyder has also compared MSI scores with structured clinical ratings of couples entering therapy (Snyder, Wills, & Keiser, 1981). These results indicated that clinicians' ratings of couples' specific marital behaviors were most closely correlated with the MSI scales designed to describe that attribute. They have also described differences in MSI results in groups previously identified as having problems in specific areas such as abuse (Snyder, 1981) and sexual dysfunction (Berg & Snyder, 1981). As a cautionary note, factor analysis of the MSI suggests that the affective nature of the marital relationship, most explicitly seen in the GDS, AFC, PSC, and TTO scales, is the primary influence on MSI results. Considerably more work is therefore required before the value of the MSI (other than as a general measure of marital satisfaction) is convincingly demonstrated.

E. Primary Communication Inventory (PCI)

1. Background

The Primary Communication Inventory (Navran, 1967) is an adaptation of an instrument developed by Locke, Sabagh, and Thomes (1956) to measure communication in marriage. The commonly held belief that the quality of communication between spouses is related to their marital satisfaction led to the need for developing this instrument. Navran wanted to be able to test the hypothesis that happily married couples are those who have developed communication skills to deal effectively with the problems that occur in marriage. In contrast, he expected unhappy marriages to be characterized by different communication styles, specifically, those which impede problem solving and contribute to the subjective experience of anger and tension (Navran, 1967).

2. Description of the Instrument

The PCI is a 25-item instrument which yields a total score, a nonverbal score, and a verbal score. Respondents indicate how often each of the behaviors occur on a 5-point Likert-type scale which varies from *never* to *very frequently*. Examples of items include ("Do you and your spouse talk over things you disagree about or have difficulties over?" and "How often can you tell as much from the tone of voice of your spouse as from what he (she) actually says?" Nine items involve making a judgment about the spouse (e.g., "How often does your spouse sulk or pout?"). For scoring purposes, rather than summing the report of self and spouse behavior, these nine items are transposed from the spouse's questionnaire. The remaining 16 items are not transposed. An individual's total score is the sum of the 16 non-transposed items from his(her) own questionnaire responses (self-report) plus the nine items rated by his(her) spouse (spouse-report). Unlike most of the other questionnaires reviewed, both husband and wife, therefore, need to complete the PCI to obtain a total score.

3. Variables Assessed

1. Quality of marital communication
2. Nonverbal communication—7 items (e.g., "Does your spouse explain or express himself (herself) to you through a glance or gestures?").
3. Verbal communication—18 items (e.g., "Do you and your spouse talk about things in which you are both interested?").

4. Psychometric Properties and Applications

Reliability. Yelsma (1984) reported internal consistency reliabilities (coefficient alpha) on a sample of 96 individuals to be .85 for the 18 verbal items and .56 for the 7 nonverbal items. Ely, Guerney, and Stover (1973), in a treatment study, reported a test–retest reliability of $r = .86$ over an 8-week period for their waiting list control group. Although promising, further evidence for reliability needs to be reported for this instrument.

Validity and Applications. The PCI has been used to compare distressed and nondistressed couples. Navran, for example, reported that his happily married couples ($N = 48$) had a mean total score of 105.3 compared to a mean of 81.4 in his unhappy couples ($N = 48$). The verbal scores were 76.1 and 58.2, while the nonverbal scores were 29.1 and 23.2 respectively. As another way of testing the relationship between communication and satisfaction, Navran correlated the PCI with the Marital Relationship Inventory (Locke & Williamson, 1958), a measure of marital satisfaction, and found a strong relationship ($r = .82$).

Ely et al. (1973) used the PCI to assess changes in communication following their "conjugal therapy" program. First, they confirmed that their sample of distressed couples reported similar scores to Navran's distressed couples. Then they found that treatment led to an improvement in PCI scores, although their posttreatment scores were not as high as Navran's happy couples.

A more recent use of the PCI has been to investigate the congruence between self and spouse reports of their communication. Beach and Arias (1983) factor analyzed the PCI and found support for two factors which were primarily defined by who did the ratings rather than by whether the communication described by the item was verbal or nonverbal. When they compared the reports of distressed ($n = 45$) and nondistressed couples ($n = 51$) they found, surprisingly, that distressed couples were more congruent than nondistressed couples.

Yelsma (1984), in another report which used the PCI to determine spouses' agreement on the perception of their communication, found that nondistressed couples ($n = 23$) were in greater agreement than distressed couples ($n = 23$). These two studies suggest possible uses of the PCI but their conflicting results make drawing substantive conclusions problematic at the present time.

F. The Sexual Interaction Inventory (SII)

1. Background

Since the pioneering work of Masters and Johnson (1970), there has been a continuing development of treatment techniques for sexual dysfunctions. Unfortunately, there has not been a serious, parallel interest in creating reliable and valid assessment instruments to help the clinician accurately identify actual sexual functioning and sexual satisfaction as well as to evaluate treatment outcome. An important exception is the work of LoPiccolo and his colleagues in developing the Sexual Interaction Inventory (SII) as part of their clinical research program with sexual dysfunction (LoPiccolo & Steger, 1974; McGovern, Stewart, & LoPiccolo, 1975; Nowinski & LoPiccolo, 1979). Their goal was to provide an easily administered paper-and-pencil inventory which could be used as a diagnostic device as well as a treatment outcome measure for assessing heterosexual couples with sexual dysfunctions. To accomplish this, the authors decided to include explicit questions regarding the couples' engagement in and satisfaction with various sexual behaviors. The sexual behaviors they included were adapted from previous work by Bentler (1968), who used a Guttman scaling procedure to develop a graduated list of sexual behaviors.

2. Description of the Instrument

The SII presents subjects with a list of 17 items covering a broad range of sexual behavior varying from minimal involvement ("The male seeing the female when she is nude") to maximal involvement ("The male and female having intercourse with both of them having an orgasm"). For each behavior, the following six questions are assessed: (a) how frequently the subject participates in a given sexual behavior; (b) how regularly the subject wishes the sexual behavior to occur; (c) how pleasurable the subject perceives this activity to be; (d) how pleasurable the subject thinks his or her partner perceives this activity to be; (e) how pleasurable the subject would like this activity to be; and (f) how pleasurable the subject would like this activity to be for his or her partner. Responses are rated using a 6-point Likert-type scale. Eleven scales are then derived for each couple; five reflecting attributes of the husband, five reflecting attributes of the wife, and one being an integration of eight of the ten scales.

3. Variables Assessed

The SII assesses the following parameters of the sexual func-

DETAILED REVIEW OF METHODS 45

tioning and sexual satisfaction of heterosexual couples:

1,2. Satisfaction with frequency—indicates the level of satisfaction with the range and/or frequency of sexual behaviors engaged in for husbands and wives, respectively.
3,4. Self-acceptance—reflects the "real self-ideal self" congruence (LoPiccolo & Steger, 1974) for husbands and wives, respectively.
5,6. Pleasure means—reflects the overall pleasure the husband and wife are deriving from their sexual activity.
7,8. Perceptual accuracy—measures the subject's knowledge concerning what gives his or her spouse sexual pleasure.
9,10. Mate acceptance—indicates the level of "real partner-ideal partner" congruence (LoPiccolo & Steger, 1974).
11. Total disagreement—a summary scale which reflects the couple's overall dissatisfaction in their sexual relationship.

4. Psychometric Properties and Applications

Reliability. A sample of fifteen couples obtained through advertising were administered the SII on two occasions, separated by a 2-week interval. Pearson product-moment correlations were computed for each of the 11 SII scale scores derived from this test–retest sample resulting in reliability values ranging from $r = .67$ to $r = .90$ for the 11 scales. These correlations were all significant at the 0.05 level or better.

Cronbach's alpha coefficient (Cronbach, 1951) was computed on the SII scores gathered from a sample of 78 couples obtained by mailing solicitation letters to 300 couples listed in official Eugene, Oregon, city records as having been married at least 2 but not more than 6 years. The reliability values, ranging from .85 to .93, were all significant at the .005 level or better.

Applications. 1. The SII has been effective at discriminating sexually satisfied couples from couples seeking treatment for sexual problems (LoPiccolo & Steger, 1974).

2. As a treatment outcome measure the SII is sensitive to

gains made in therapy as well as to changes reported during follow-up periods (De Amicis, Goldberg, LoPiccolo, Friedman, & Davies, 1985; McGovern *et al.*, 1975; Morokoff & LoPiccolo, 1986). Since its development, the SSI has been the primary questionnaire for assessing the general level of sexual functioning in this area of research.

G. Relationship Belief Inventory (RBI)

1. Background

The Relationship Belief Inventory (RBI) was designed by Epstein (Eidelson & Epstein, 1982; Epstein & Eidelson, 1981) to systematically evaluate five dysfunctional beliefs that might negatively affect marital relationships. It evolved out of the increasing interest in cognitive factors that may influence the development or maintenance of stressful relationships (Drydon, 1981; Epstein, 1982). The underlying premise in this literature is that holding certain relationship beliefs may both impair marital satisfaction and reduce the possibility of achieving improvement in this domain during treatment.

As a first step in the development of the RBI, 20 marital therapists were asked to list those beliefs that seemed to cause the most serious difficulties for their clients. A pool of 128 items was then developed to measure five of the most important dysfunctional beliefs. This inventory was given to a sample of 47 couples beginning therapy. Twelve items were then selected to represent each of the five belief scales on the basis of individual item variances, item-total correlations, and Epstein's judgment of clarity of meaning. These 12-item scales were then administered to a second sample of 100 couples (48 clinical and 52 nonclinical) and were subsequently refined to eight items each on the basis of item-total correlations.

2. Description of the Instrument

The RBI includes five, eight-item scales. Spouses respond to each item using a 6-point Likert type scale which ranges from "I strongly believe that this statement is true" to "I strongly believe that this statement is false." For each scale, approximately one half of the items are positively keyed and one half are negatively keyed. Total scores for each scale are calculated by summing all item scores after reversing the negatively-keyed items.

3. Variables Assessed

The five unrealistic beliefs about intimate relationships measured by the RBI are the following:

1. Disagreement is destructive (D)—assesses the extent to which spouses believe that having any disagreements indicates that they have major problems and that their relationship is seriously threatened. Previous investigators have suggested that individuals who possess this belief try to avoid direct communication when attempting to solve their relationship problems (Raush, Barry, Hertel, & Swain, 1974; Satir, 1967).
2. Mindreading is expected (M)—measures the degree to which spouses believe that if their partner cares for and understands them, he or she should know how they feel and think without being told.
3. Partners cannot change (C)—assesses the extent to which spouses believe that neither their partner nor the quality of their relationship can be changed.
4. Sexual perfectionism (S)—measures the belief that one must be a perfect sexual partner.
5. The sexes are different (MF)—assesses the belief that men and women feel, think and act differently and that they have very different relationship needs.

4. Psychometric Properties and Applications

Reliability. Cronbach's alpha coefficients were computed on the five scales with results ranging from 0.72 to 0.81.

Validity and Applications. Validation of the RBI was performed on a sample of 52 nonclinical (MAT > 100) couples and 48 distressed couples (beginning treatment) who completed the Marital Adjustment Test (MAT, Locke & Wallace, 1959) and the Irrational Belief Test (IBT; Jones, 1968) which measures irrational beliefs about the self. The clinical couples also completed a therapy goals and expectations questionnaire (Epstein & Eidelson, 1981).

Convergent validity was determined by examining the correlations between the RBI and the IBT. The results demonstrated that all of the RBI scales except the MF scale were significantly positively correlated with the IBT, although the absolute magnitude of the relationships were not very strong. The correlations of the D, M, C, and S scales of the RBI with the IBT were .31, .21, .14, and .28, respectively ($N = 200$, $p < 0.05$).

Construct validity was assessed by comparing the RBI scales and the MAT, and within the clinical sample by comparing the RBI to subjects' attitudes about therapy. Results indicated that for the combined sample of clinical and nonclinical couples, all five RBI scales were significantly and negatively correlated with MAT scores. The correlations ranged from −.57 for the D scale to a low of −.18 for the S scale. When similar correlations were calculated separately for each group, all except the C scale in the nonclinical group remained significantly negatively correlated to the MAT. The major difference between the two groups occurred in the correlation between the C scale and the MAT, which was statistically significant ($r = -.53$) for the clinical group but was nonsignificant ($r = .00$) for the nonclinical group. The observed relationship between the MAT and the RBI scales supports the hypothesis that the assessed beliefs are associated with marital dissatisfaction. Additionally, further support for this construct was found in the clinical sample where higher scores on the D, M, and C scales were related to decreasing levels of belief regarding whether therapy was desirable, whether therapy would be effective, and whether it should be conducted in a conjoint manner.

Although more extensive psychometric evaluations of this instrument are needed, it is a promising instrument for assessing potentially important variables in an area of increasing interest.

H. Conflict Tactic Scales (CT)

1. Background

Describing the process by which family members attempt to resolve interpersonal differences has assumed an increasingly important position in marital and family research. Observations of actual problem-solving behavior have been conducted, for example, with this purpose in mind (Jacob, Ritchey, Cvitkovic, & Blane, 1981). Although offering important information concerning this question, a need exists for additional forms of data collection so that larger samples of couples or families can be studied and because certain types of family behavior are unlikely to be displayed in laboratory settings. The use of violence to solve family problems is a particular strategy for which questionnaires are a better suited assessment strategy than observational methods. Concurrently, there has been a growing interest in the epidemiology of family violence.

The Conflict Tactic (CT) scales were developed by Straus (1979) to allow for the assessment of a broad sample of family members regarding the diverse strategies they use to resolve conflicts in their families. He incorporated into his scales three basic approaches family members could take in their attempts to resolve their conflicts including the use of reasoning, verbal aggression, and violence or physical aggression. These scales have subsequently been used in studies attempting to further our understanding of the extent to which certain tactics, and in particular violent tactics, are used and what influences the choice of these particular approaches.

2. Description of the Instrument

Straus developed two versions of the CT scales: Form A, containing 14 items, which was designed to be completed as a paper-and-pencil test, and Form N, containing 19 items, which was designed to be administered in an interview format. They both contain a graduated series of items which describe the types of actions a person might take in attempting to resolve a conflict.

They begin with the least coercive strategies, such as "I tried to discuss the issue relatively calmly" and become increasingly more aggressive toward the end where behaviors such as "I hit (or tried to hit) him or her with something hard" occur. Additionally, Form N includes several more items which describe even more extreme behaviors including "used a knife or gun." Subjects respond to each item by indicating, on a scale ranging from "never" to "more than once a month" on Form A or "never" to "more than 20 times" on Form N, how frequently a particular behavior was engaged in during the past year. The individual first answers questions regarding his or her own behavior toward a particular family member and then is asked to answer the same questions with regard to the same family member's behavior toward him or her. The CT scales can be completed by a subject with regard to any family member so that marital, parent–child and sibling–sibling relationships can be assessed.

3. Variables Assessed

1. Reasoning—the use of rational discussion, argument, and reasoning to resolve conflicts.
2. Verbal aggression—the use of verbal and nonverbal acts which symbolically hurt the other, or the use of threats to hurt the other for the purpose of resolving conflicts.
3. Violence—the use of physical force against the other to resolve conflicts.

4. Psychometric Properties and Applications

Reliability. In support of the reliability of Form A, Straus reported that the mean correlations of items to their respective scales for husbands and wives reports on the CT ranged from .70 to .88. On Form N, he reported coefficient alpha's for the three subscales across all family dyads ranged from .50 to .88. The reasoning scale, which only has three items in this form, accounted for almost all of the low alpha coefficients.

Applications. 1. Factor analysis of both Form A and Form N reveal three factors corresponding to the expected dimensions of reasoning, verbal aggression and violence. In addition, a fourth factor, corresponding to the extreme violence items, was found for Form N (Straus, 1979).

2. The CTS has been used in studies which have employed national samples in attempts to document the extent to which violence is used by American families as a conflict resolution strategy (Straus, Gelles, & Steinmetz, 1980). Data from these studies has subsequently been used to clarify etiological factors in family violence. For example, Kalmuss (1984) has attempted to identify factors that affect the development of marital aggression across generations. Her analysis suggested that observing aggression between one's own parents is more strongly related to the subsequent development of violent marriages than is being the recipient of violent behavior as a child. Other investigators have applied the CTS in studies of family styles in particular subcultures. Brutz and Ingoldsby (1984), for example, have compared the rates of violence in Quaker families to the national rates.

I. Other Marital Scales

The search for better methods of assessing marital satisfaction and related concepts continues at a vigorous pace with each new instrument attempting to add a novel assessment procedure into this already saturated area. Roach, Frazier, and Bowden (1981), for example, developed the Marital Satisfaction Scale, for assessing subjects' perception of their marriage—a procedure which is characterized by the use of a standard response format for all items (6-point Likert scale), good reliability, and the inclusion of items that have the possibility of changing across treatment for marital problems.

Several other measures have potential strength and interest in light of the clear explication of a theoretical base on which the instrument was developed. Sabatelli (1984), for example, developed the Marital Comparison Level Index (MCLI) based on the social exchange theories of Thibaut and Kelley (Kelley & Thibaut, 1978; Thibaut & Kelley, 1959). Rather than have spouses rate their level of satisfaction with various aspects of their marital relationship, these authors use a response format that asks spouses to compare what they perceive they have with what they expect to have in their relationship. In this way, a more idiosyncratic description of marital satisfaction is derived which emphasizes the issues that spouses themselves perceive to be important.

Another scale influenced by exchange theory is the Marital Alternatives Scale (MA; Udry, 1981). Stimulated by the theories of Levinger (1965, 1979) and Farber (1964) the MA scale, rather than assessing satisfaction, assesses subjects' perceptions regarding how they would be affected by not having their spouse and how probable it is that a new spouse of equal or better quality could be found. By focusing on the subject's perceived alternatives, Udry suggests that she is able to measure an important construct related to marital stability but separate from marital satisfaction.

Finally, scales have been developed for documenting the extent to which a spouse has considered or acted on a desire to obtain a divorce (O'Farrell, Harrison, Schulmeister, & Cutter, 1981; Weiss & Cerreto, 1980). This is another side of the marital "satisfaction" issue, one that may have practical significance for prediction of marital dissolution and may offer another way of describing samples and assessing the severity of marital problems.

IV. Relationship Assessments: Questionnaires Regarding Parent–Child Relationships

Although the parent–child dyad has been considered critical in understanding the family's role in child psychopathology, "recommendable" assessment procedures focused on parent–child relationships are far from plentiful. Simply put, most instruments found within this domain are characterized by weak psychometric underpinnings and/or limited use (Olson, 1976; Straus & Brown, 1978). As such, the selection of procedures for review was as often based on their promise and relevance as on their established status as a reliable and valid assessment technique. Notwithstanding the particular importance of this subgroup of measures, we were simply not comfortable in presenting additional instruments that we could not recommend with much enthusiasm.

Included among the four instruments selected for detailed review is Lorna Benjamin's (1974) Structural Analysis of Social Behavior (SASB) as applied to the parent–child relationship; a current and useful revision of Schaeffer's Child Report of Parent Behavior Inventory (Margolies & Weintraub, 1977); and two relatively new instruments for assessing parent–child communication (Barnes & Olson, 1982) and parent–child satisfaction in regard to specific areas of concern (Jacob & Seilhamer, 1985). These four instruments represent considerable diversity regarding conceptual foundations, assessment targets, and usefulness in studies of etiology, course, and treatment.

A. Structural Analysis of Social Behavior (SASB)

1. Background

The Structural Analysis of Social Behavior (SASB) is based on a theory of interpersonal behavior rooted in several interpersonal circle or circumplex models that were first described in the late-1950s (Leary, 1957; Schaefer, 1959). At the core of such models are two perpendicular dimensions and the assumption that personality and interpersonal descriptions must incorporate the nature and degree of deviation on both dimensions. In Leary's model, "dominate and submit" define poles of the vertical axis, and "love and hate" are opposite points on the horizontal axis. In this framework, boast was placed on the hate side of dominate and teach appeared on the love side of dominate.

The full version of the SASB model consists of three diamond-shaped surfaces, each corresponding to a distinct focus: (a) *focus on other* reflects an action directed toward another person and is deemed parent-like, (b) *focus on self* involves a reaction to the other person and is deemed childlike, and (c) *intrapsychic* reflects introjected experiences from others turned inward towards the self.

For all three foci (surfaces), there are two central dimensions. Affiliation is on the horizontal axis and ranges from friendly to hostile, whereas interdependence is on the vertical axis and extends from domination to emanicipation. Each surface has four points representing extremes on these two dimensions. All the points in between the four poles are comprised of combinations of varying degrees of affiliation and dominance. A numerical system allows for representation of each point by a three-digit number. SASB theory holds that the three dimensions of focus, affiliation and dominance are all that are sufficient to characterize a range of interpersonal and intrapsychic events. The various combinations of the above three dimensions yield 108 different points since there are 36 points on each of these surfaces.

2. *Variables Assessed*

1. Weighted affiliation score—is the degree to which a set of ratings is centered on the affiliation axis. A summary score is derived by multiplying each item score by a weight that reflects its closeness to the affiliation pole, and then summing these products.
2. Weighted interdependence score—the degree to which a set of ratings is centered on the interdependence axis. This summary is derived by multiplying each score by a weight that reflects its closeness to the interdependence pole and then summing these products.
3. Series A ratings—questionnaire items that consist of subject ratings of significant other on the SASB grid. These ratings are equivalent to the grid termed "focus on the other."
4. Series B ratings—questionnaire items that consist of subject ratings of himself or herself in relation to another person, and they are equivalent to the SASB grid termed "focus on self."
5. Series C ratings—questionnaire items that allow raters to score themselves on the SASB, and they are equivalent to the grid termed "intrapsychic."

3. *Description of Instrument*

Ratings of self and significant others are possible using the SASB. Questionnaire items are available for each of the 108 points in the full scale version of the SASB. A set of questionnaires,

DETAILED REVIEW OF METHODS 55

called the Intrex Questionnaires, allows the respondent to describe a particular relationship, such as a child describing his/her parents. For example, the questionnaire item describing the grid point *Dominate* reads:

> My ———— is the boss of our relationship, always "on top," in control of, in charge of how we use the available time, space, and supplies. He/she insists, I comply with him/her quickly and quietly "just because he/she said so.

Items are randomly ordered and are rated on a 0–100 scale, with 10-point intervals marked and anchor points labeled Not At All = 0, Moderately = 50, Perfectly = 100. Series A ratings consist of subject ratings of significant others, such as parents' ratings of their children. Series B ratings reword the items so that the individual rates himself or herself in relation to the other person. Series C allows raters to score themselves "in general terms" on each of the 108 items, such as the item for "I am my own master" reads: "I am responsible for, in control of, what happens to me. I plan ahead, look back, set my bearings and set sail. I am captain of my ship, the master of my life." In effect, Series A, B, and C ratings are equivalent to the three surfaces of the SASB—other, self, and intrapsychic.

A "short-form" of the questionnaire is available in which each point is represented by a brief phrase. In the short-form series, ratings are made on a 5-point scale labeled: 0–25–50–75–100. The short-form can be completed in less than 1 hour; the longer form takes considerably more time.

There is a cluster version of the model which consists of eight clusters on each of the three surfaces. Each cluster consists of 4–5 points from the full model.

A *map* is generated by tabulating all items that receive sums above the median score. These items, their scores, and brief descriptions are laid out along the diamond shaped grid. This allows for a quick visual profile or map of a respondent's critical ratings. "The degree to which a given map is centered on the affiliation axis is summarized by the *weighted affiliation score* for each of the surfaces mapped" (Benjamin, 1977, p. 396). Each item score is multiplied by a weight that reflects its closeness to this affiliation pole, and then these products are summed. The same is done for the autonomy–dominance pole. The result is an "affiliation–autonomy vector" that summarizes a set of ratings' relative position on the two major dimensions of the SASB. For example, a mother might rate her son's hostile behavior towards her as −124.0. The −124 indicates ratings on the affiliation axis near the "attack" pole. The 0 suggests no clear direction on the autonomy axis.

Both real–ideal and self–other discrepancy ratings can be generated. For example, a mother and daughter questionnaire data could yield information on how daughter sees herself in relation to mother and how mother sees daughter in relation to herself. Daughter might rate herself as primarily "friendly" towards mother, while mother rates daughter as primarily "autonomous" in relation to mother.

Benjamin discusses questionnaire data for a subject as young as age 15. College students have also been used as raters. Because of the length and sophistication of the questionnaire items, it is unlikely, in our opinion, that children below the age of 10 to 12 could complete the questionnaires. Targets of the questionnaires typically include ratings of parents by children and vice versa and include both normal and disturbed families.

4. Psychometric Properties and Applications

Reliability. Autocorrelations were computed to check on the degree of relationship between SASB ratings of items in close proximity. Correlations are, as expected, higher for adjacent items than for items two steps apart. Computing correlations for items at successive steps apart typically yields an inverted normal curve. According to Benjamin (1974), the correlation between the derived autocorrelation curves and an inverted normal curve

> can be regarded as a coefficient of internal consistency, since it reflects the degree to which raters give similar ratings to items sampling chart points hypothesized to be adjacent; the degree to which they gave opposite ratings to items sampling chart points hypothesized to be adjacent; the degree to which they gave opposite ratings to items sampling points hypothesized to be opposite; and the degree to which they showed no relations among items hypothesized to sample orthogonal points. (p. 403)

Internal consistency for the long and short form is exceptionally high ($r = .90$; Benjamin, 1974). Test–retest reliability is also high in normal samples ($r = .87$), and varies meaningfully in less stable psychiatric populations.

Validity and Applications. 1. Factor analysis of questionnaire ratings have consistently yielded four factors that correspond to the four "poles" of attack versus tender embrace and emancipate versus dominate. In one sample of 110 persons who rated their recall of their mothers' behavior when the raters were between 5 and 10 years old, the four derived factors accounted for 64% of the variance (Benjamin, 1977). These same four factors almost always emerged in the different samples studied. The only exception is the factor analysis of Series C, items that require raters to view themselves in general terms. These analyses have not yielded clearly identifiable factors relating to the underlying dimensions of affiliation and interdependence.

2. More recently, the author reports that SASB ratings can clearly discriminate between the ratings of different diagnostic groups, such as borderlines versus major affective disorders. Furthermore, SASB ratings are reported to be better predictors of DSM-III diagnoses than MMPI and SCL-90 scores (Benjamin, 1985).

3. The SASB has been used with normal families and with families in psychiatric treatment. With the SASB, family relationships can be "mapped our" at the beginning, middle, and end of treatment. Benjamin uses SASB ratings to show family members how their ratings of each other replicate earlier patterns in the family. She uses the grid "maps" to plot therapeutic interventions designed to correct an excessive orientation on one of the SASB dimensions.

4. Finally, SASB ratings are reported to be useful with clinical groups who frequently demonstrate family pathologies, such as eating disorders (Humphrey, 1986; Humphrey, Apple, & Kirschenbaum, 1985).

B. Child Report of Parental Behavior Inventory (CRPBI)

1. Background

Inventories designed to measure children's perceptions of parental behavior include the Cornell Parent Behavior Inventory (CPBI) developed in 1962 by Devereux and Bronfenbrenner

(Seigelman, 1965); the Parent Perception Inventory (PPI) developed recently by Hazzard, Christensen, and Margolin (1983); and the Child Report of Parental Behavior Inventory (CRPBI) developed by Schaefer (1959, 1965a,b). Each of these instruments taps similar constructs and components of parent behavior. However, the CRPBI, developed by Schaefer, is the most frequently cited and used by researchers and is the focus of this review.

Schaefer developed the CRPBI from two sources: (a) the developmental literature that indicated that both the quality of the parent–child relationship and the total pattern of a child's experience (rather than specific infant-care practices) were important components in the evolving personality of the child, and (b) an empirical evaluation of previous studies of parental behaviors. Initial development of the instrument focused on using a circumplex model by which data describing molar social and emotional interactions between mother and child were ordered into two major dimensions of maternal behavior—love versus hostility and autonomy versus control (Schaefer, 1959, 1961, 1965a). Subsequent studies (Margolies & Weintraub, 1977; Renson, Schaefer, & Levy, 1968; Schaefer, 1965b; Teleki, Powell, & Dodder, 1982) revealed three orthogonal dimensions—acceptance versus rejection, psychological autonomy versus psychological control, and firm control versus lax control.

The CRPBI has been a flexible instrument in the hands of the researcher. Various investigators have revised the original 260-item instrument into shorter versions that retain the original conceptual foundation as well as many of its scales and items. Margolies and Weintraub (1977) have published results of the most recent, shortest version of the CRPBI, here described in some detail.

2. *Variables Assessed*

   1. Acceptance versus rejection—assesses the degree to which the child perceives positive involvement versus hostile detachment in his or her parents.
   2. Psychological autonomy versus psychological control—describes the degree to which the child perceives his or her parents covert use of control through guilt, intrusiveness, and parental direction.

3. Firm control versus lax control—describes the degree to which the parents make rules and enforce them.

3. Description of the Instrument

Margolies and Weintraub's 56-item CRPBI consists of six scales measuring parental behaviors. The child indicates whether his or her parent is "like," "somewhat like," or "not like" each of the items described. He or she completes separate, but identical, forms for the mother and the father. The six scales in the 56-item revision are as follows:

1. Acceptance
2. Child-centeredness
3. Nonenforcement
4. Instilling persistent anxiety
5. Controlling through guilt
6. Lax discipline

Items on the original 260-item instrument were generated from a factor analysis of psychologists' ratings of parental behaviors (Schaefer, 1965a). Approximately 520 items were written from which the final 260 items were chosen, based on psychologists' ratings of clarity of description, relevance, applicability to both father and mother, and high predicted item variance. The 56-item instrument, a revision of the original 260-item form, has been found to closely approximate the accuracy of the original instrument (Margolies & Weintraub, 1977). Each item describes relevant, specific, and observable parental behaviors.

4. Psychometric Properties and Applications

Reliability. For the three-factor score, Margolies and Weintraub (1977) report test-retest reliabilities on the 56 item CRPBI as ranging from .66 to .93 at 1-week and 5-week intervals. These correlations were based upon data from 120 children, from 9 to 11 years of age. Although Margolies and Weintraub (1977) do not report on the internal consistency of the 56 item instrument, Schaefer (1965a) reports internal consistency (KR-20) of the original 26 scales ranged from .60 to .90 (median = .76).

Factor analysis of the 56-item version found that Factors I and II (acceptance versus rejection and psychological autonomy versus psychological control) held up very well. Factor III (lax control versus firm control) was less stable than the other two factors (Margolies & Weintraub, 1977). No norms have been published for any version of the instrument.

Validity and Applications. 1. The 56-item version has been used in a study of children from single-parent families and children living in intact families (Teleki *et al.*, 1982). Three factors emerged for children's reports of married mothers, married fathers, and divorced fathers. However, only two factors emerged for children's reports of divorced mothers.

2. A study by Droppleman and Schaefer (1963), using the original 260-item instrument, found that normal boys and girls reported mothers as more nurturant and indirectly controlling than fathers.

3. Further evidence of the discriminative validity of the original 260-item instrument was reported by Schaefer (1965a). Responses to parental behavior items discriminated normal from delinquent boys. In addition, each group of boys described significantly different patterns of maternal and paternal behavior.

4. The Parent Perception Inventory (PPI), an instrument derived from Schaefer's CRPBI and Bronfenbrenner's Parental Behavior Questionnaire, is composed of four subscales: the child's perception of positive maternal behavior, negative maternal behavior, positive paternal behavior, and negative paternal behavior (Hazzard, *et al.*, 1983). Tests of the instruments convergent validity indicated expected and significant correlations between PPI scores, child's self-concept, and parents' reports of the child's conduct disorder. Evidence for the instrument's discriminant and construct validity are also described by Hazzard *et al.* (1983).

C. *Parent–Adolescent Communication Scale (PAC)*

1. *Background*

The Parent–Adolescent Communication (PAC) Scale, developed by Barnes and Olson (1982), assesses adolescents and their parents regarding their perceptions and experiences of communicating with each other. Specifically, the questionnaire measures both positive and negative aspects of communication as well as the content and process of the parent–child interactions.

Communication is one of the most crucial components of interpersonal relationships, and is a central construct in both the family development framework and the systems theory perspective. According to Olson, evidence supporting the importance of communication to family relationships comes from the writings of marriage and family therapists, particularly those who emphasize communication skills training in their efforts to improve family life. Within the context of the family, communication appears to be particularly important for the adolescent and his or her parents. During this turbulent period, parent–child relationship is subjected to challenge, and is changing, and effective parent-child communications are essential to the successful negotiation of these changing developmental needs.

Of particular relevance to the PAC Scale, communication is an important component in the theoretical model of marital and family systems developed by Olson *et al.* (1980). Their circumplex model, which focuses on the dimensions of family cohesion and family adaptability, hypothesizes that effective communication facilitates movement of families on the other two dimensions (cohesion and adaptation) of the model. Further, ineffective communication may impede movement toward balanced levels of adaptability and cohesion.

The PAC Scale, in attempting to assess the views that parents and adolescents have about communicating with each other, focuses on the freedom to exchange ideas, intergenerational information and concerns, trust between each other, and the positive or negative emotional tone of the interaction.

2. Variables Assessed

1. Open family communication—assesses the freedom with which parent and adolescent child exchange information and the understanding and satisfaction derived from their exchanges.
2. Problems in family communication—assesses constraints

on exchanging information, such as selectively choosing what will be communicated.

3. Description of the Instrument

The PAC Scale, consisting of 20 items, is easily administered to adolescents (12 years of age and older) and their parents. The response format ranges from "strongly disagree" to "strongly agree" on a 5-point Likert-type scale. The separate forms for adolescent, mother, and father are intended to be answered by all three members of the family. A total score is obtained by simply summing all the items, although care must be taken to reverse the point value of the 10 items on the problems in family communication subscale.

There are two subscales, each of which taps both content and process issues:

Open family communication—This subscale, consisting of 10 items, assesses positive aspects of parent–adolescent communication. As noted by Olson,

> the focus is on the freedom and free flowing exchange of information, both factual and emotional as well as on the sense of lack of constraint and degree of understanding and satisfaction experienced in their interactions. (p. 37)

Example: When I ask questions, I get honest answers from my mother/father.

Problems in family communication—This subscale, also consisting of 10 items, focuses on "the negative aspects of communication, hesitancy to share, negative styles of interaction, and selectivity and caution in what is shared" (p. 37). Example: When talking with my (mother/father) I have a tendency to say things that would better be left unsaid.

Development of the PAC Scale occurred in two phases. First, the literature relevant to parent–adolescent communication was reviewed and a 35-item pool of statements was generated. These items were piloted on 433 normal high school and college adolescents (16 to 20 years of age). Three factors emerged from data analyses: open family communication, problems in family communication, and selective family communication. On the basis of this factor analysis, the scale was reduced to two subscales, each consisting of 10 items—open family communication and problems in family communication (formerly Factors II and III).

4. Psychometric Properties and Applications

Reliability. Norms are available from families participating in a large national survey ($N = 998$ adults, 417 adolescents). Internal consistency estimates (Cronbach's alpha) were .87 (open family communication), .78 (problems in family communication), and .88 (total scale). Test–retest reliabilities (4- to 5-week interval) ranged from .60 to .78 (Olson et al., 1982).

Validity and Applications. The PAC Scale was used in a study of the relationship between parent–adolescent communication and the circumplex model (Barnes & Olson, 1985). Results indicated that while parents' responses supported the main hypothesis that balanced families have higher communication scores reflecting more open and problem-free communication, adolescents' responses contradicted this hypothesis. Barnes and Olson (1985) themselves note: "A family level analysis indicated a more linear relationship between communication and family cohesion and adaptation" (p. 445) than is predicted by the Circumplex Model.

D. Parent–Child Areas of Change Questionnaire (PC–ACQ)

1. Background

Analogous to the marital ACQ developed by Weiss (Weiss, et al., 1973) and his colleagues in the early 1970s (described on page 36), the Parent–Child Areas of Change Questionnaire (PC-ACQ) was developed for the purpose of evaluating parent–child relationships and specifying problem areas in them (Jacob & Seilhamer, 1985). Like the marital form, the PC–ACQ has potential application in various clinical-research endeavors. Of particular note, the PC–ACQ provides a systematic method for the collection of normative data concerning parent–adolescent behavioral exchanges. Although it generally has been assumed that some degree of conflict is inherent in relationships between parents and independence-seeking adolescents, there is little empirical data regarding how such global concepts as "conflict" or "satisfaction/dissatisfaction" are behaviorally expressed in these relationships. The PC–ACQ can provide detailed information about parent–child problem areas and about the congruence in perceptions of these relationships. Additionally, the PC–ACQ can be used as a criterion variable for selection and classification of distressed and nondistressed families. It can also provide convergent validity for other assessment measures. In clinical treatment studies, the PC–ACQ can provide a quantitative measure of distress and can identify specific conflict areas to be targeted for intervention. Finally, the instrument can be a catalyst for discussion of family-relevant problem areas that are recorded and subsequently assessed through detailed coding systems.

2. Description of the Instrument

In writing items for the PC–ACQ, the authors tried to tap domains in the marital ACQ that are also relevant to parent–child relationships (e.g., household management, affectional, companionship areas). Also, items were generated that were assumed to be behavioral indicators of parent–adolescent conflict, namely, items that reflect such issues as autonomy and independence. (A companion form for the ACQ asks each spouse to predict the extent to which he or she believes that his or her partner desires change in the respondent's behavior. Such an alternate form was not developed for the PC-ACQ.)

The final PC-ACQ consists of a 34-item parent form on which the mother or father reports on the child and a 32-item form on which a child reports on the parent. Items on the child form are geared to the preadolescent to adolescent child and are written so that they can be understood by individuals with a fifth grade reading level. As with the ACQ, respondents are asked to rate items on a 7-point scale ranging from "much less" (-3) to "no change" (0) to "much more" ($+3$). Examples: "I want my child to keep his/her room clean and neat." "I want my child to spend time at home with the family." "I want my father/mother to help me with my homework." "I want my father/mother to let me dress the way I like."

3. *Variables Assessed*

- Desire for change—degree to which parent (child) desires change from his or her child (parent) in regards to a range of relationship-relevant issues.

4. *Psychometric Properties and Applications*

The PC–ACQ was initially designed to gather information on areas of parent–child conflict in families participating in a larger study of family interaction (Jacob, 1987). Similar to Jacobson's (1984) use of the marital ACQ, the PC–ACQ was used to generate discussions among family dyads (mother–child, father–child) and the family triad (mother–father–child) in a laboratory setting.

Three groups of families participated in the study, all of which had been classified on the basis of the father's psychiatric status. In total, 130 intact families were included—a total consisting of families in which the father had been identified as alcoholic ($N = 43$), depressed ($N = 43$), or normal control ($N = 44$). Participating children were 10 to 17 years of age. Evaluation of PC–ACQ responses for these 130 families provided the instrument's preliminary reliability and validity data (Jacob & Seilhamer, 1985).

Reliability. As a measure of internal consistency, Cronbach's Alpha (Cronbach, 1951) was computed for the parent version and the child version of the PC–ACQ and for each of the four types of dyadic reports; that is, mother → child, child → mother, father → child, and child → father. For these four forms, alphas were 0.91, 0.93, 0.93, and 0.94, respectively.

Validity and Applications. 1. A total "desire for change" score (DC) was computed by summing the absolute values of responses on the PC–ACQ for each of the four dyads and then comparing DC scores across groups. Results indicated significant differences in mean DC scores between distressed (alcoholic, depressed) groups and the nondistressed (normal) group for the father–child relationship (father's report on child and child's report on father), and the mother–child relationship (mothers in the alcoholic group reported higher DC scores on children than mothers in the depressed or normal groups).

2. To assess the instrument's concurrent validity, parents' reports on the PC–ACQ were correlated with their reports on the Child Behavior Checklist (CBCL; Achenbach, 1978; Achenbach & Edelbrock, 1979). Results indicated that high DC scores were positively and significantly associated with scores on the internalizing and externalizing scales and negatively and significantly related to scores on the three competency scales. This pattern of results held for mothers' and fathers' scores, the different diagnostic groups, and male versus female children.

3. To determine how PC–ACQ reports relate to marital satisfaction, DC scores were correlated with father reports and mother reports on the Dyadic Adjustment Scale (DAS; Spanier, 1976). For the total sample, mothers' DAS scores correlated significantly with mothers' DC for sons and daughters combined and also separately for sons and for daughters. For fathers' DAS scores, the correlation with DC on sons and daughters combined and sons separately are significant. Child DC scores on either parent were not significantly related to measures of their parents' marital satisfaction.

V. Relationship Assessments: Questionnaires Regarding Sibling Relationships

Although the study of sibling relationships has received increasing attention since the mid-1970s, (Bank & Kahn, 1982; Dunn & Kendrick, 1982; Lamb & Sutton-Smith, 1982), recent empirical efforts have focused primarily on very young children and have employed direct observation methodologies (Dunn & Kendrick, 1981). Notwithstanding such emerging interests, the identification and measurement of core dimensions of sibling relationships— for latency age children through adolescents—is just beginning to surface in the literature. Only one instrument for the assessment of sibling relationships seemed sufficiently developed to justify a detailed review.

A. The Sibling Relationship Questionnaire

1. Background

The Sibling Relationship Questionnaire (Furman & Buhrmester, 1985a) is an extension of the authors' previous work on children's perception of their social networks (Furman, Adler, & Buhrmester, 1984; Furman & Buhrmester, 1985b). In particular, an earlier study by Furman et al. (1984) had examined common underlying dimensions across different relationships. To study children's relationships with mothers, fathers, siblings, grandparents, teachers, and friends, these investigators administered a Children's Relationship Questionnaire and developed separate questionnaires for siblings, friends, and parents. Most effort was directed toward the development of the sibling questionnaire.

Development of a sibling relationship questionnaire was motivated by the investigators' interest in a global, multidimensional, cross-situational assessment of sibling relationships for which no current method was satisfactory. The authors were particularly interested in capturing the child's view of his or her relationships rather than an outsider's judgment. (According to Furman and Buhrmester (1985a):

> An insider's description of a relationship, as might be obtained in an interview, can provide a rich picture of the history and current status of a relationship. An insider is also sensitive to the private meaning of a behavior and can interpret behaviors within the broad context of the relationship. (p. 449)

In Study 1, children were interviewed to capture the facets they perceived to be most important and/or common in sibling relationships. The most commonly reported variables were used to construct self-report rating scales. These rating scales were then administered and factor analyzed to identify underlying dimensions.

2. Description of the Instrument

The qualities coded from childrens' interviews were intimacy, prosocial behavior, companionship, similarity, nurturance by sibling, nurturance of sibling, admiration by sibling, admiration of sibling, affection, dominance by sibling, dominance over sibling, quarreling, antagonism, competition, parental partiality, and general relationship evaluation (Furman & Buhrmester, 1985a, p. 451, Table 1).

A scale was then developed for each of these qualities except for general relationship evaluation. As noted by Furman and Buhrmester (1985a):

> The remaining quality, "general relationship evaluation," served as the basis for two scales: (a) satisfaction with the relationship, and (b) importance of the relationship. Each scale consisted of three items. A 5-point Likert format (1 = Hardly at all and 5 = Extremely much) was used for all scales except the parental partiality scale. In that case, response choices ranged from "almost always him/her [favored]" to "almost always me [favored]," and scores were based on deviations from the midpoint of "about the same." Thus, the scale was a measure of absolute partiality rather than a measure of the direction of partiality for the subject or sibling. (p. 452)

An attempt was made to preface every fifth item with a statement that would make response alternatives less susceptible to social desirability.

The questionnaire consists of 51 items. The subject answers items regarding his or her relationship with one specific sibling. Furman and Buhrmester administered the questionnaire to fifth and sixth graders where the questionnaire was read orally to groups of children.

A principal components analysis revealed four underlying dimensions which accounted for 71% of the variance: warmth/closeness, relative status/power, conflict, and rivalry.

3. *Variables Assessed*

   1. Warmth/closeness—the rating scales which have the highest factor loadings on warmth/closeness include intimacy, prosocial behavior, companionship, similarity, admiration by sibling, admiration of sibling, and affection.
   2. Relative status/power—nurturance of sibling and dominance over sibling have the highest positive factor loadings on relative status/power; nurturance by sibling and dominance by sibling have the highest negative factor loadings on relative status power.
   3. Conflict—quarreling, antagonism, and competition have the highest factor loadings on conflict.
   4. Rivalry—rivalry is largely composed of parental partiality, but competition has a weak positive-factor loading.

4. Psychometric Properties and Applications

Reliability

> Scores were computed for each of the 17 scales by averaging the three items designed to assess the quality. The internal consistency coefficients (Cronbach's alpha) for those composites all exceeded .70 except for the competition scale (.63) (M = .80). . . . The questionnaire has been administered twice (10 days apart) to another sample of 94 children, and test-retest reliabilities for the three-item scales were found to be high, mean $r = .71$, ranging from .58 to .86. (Furman & Buhrmester, 1985a, p. 452)

Validity and Applications. 1. To determine the association between sibling relationship variables and family constellation factors (sex of subject, sex of sibling, relative age—older or younger sibling, age difference, and family size), a series of multiple regression analyses were conducted. For each such analysis, variation on a sibling relationship score was predicted from the five family constellation variables.

> The Relative Status/Power scores could be predicted quite accurately from the equation of the constellation variables ($R = .84$), principally because of the inclusion of relative age, $R = .81$. In contrast, the equations of constellation variables did not account for more than 20% of the variance on the three other factors. (Furman and Buhrmester, 1985a, p. 456)

2. Principal components analysis of the Sibling Relationship Questionnaire, the Friendship Questionnaire Scale, and the Parent Relationship Questionnaire revealed similar, although not identical, underlying factors. The Sibling Relationship Questionnaire produced factors for warmth/closeness, relative status/power, conflict, and rivalry, whereas factors identified from the Friendship Questionnaire Scale were warmth/closeness, conflict, and exclusivity. Factors from maternal self-report form included warmth, conflict/punishment, egalitarian closeness, and protectiveness (Furman *et al.*, 1984).

Thus far, this measure has mainly been used to understand which facets of sibling relationships are perceived as most important by normal subjects. No studies have yet been reported in which the instrument has been related to psychopathology, treatment outcome, or clinical-theoretical interests.

VI. Relationship Assessments: Questionnaires Regarding Whole Families

Since 1980, a considerable number of "whole family" assessment procedures have emerged within the family field. In contrast with other subsets of measures, a great deal of time and effort has been devoted to the development of these instruments, involving relatively careful and systematic attempts to build psychometrically-sound and theoretically-relevant procedures. Several recent reviews of this material can be found in Forman and Hagen (1983, 1984), and Skinner (1987).

Three of the instruments selected for review—the Family Environment Scale (FES), the Family Adaptability and Cohesion Scales (FACES), and the Family Assessment Measure (FAM)—are solid instruments deserving the serious attention of the clinical researcher. Each approaches the family from somewhat different theoretical, clinical, and empirical perspectives, resulting in considerable uniqueness associated with each procedure. The fourth measure, the Family Crises-Oriented Personal Evaluation Scales (F-COPES), is a new, yet promising instrument which addresses the interface between the family and the larger environment; namely, the family's pattern of coping with internally or externally generated difficulties.

A. Family Environment Scale (FES)

1. Background

The Family Environment Scale (FES) was one of the first instruments developed specifically for family assessments. Representing one of several social climate scales developed by Moos during the 1970s, the instrument is composed of 10 rationally derived subscales assessing three broad domains: the interpersonal relationships among family members, personal growth characteristics emphasized by the family, and the system organizational features of the family.

The FES arises from an interactionist perspective which, first and foremost, contends that behavior is best understood as a joint function of the person and the environment (Bowers, 1973; Mischel, 1973; Endler & Magnusson, 1976). As described by Skinner (1987):

> Personality assessment has traditionally tended to focus upon the person with the measurement of personality traits. However, a growing body of evidence has shown that a substantial proportion of variance in behavior can be accounted for by situational and environmental factors. The measurement of social climate is one of the main ways in which human environments may be characterized. This perspective assumes that environments have unique 'personalities' just as individuals do. Thus, the Family Environment Scale was developed to measure the social climate of the family according to relationship, personal development and system maintenance dimensions. (p. 433)

2. Description of the Instrument

The FES assesses the family in regards to three primary domains, each of which is composed of two or more dimensions: (a) relationship dimensions (cohesion, expressiveness, conflict); (b) personal growth dimensions (independence, achievement orientation, intellectual-cultural orientation, active recreational orientation, moral-religious emphasis); and (c) system maintenance dimensions (organization, control).

Development of an initial item pool ($n = 200$) was achieved through interviews with families as well as from other social clinical scales developed by Moos (1974). This early form was administered to a large and heterogeneous sample of families (1,000 people within 285 families). Ninety items were subsequently selected which satisfied the following criteria: high item to total-score correlations, equal number of items scored true and false to avoid acquiescence response set, low to moderate subscale correlations, maximum item and subscale discrimination among families, and an overall even split in item response frequency to avoid items characteristic of only extreme families. The final form consists of 90 items; each of the 10 subscales is composed of 9 items.

Currently, the FES can be used in three different forms: the Real form (Form R), the Ideal form (Form I), and the Expectations form (Form E). All forms have a true–false format and scoring can be completed by means of templates that are provided. Although the authors do not indicate a minimum age for respondents, it is our opinion that children should be at least 10 years old.

3. *Variables Assessed*

   Relationship Dimension

   1. Cohesion—the degree of commitment, help, and support family members provide for one another.
   2. Expressiveness—how much family members are encouraged to act openly and to express their feelings directly.
   3. Conflict—the amount of openly expressed anger, aggression, and conflict among family members.

   Personal Growth Dimension

   1. Independence—the extent to which family members are assertive, self-sufficient, and make their own decisions.
   2. Achievement orientation—the extent to which activities (such as work) are cast into an achievement-oriented or competitive framework.
   3. Intellectual-cultural orientation—the degree of interest in political, social, intellectual, and cultural activities.
   4. Active-recreational orientation—the extent of participation in social and recreation activities.
   5. Moral-religious emphasis—the emphasis on ethical and religious issues and values.

   System Maintenance Dimension

   1. Organization—the importance of clear organization and structure in planning family activites and responsibilities.
   2. Control—the extent to which set rules and procedures are used to run family life.

4. *Psychometric Properties and Applications*

   Reliability. Across the 10 subscales, coefficient alpha ranges from .61 to .78 (Moos & Moos, 1981). As reported by Bagarozzi

(1984), average test–retest reliabilities were quite satisfactory at 8 weeks ($r = .78$), 4 months ($r = .74$) and 12 months ($r = .73$). Intercorrelation among the various subscales are in the low to moderate range with an average value of $r = .25$ (Billings & Moos, 1982). Finally, detailed normative data are available on a normal family sample ($N = 1125$), a sample of distressed families ($N = 500$), and on subgroups varying in terms of family size and age of parent, single- versus two-parent status, and family ethnic status (black and Mexican Americans).

Validity and Applications. Since 1980, the FES has been used in a wide range of studies, the results from which bear upon the instrument's validity and applicability in various areas of clinical research.

1. The most extensive use of the FES has been associated with Moos' programmatic treatment outcome studies of alcoholism in which various FES subscales have been related to family functioning and alcohol consumption at 6-month and 2-year follow-up (Finney, Moos, & Newborn, 1980; Finney, Moos, Cronkite, & Gamble, 1983; Moos & Moos, 1984; Moos, Bromet, Tsu, & Moos, 1979; Moos, Finney, & Chan, 1981; Moos, Finney, & Gamble, 1982).

2. Various studies, supporting the instrument's predictive validity, have also been reported (Moos & Moos, 1981). For example, parents receiving treatment had higher cohesion and support scores than a no-treatment control group (Karoly & Rosenthal, 1977); families who completed as opposed to dropped out of a treatment program for their delinquent children had higher scores on the intellectual-cultural orientation subscale; and depression in men and women was predicted from various FES subscale scores (Wetzel & Redmond, 1980).

3. The instrument's construct validity has received support from various studies in which FES scores have discriminated disturbed families from "normal" families (Moos & Moos, 1981), including experimental groups with maritally distressed couples (Scoresby & Christensen, 1976); schizophrenics (Janes & Hesselbrock, 1976; White, 1978); heroin users (Penk, Robinowitz, Kidd, & Nisle, 1979); adolescent runaways (Steinbock, 1978); and alcoholics (Moos & Moos, 1981). Most recently, Wald, Greenwald, and Jacob (1984), reported on differences in children's (age 10–18

years old) FES scores as a function of parents' diagnostic status (alcoholic, depressed, and normals).

4. Several case studies have explored the clinical utility of the FES (Fuhr, Moos, & Dishotsky, 1981; Moos & Fuhr, 1982). Fuhr *et al.* (1981), for example, compared Form R (real) and Form I (ideal) responses, identified areas of disagreement, and integrated this information into the therapeutic process.

5. Based on FES data, Moos' studies of family typologies have identified six types of family environments—three oriented toward personal growth, two focused on interpersonal relationships, and one directed toward system maintenance (Billings & Moos, 1982; Moos & Moos, 1976).

6. Additional studies using the FES have focused on adult career patterns, family role and social functioning, and adolescent personality (Forman & Hagan, 1984; Moos & Moos, 1981) as well as the relationship between the Parental Attitude Research Instrument (PARI; Schaefer & Bell, 1958) and various FES subscales (Ollendick, LeBerteaux, & Howe, 1978).

B. *Family Adaptability and Cohesion Scales II (FACES II)*

1. *Background*

The Family Adaptability and Cohesion Scales (FACES), developed by Olson and colleagues, operationalizes the two primary dimensions of the Circumplex model of marital and family systems (Olson, Sprenkle, & Russell, 1979). Development of the circumplex model began in 1976 when it became apparent that the dimensions of cohesion and adaptability were salient features in family therapy, family sociology, and small group research. The Circumplex model was intuitively derived, and attempts to integrate the theoretical concepts and empirical studies found in the marital and family process literature.

Family cohesion in this model has two components: "the emotional bonding members have with one another and the degree of individual autonomy a person experiences in the family system" (Olson *et al.*, 1979, p. 5). There are four levels of family cohesion which range from disengagement (extreme, low cohesion) to separated (moderate, balanced cohesion) to connected (moderate, balanced cohesion) to enmeshed (extreme, high cohesion). Family adaptability, "the ability of a marital/family system to change its power structure, role relationship rules in response to situational and developmental stress" (Olson *et al.*, 1979, p. 22) assumes that a well-functioning family system requires the ability to maintain stability while being flexible enough to change when crises occur. Family adaptability ranges from rigid (extreme, low adaptability) to structured (moderate, balanced adaptability) to flexible (moderate, balanced adaptability) to chaotic (extreme, high adaptability).

Sixteen types of marital and family systems can be identified and described by combining the four levels of the cohesion dimension with the four levels of the adaptability dimension in a curvilinear fashion. Effective family functioning will be found in families with *balanced levels* of cohesion and adaptability; that is, flexible separateness, flexible connectedness, structural connectedness, and structural separateness. The *least* effective family functioning will be found in families with extreme levels of cohesion and adaptability—chaotically disengaged, chaotically enmeshed, rigidly enmeshed, and rigidly disengaged. There are, in addition, eight other combinations of the two dimensions.

A third dimension in the Circumplex model, "family communication," is hypothesized to facilitate movement to and maintenance of the balanced levels of the two major dimensions in the model. Ineffective communication prevents movement toward the desired balanced levels of the two dimensions.

The model is dynamic in that it assumes changes in family type can and will occur over the span of the family life cycle. Families are free to move in any direction on the two major dimensions as the changing requirements of the family demand. FACES II, a modification of the original FACES, was developed to empirically test this model.

2. Variables Assessed

1. Family cohesion—assesses the degree to which a family member feels connected (bonded) and separated (autonomous) from other family members.

2. Family adaptability—assesses the flexibility of the family system in response to stress.

3. Description of the Instrument

FACES II is a 30-item instrument which taps the dimensions of *cohesion* (16 items) and *adaptability* (14 items). Within each dimension there are specific concepts used to measure the dimension. Eight concepts are used for the cohesion dimension: emotional bonding, family boundaries, coalitions, time, space, friends, decision making, and interests and recreation. For the adaptability dimension (the ability of a marital or family system to change its power structure, role relationships, and relationship rules in response to situational and developmental stress) six concepts are used: assertiveness, leadership, discipline, negotiation, roles, and rules.

FACES is designed to be administered twice to family members to obtain a measurement of the individual's perceived family (how would you describe your family now), and his ideal family (how would you like your family to be). There is a 5-point Likert response scale to indicate how applicable the statements are to the respondent's family. FACES II can be easily revised for use with couples and single parent families. Hand scoring is quick, and a profile can be plotted to facilitate interpretation. An individual's level of satisfaction with his or her current family system can be assessed by comparing the perceived—ideal discrepancy score. Olson indicates that 12-year-olds can comprehend and respond to FACES items.

Development of the Instrument. The original version of FACES, developed in 1978, was a 111-item instrument designed to measure cohesion and adaptability. An initial version of FACES II was developed in 1981 to correct some of the limitations in the earlier version. It was shortened to 50 items, simple sentences were constructed so that it could be used by children, a 5-point response scale was developed and the independence scale from cohesion was dropped. On the basis of factor analysis and reliability checks, the final version of FACES II was constructed.

Work is underway on another version—FACES III, in which a third dimension, *communication*, is included and construct validation studies comparing FACES III with therapists' observations are in progress. Both FACES II and III are available for use on the IBM-PC microcomputer.

4. Psychometric Properties and Applications

Reliability. Olson et al. (1982) report internal consistency (coefficient alpha) of .87 for cohesion, .78 for adaptability, and .90 for the total scale. Test–retest reliabilities are not reported for FACES II. Normative data for FACES was obtained from a national sample of Caucasian Lutherans (2082 adults and 416 children) at different stages in the life cycle.

Factor analysis limited to two factors had cohesion items loading on Factor I (median loading of .49; range from .35 to .61), and adaptability items loading on Factor II (median loading of .41; range from .10 to .55).

Validity and Applications. 1. Balanced and extreme families, defined by FACES II, were found to differ in terms of other relevant couple and family variables (Olson & Portner, 1983).

2. Barnes & Olson (1985) used FACES II in conjunction with an instrument assessing parent–adolescent communications. For parents, effective (high) communication was associated with the *balanced* family type and low communication was overrepresented in the *extreme* family type. For adolescents, however, low communication was indicative of the balanced family type, and effective (high) communication was associated with the extreme family type.

3. Lack of agreement among family members in their FACES II scores was reported by Olson and Portner (1983). This raises the question of which member's report is most useful for what purpose, as well as demonstrating the importance of obtaining scores from as many family members as possible to gain a realistic picture of the family system.

4. Finally, Olson and Portner (1983) report data from a large national sample showing significant differences on the Cohesion

and Adaptability dimensions of FACES II at different stages in the family life cycle.

C. Family Assessment Measures (FAM)

1. Background

The Family Assessment Measure, FAM III, (Skinner, Steinhauer, & Santa-Barbara, 1983) was developed to discriminate areas of family strengths and weaknesses, as well as to differentiate families that are coping successfully from those whose coping styles are dysfunctional. FAM III provides indices of family process rather than family structure, and is an extension of the Family Categories Schema (Epstein, Rakoff, & Sigal, 1968).

FAM III is based on the Process Model of Family Functioning (PMFF; Steinhauer, Santa-Barbara, & Skinner, 1984) which posits that family members share common goals without which the family would not exist. These common objectives are "to provide for the biological, psychological, and social development and maintenance of family members." (Steinhauer, Santa-Barbara, & Skinner, 1984, p. 78). In order to achieve these family goals, certain tasks must be carried out. During the course of the family life cycle the tasks may change, but they always involve the same basic skills and similar processes regardless of when they are accomplished.

The overarching goal of family functioning then, is to successfully accomplish a variety of tasks (*task accomplishment*). Some of these tasks are unique to each family while others are culturally defined; both are determined by a family's values and norms. Task accomplishment is the most important dimension in the process model. When it is successful, the family can accomplish the major basic, developmental, and crisis tasks necessary for healthy functioning. To facilitate accomplishment of these tasks, *role performance* and *communication* are necessary, related processes. Role performance involves carrying out prescribed specific behaviors by each family member. Communication is required for effective role performance and task accomplishment.

Three additional dimensions complete the PMFF. Affective involvement (the degree and quality of family members' concern and interest for one another) determines whether relationships are nurturant and supportive or destructive and self-serving. Control refers to the techniques family members use to influence each others' behavior and may be characterized as rigid, flexible, laissez-faire, or chaotic. Finally, values and norms are reflected directly or indirectly in every aspect of the family's functioning.

The PMFF is a dynamic model which attempts to identify dimensions that are descriptive of family health or pathology as well as to define the processes by which families operate. The model, with its emphasis on how basic dimensions of family functioning interrelate, stimulates assessment at both the total family system and individual intrapsychic levels (Steinhauer & Tisdall, 1984).

2. Description of the Instrument

FAM III is a 134-item self-report instrument which mother, father, and all children 10 years of age and older may complete in approximately 45 minutes. Scores can be graphed onto a profile sheet for ease in interpretation. Items are organized around three different response formats: (a) *general scale* (50 items focused on the health/pathology of the family as a whole); (b) *dyadic relationship scale* (42 items, for each dyad assessed, focused on relationships between specific members); and (c) *self-rating scale* (42 items focused on the individual's perception of his or her functioning in the family).

Within each response format, scores are obtained on the FAM's seven primary dimensions and on an overall rating of family functioning; for the general scale, additional scores are obtained regarding measures of social desirability and denial/defensiveness. Although the scales can be used separately, the most complete assessment of family functioning is provided by the combined scales.

A preliminary version of the FAM was developed according to a construct validation paradigm. Following initial item generation, 30 items for each construct were administered to 433 individuals representing 182 clinical and nonclinical families. Median internal consistency reliability was .87 for the best 10 items selected for each subscale. FAM significantly differentiated between clinical and nonclinical families. FAM II, developed from these analyses is a briefer, 115 item instrument. Finally, in response to feedback from users of FAM II and statistical analysis of its measurement properties, FAM III was developed to provide more differentiated information about areas of family functioning. Specifically, FAM III assesses the family from the three different levels described above and provides the clinician or researcher with an indication of family members' perceptions of strength and weakness within specific areas of functioning.

A prototype version of FAM III has been developed for administration using an IBM-PC microcomputer.

3. Variables Assessed

FAM III has seven subscales to assess constructs, and two subscales to assess response style biases. They are:

1. Task accomplishment—successful achievement of a variety of basic, developmental, and crisis tasks.
2. Role performance—includes three operations: "(1) allocation or assignment of specified activities to each family member; (2) agreement or willingness of family members to assume the assigned roles; and (3) actual enactment or carrying out of prescribed behaviors" (Skinner *et al.*, 1983, p. 93).
3. Communication—this construct assesses whether family members send clear messages and are open to the messages they receive.
4. Affective expression—describes the range, quality, and appropriateness of affective communications.
5. Affective involvement—"degree and quality of family members' interest in one another" (p. 93).
6. Control—"process by which family members influence and manage each other" (p. 93).
7. Values and norms—how tasks are defined and how the family proceeds to accomplish them may be greatly influenced by the specific culture and family background.

8. Social desirability
9. Denial/defensiveness

4. Psychometric Properties and Applications

Reliability. Norms on normal families (247 adults and 65 adolescents) are published in the *FAM III Administration and Interpretation Guide* (Skinner, Steinhauer, & Santa-Barbara, 1983) and norms on clinical families are available by contacting Harvey Skinner. Internal consistency estimates (coefficient alpha) from analyses of 475 families are .93 for the general scale, .95 for the dyadic relationship scale, and .89 for the self-rating scale. Intercorrelations among subscales ranged from .39 to .70 (general scale), .63 to .82 (dyadic relationship scale), and .25 to .63 (self-rating scale).

Validity and Applications. 1. The ability of FAM III to differentiate problem from nonproblem families was assessed with the sample of 475 families described above. Problems in the area of control, values and norms, and affective expression served to differentiate children from adults with the children reporting more problems. Problem families tended to report more dysfunction in the areas of role performance and involvement than nonproblem families (Skinner, 1987).

2. Steinhauer (1984) discusses the potential usefulness of FAM III for clinicians involved in family therapy. The profile generated from each family members' scores can be used to confirm and amplify a clinical assessment and to demonstrate how each family member perceives family functioning.

3. Currently, a number of research studies are addressing the external validity of FAM III. Developmentally delayed preschoolers are being investigated in separate studies by Markovitch and Cohen; youths "at risk" for psychiatric disorders are being studied by Martin, and parent–infant interactions of infants with cystic fibrosis are being studied by Simmons (Skinner, 1987). Finally, Jacob has been using the FAM in studies of families with alcoholics, depressives, and normal controls (Jacob, Rushe, & Seilhamer, in press).

D. Family Crisis-Oriented Personal Evaluation Scales (F-COPES)

1. Background

F-COPES is aimed at identifying problem-solving behaviors in families as they respond to difficulties or crises. The scales on this inventory are derived from the Double ABCX model of family stress theory (McCubbin & Patterson, 1981), which is an extension of an early family crisis model, the ABCX model, advanced by Hill (1949, 1958). Hill's ABCX model "attempted to identify which families, under what conditions, using what resources and coping behaviors were able to make positive adaptations to stressful events" (p. 7). This framework focused on *precrisis* variables such as the stressor event, the family's resources to meet the event, and the definition the family made of the event.

The Double ABCX model, conceptualized and developed by McCubbin and Patterson (1981), emerged from studies of families in war-induced crises. Their conceptualization adds to the early ABCX model's *postcrisis* variables in an effort to describe

> the additional life stressors and changes which may make family adaptation more difficult to achieve, (b) the critical psychological and social factors families call upon and use in managing crisis situations, (c) the processes families engage in to achieve satisfactory resolution, and (d) the outcome of these family efforts. (p. 9)

F-COPES operationalizes the coping dimensions of the Double ABCX model and focuses on two levels of interaction: *internal*—the ways in which the family handles difficulties and problems which arise between family members, and *external*—the ways in which the family handles problems or demands which come from the social environment but which affect family members. For example, a male adolescent's need for independence must be balanced with the family's need for his completing his chores or for his participation in shared family activities. This requires an internal adaptation to problems. An external situation arises when, for example, the wife-mother enters or returns to the work force. The family must handle the problems which arise from this new commitment which takes her outside the family and does this most effectively by establishing a balance between the ongoing family demands and the new work demands.

It is hypothesized that adaptation to stressful situations will be more effective in families which have coping behaviors on both levels of interaction.

2. Description of the Instrument

The F-COPES is a 29-item, 5-subscale inventory, and can be easily administered to family members above 12 years of age. Respondents select from Likert-type responses of strongly disagree, moderately disagree, neither agree nor disagree, moderately agree, and strongly agree. The prefix for all items is, "When we face problems or difficulties in our family, we respond by [item]". A summary score can be obtained for each subscale and a total score by simply summing the items. The five subscales measured are (from McCubbin et al., 1982):

1. Acquiring social support (9 items). "Measures a family's ability to actively engage in acquiring support from relatives, friends, neighbors, and extended family" (p. 104). For example: When we face problems or difficulties in our family, we respond by sharing our difficulties with relatives.
2. Reframing (8 items). "Assesses the family's capability to redefine stressful events in order to make them more manageable" (p. 104). For example: When we face problems or difficulties in our family, we respond by knowing we have the strength within our own family to solve our problems.
3. Seeking spiritual support (4 items). "Focuses on the family's ability to acquire spiritual support" (p. 104). For example: When we face problems or difficulties in our family, we respond by participating in church activities.
4. Mobilizing family to acquire and accept help (4 items). "Measures family's ability to seek out community resources and accept help from others" (p. 104). For example: When we face problems or difficulties in our family

we respond by seeking professional counseling and help for family difficulties.
5. Passive appraisal (4 items). "Assesses the family's ability to seek out community resources and accept help from others" (p. 104). For example: When we face problems or difficulties in our family we respond by knowing luck plays a big part in how well we are able to solve family problems.

Development of the instrument began with a review of the literature of coping strategies. The pilot instrument consisted of 49 items relating to coping as well as some items the authors deemed important. One hundred and nineteen family members representing all stages of the family life cycle completed the questionnaire. Data analysis reduced the list to 30 items. The eight factors (scales) grouped on two dimensions, internal and external family coping patterns, emerged from factor analysis.

The 30-item scale was administered to a large national sample ($N = 2740$) and from factor analysis emerged the final version of F-COPES—a 29-item inventory consisting of five factors (scales).

3. Psychometric Properties and Applications

Reliability. Norms are available for male and female adults and adolescents. Internal consistency (Cronbach's alpha) of the five factors range from .63 to .83 with the total scale being .86. Test–retest reliabilities (4 week) for the five factors range from .61 to .95 with total scale being .81 (Olson, McCubbin, Barnes, Larsen, Muxen, & Wilson, 1982).

VII. Relationship Assessments: Structured Interviews

In contrast with questionnaires and objective test procedures, structured interviews involve direct, face-to-face contact between the researcher/clinician and the subject/patient. As a result, there is increased potential for examining and elaborating the meaning of complex family processes, as well as members' beliefs and attributions regarding such phenomena. Notwithstanding the associated potential for biased responses through subtle interpersonal cues, various investigators believe that some family data (at least during an early stage of understanding) can only be acquired and made meaningful through extended, in-depth interviews. Hence, the need for the personal interview format.

The two procedures selected for review come from very different theoretical perspectives and address quite different aspects of psychopathology—the focus of *expressed emotion* concerning the impact of negative family communications on the course of schizophrenia and the assessment of *family rituals* emerging from anthropological foundations and concerned with the transmission of alcoholism across generations. The potential applicability of both instruments, however, seems to go far beyond their original interests, so that psychopathologists from diverse backgrounds would be encouraged to learn more about each of these procedures.

A. Expressed Emotion

1. Background

Expressed emotion (EE) is a measure of critical comments made by a psychiatric patient's relatives about the patient at the time the patient is admitted to the hospital. More generally, EE is aimed at measuring negative aspects of the family environment that have been related to the course, and more recently, the onset of schizophrenic disorders.

EE is descended from the work of Brown and associates at the social psychiatry unit of the Institute of Psychiatry in London. Major interests of this research group involved the presence of institutionalization and subsequent treatment and rehabilitation, and the influence of family members on the course of schizophrenic disorders. An initial follow-up of 156 patients showed the risk of readmission to be related to the discharge living arrangements (Brown, Carstairs, & Topping, 1958). The concept of EE was further developed in a follow-up of the living arrangements of 128 schizophrenic men (Brown, Monck, Carstairs, & Wing, 1962).

The Camberwell Family Interview Schedule (CFIS), a semistructured interview, was developed as a way of eliciting material for EE ratings, and was used in a study by Brown, Birley, and Wing (1972). Subsequently, the CFIS was abbreviated by Vaughn and Leff (1976a,b) and used in a replication study of the original work by Brown.

In recent years, American investigators have used the British criteria for measuring EE, although Valone, Norton, Goldstein, and Doane (1983) use the UCLA Parent Interview, a semistructured interview, to elicit material for measuring EE. In addition, attempts have been made to devise briefer methods for measuring EE. Mugana, Goldstein, Karno, Miklowitz, Jenkins, & Falloon (1986), for example, describes the five-minute speech sample, which involves,

> a five minute reply by a relative to the interviewer's statement: I'd like to hear your thoughts about _____, in your own words and without interrupting you with questions or comments. When I ask you to begin, I'd like you to talk for five minutes, telling me what kind of person _____ is and how you get along together. (p. 205)

2. Variables Assessed

- Critical comments—remarks by relatives about the patient that are judged to be statements of "resentment, disapproval, or dislike."
- Hostility—defined as a remark "indicating the rejection of someone as a person."
- Emotional overinvolvement—statements made by relatives that indicate "unusually marked concern about the patient."

3. Description of the Instrument

In the initial study by Brown et al. (1962), three scales were developed to assess relatives' attitudes toward the patients: expressed emotion, hostility, and dominant or directive behavior. The scales for hostility and expressed emotion were used to dichotomize the group into high and low EE groups.

In the next elaboration of EE, Brown et al. (1972) used the

CFIS, developed by Brown and Rutter (1966) to elicit information from the relative about the patient. In this work, EE was based on an index derived from the number of critical comments, a rating of hostility, and a rating of emotional overinvolvement of parents. (Two other scales for warmth and dissatisfaction were rated, but were not used to derive the EE index.) Critical comments were judged "either by tone of voice or by content of what was said—for a remark to be judged critical, there had to be a clear and unambiguous statement of resentment, disapproval or dislike" (p. 243). Hostility was rated as present or absent (Brown et al. 1972) and was defined as present "if a remark was made indicating the rejection of someone as a person" (p. 243). Emotional overinvolvement "was designed to pick up unusually marked concern about the patient" (p. 243). Subsequent studies by Vaughn and Leff (1976a,b) and others have used these three scales to derive a level of EE for each relative.

The derivation of an index of expressed emotion for each subject is based on material gathered in a face to face interview with the patient's relative. In the original Brown et al. (1962) study, the "key relative" was defined as the most closely related female living in the household, typically a wife or mother. Patient and relative were seen together. In the later study by Brown et al. (1972), relatives were interviewed at home while the patient was in the hospital, and if both parents were available, they were seen separately. This same procedure was followed in the Vaughn and Leff (1976a,b) replication.

In most studies, ratings on three scales are used to derive an EE index for a subject: the number of critical comments made about the patient, a dichotomous rating of hostility, and a rating of emotional overinvolvement. Typically, hostility is highly related to critical comments so that the former is not used. A cut-off score of seven critical comments (Brown et al., 1972), and more recently six (Vaughn & Leff, 1976a,b), is used to place a subject in the high EE group. Relatives who displayed "marked" emotional overinvolvement or a rating of 4 to 5 on a 5-point scale were also included in the high EE group. Although the original interview to gather data on family attitude took between 4 and 5 hours (Brown et al., 1972), the abbreviated version takes between 1 and 2 hours to complete (Vaughn & Leff, 1976a,b).

Training. Psychologists and psychiatrists have been trained to make the ratings (Vaughn & Leff, 1976a,b) and "several months" are necessary to learn the interview scales. Other studies do not describe who the raters were but do note that "extensive training" in the coding system is necessary (Valone et al. 1983). In several studies it appears that ratings are done in real time. In the Valone et al. (1983) study, audiotapes of the interview were used to make EE ratings. If permanent records are kept, they are in the form of audiotapes.

4. Psychometric Properties and Applications

Reliability. Interrater reliability has been consistently high for the categories that comprise the EE index. In the original Brown et al. (1962) study, percentage of agreement was well over 90% and in the subsequent Brown et al. (1972) study, no category used to derive EE fell below a product moment correlation of $r = .80$. In more recent work, interrater reliability remains high, for example, $\kappa = 1.00$, $p < .0001$ for emotional overinvolvement, $\kappa = .86$, $p < .0001$ for criticism and $\kappa = .83$, $p < .0001$ for hostility (Valone et al., 1983). No data are available on test–retest or internal consistency measures.

Validity and Applications. 1. Support for the predictive validity of the EE construct comes from a number of studies in which high EE predicts relapse in both schizophrenic and depressed patients once they return home from the hospital (Brown et al., 1962, 1972; Vaughn & Leff, 1976a,b). Although one study did not find a relationship between EE and relapse (Kottgen, Sonnichsen, Mollenhauer, & Jurth, 1984), these authors noted sampling issues that might have influenced their results.

2. EE has also been related to the onset of schizophrenia. Doane et al. (1982), used a measure of parental communication deviance and a measure "somewhat similar to EE" to predict outcomes for a sample of disturbed adolescents who were assessed prior to the onset of severe psychopathology. The measure related to EE added a good deal of precision to the outcome pre-

diction compared to the use of the communication deviance measure alone.

3. Evidence for the construct validity of EE was presented in two studies that showed patterns of high arousal in both high and low EE patients when a key relative was not in the room. When the relative entered the room, low EE patients displayed decreases in arousal, measured by habituation of the (GSR) response. High EE patients did not show decreases in arousal, however, suggesting possible differences in high and low EE parental behavior (Sturgeon, Kuipers, Berkowitz, Turpin, & Leff, 1981; Tarrier, Vaughn, Lader, & Leff, 1979).

4. In the UCLA sample of disturbed adolescents at risk for serious psychopathology, high EE parents displayed significantly more mild and harsh criticisms when in direct interaction with their child (Valone *et al.*, 1983). In another study, ratings were made of both patients and their parents when interacting together. It was hypothesized that acutely ill schizophrenic patients would manifest more avoidance behaviors when interacting with their high EE parents, although little support was found for this hypothesis. On the other hand, high EE parents were found to spend more interview time talking and less time looking at patients, suggesting that high EE relatives were intrusive and low EE relatives were supportive of the patient (Kuipers, Sturgeon, Berkowitz, & Leff, 1983).

5. Preliminary findings from a study by Berkowitz, Kuipers, Eberlein-Frief, and Leff (1981) suggest that a psychoeducational program for parents can reduce the risk of relapse in high EE households and even lower the level of EE in these households.

B. Family Ritual Interview

1. Background

Wolin's Family Ritual Interview is a structured, individual interview that was designed to study the relationship between disruption of family rituals and the transmission of alcoholism. The interview covers two main areas: identification of rituals present before heavy drinking, and the impact of heavy drinking on those rituals. The interview has been used in two studies: Wolin, Bennett, and Noonan (1979) and Wolin, Bennett, Noonan, & Teitelbaum (1980).

Working within a family-systems framework, the authors assume that alcoholism is a family problem and that the transmission of alcoholism across generations is in part caused by the family environment. Family rituals, defined as patterned behavior that family members perceive to have symbolic meaning, are believed to be particularly important to the family identity. Rituals are repetitive, secular interactions that have received anthropological attention for their impact and enhancement of a group's identification. Rituals often surround celebrations, traditions, and patterned interactions. The performance of rituals allows for symbolic expression of the rules, roles, expectations, and values which are important to the family. Rituals clarify the family's sense of being a group, and distinguish the members from external social forces.

Often, the importance of rituals is difficult for the family to articulate; they see their rituals as subtle, accepted patterns. Because rituals have such an important role in the definition of familial values which are likely to be accepted by the next generation, disruption of rituals can have profound, lasting effects on family members.

The focus of their work has been to examine the effect of disruption of family rituals by alcoholism and the transmission of alcoholism. They expected that families who protected rituals from the impact of alcoholism would be less likely to produce children who became alcoholics. Families who allowed alcohol to disrupt important rituals were more likely to transmit alcoholism to the children.

2. Description of the Instrument

The Family Ritual Interview is conducted by an experienced clinician who is instructed to answer 12 questions about each of seven family occasions: dinnertime, holidays, evenings, weekends, vacations, visitors in the home, and discipline.

The first five questions the interviewer answers determine

whether the family has rituals in each of the above areas. For each area, several aspects were assessed: the meaning of the event (either positive or negative), the amount the event changed over time, the relationship to the family, and the origin of the ritual (Wolin, Bennet, Reiss, & Conners, 1979). Questions 6 through 12 relate to characteristics of drinking periods; that is,

> presence of the alcoholic parent, intoxication of the alcoholic parent, response of the family to the intoxication, change in level of participation of the alcoholic parent when intoxicated, response of the family to that change, and overall change during the period of heaviest drinking. (Wolin et al., 1979, p. 590)

The structured interview format and the 12 questions coded are not published, although the materials may be obtained from the authors. Training and qualifications for interviewers are not described. The interview is used with parents and children and scored separately for each member.

The answers from questions 6 through 12 are used to classify the family into one of three types: distinctive, intermediate subsumptive, and subsumptive. Distinctive families are families whose rituals are not interrupted or disrupted by alcohol. In subsumptive families, all rituals are affected by the alcoholic member's drinking. Intermediate subsumptive families are those in which approximately half of the rituals were affected by drinking.

3. Psychometric Properties and Applications

Reliability. To check reliability, a staff member, blind to the family's diagnostic status, coded the data from six families. There was 88% agreement on whether the family exhibited patterned behavior, and 83% agreement on whether the patterned behavior qualified as a ritual (Wolin et al., 1979). Interrater agreement on questions 6 through 12 ranged from 67% to 100%; rater reliability from .67 to 1.00.

Validity and Applications. Wolin et al. (1979) found that subsumptive families were significantly more likely to have children with alcohol problems. This was particularly true for families in which holiday rituals were disrupted by alcohol use.

VIII. Relationship Assessments: Quasi-Observational Procedures

The family unit not only offers the investigator a rich and varied range of assessment targets, but the opportunity for collecting observational data from members themselves. In particular, family members can be asked to observe and record the behavior of other family members and, in so doing, important relational data can be gathered that would otherwise be unavailable to outsiders. This strategy has been called "quasi-observational" by Weiss (Weiss & Margolin, 1986) who places this method along a continuum ranging from the highly objective, nonparticipant observation data obtained from "professional" coders to the global, retrospective, self-report data obtained from family members about intrafamilial relationships. (Furthermore, both quasi-observations and nonparticipant observations differ from participant observations. In the latter approach, investigators actually join and interact with families and, in so doing, collect and report on their observations of family relationships. Examples of such approaches as applied to family studies include the work of Henry (1967) and Kantor and Lehr (1975).

Thus far, quasi-observational approaches have been developed primarily as part of the assessment procedures utilized in behavioral treatment programs (Margolin, 1987). For example, the Parent Daily Report (PDR; Chamberlain, 1980; Patterson, Reid, Jones, & Conger, 1975), which requires parents to keep track of their children's behavior, was created as part of the treatment program for aggressive children developed by Patterson and his colleagues. Another important quasi-observational instrument, the Spouse Observation Checklist (SOC; Wills, Weiss, & Patterson, 1974), was created as part of a program for the treatment of marital distress (Weiss & Perry, 1979). Although the PDR and the SOC have been the most frequently used quasi-observational instruments, extensive developmental work on two new quasi-observational procedures has recently been initiated: the Parent–Child Observation Schedule (PCOS; Grounds, 1985), which is completed by parents and their adolescent children, and the Sibling Observation Schedule (SOS; Seilhamer, 1983) designed to provide information on the sibling relationships of adolescent-age children. When combined with the SOC, the PCOS and the SOS allow for a relatively comprehensive assessment of a range of family subsystems. Although still quite new, the PCOS and SOS will be briefly described in order to provide a more complete perspective on the potential value of quasi-observational approaches to the assessment of family factors and child psychopathology.

A. Parent Daily Report (PDR)

1. Background

The use of telephone interviews for gathering short-term, retrospective reports of family behavior has been an effective data collection procedure for assessing naturally occurring family behaviors, especially those that are infrequent or covert. These procedures have been successfully utilized in studies evaluating hypotheses concerning family behavior (e.g., Montemayor, 1982), although their primary application has been found in clinical research studies. The prototype instrument selected for review, the Parent Daily Report (PDR) has a relatively lengthy history, and has been utilized more frequently and has been subjected to more psychometric evaluations than other related instruments (Jones, 1974).

The PDR was originally developed as part of the integrated treatment and assessment program for aggressive children created by Patterson and his colleagues (Jones, 1974; Patterson, 1974; Patterson et al., 1975). The PDR gave therapists daily descriptions of child problem behaviors that were of concern to parents and not likely to be seen by trained observers during structured observation sessions. Therefore, collection of such data was useful for the development and evaluation of treatment programs.

2. Description of the Instrument

The PDR is a brief telephone interview which asks parents to report on the problem behaviors engaged in by their child during the previous 24 hours. Depending on the study, interviewers have either inquired about specific targeted problem behaviors selected from the 35-item PDR checklist, or all 35 behaviors have been covered. The parent is asked to indicate whether a behavior did or did not occur rather than the total frequency of occurrence.

3. Variables Assessed

Both the total number of negative behaviors and the total number of targeted problem behaviors can be assessed with the PDR. Additionally, if a finer breakdown is desired, Chamberlain (1980) found that PDR items clustered into four groups that she named aggression, unsocialized, immaturity, and retaliation.

4. Psychometric Properties and Applications

Reliability. In general, interviewers agree with reliability checkers who only listen to the PDR being administered. For example, Jones (1974) reported perfect agreement on 85% of the behaviors, and Chamberlain (1980) reported 98% agreement. Furthermore, Chamberlain conducted the PDR interview with both the mother and father in 10 families to assess interparent agreement. She found that agreement levels were high for behaviors identified as being a problem ($r = .89$) but low for the total score ($r = .02$) which included many nonsalient child behaviors. Finally, Chamberlain (1980) found that the first half and last half of a 12-day data collection period were significantly correlated ($r = .81$).

Validity and Applications. The PDR has been used as an ongoing assessment procedure and outcome measure in investigations of behaviorally oriented family therapy. In such studies it has been sensitive to changes in child behavior (Forgatch & Toobert, 1979; Patterson, 1974; Patterson & Reid, 1973; Webster-Stratton, 1984). It has also been used in normative studies to describe the rate of occurrence of problem behaviors in children from nonclinic families (Chamberlain, 1980).

B. Spouse Observation Checklist (SOC)

1. Background

As part of the development of behavioral marital therapy programs during the late 1960s and early 1970s, various assessment procedures, including the Spouse Observation Checklist (SOC; Weiss & Perry, 1979), were constructed. The behavioral and social exchange theories that guided this work suggested that the daily behaviors of spouses—how they acted and reacted toward one another—would be related to specific and global measures of marital satisfaction. In order to gather data relevant to this hypothesis, Weiss and his colleagues attempted to develop a "universal" list of pleasing and displeasing behaviors. Initially, behaviors were drawn from the two major domains of instrumental and affectional events and later expanded to include companionship activities as well. With SOC data, strengths and weaknesses of a couple's relationship, corresponding to the occurrence or nonoccurrence of specific behaviors, can be identified and the continuing daily use of the SOC by a couple can help document changes that occur in their interactions.

The use of the SOC was first presented in clinical reports by researchers at the University of Oregon and the Oregon Research Institute (Margolin, Christensen, & Weiss, 1975; Patterson & Hops; 1972; Weiss, et al., 1973). A more formal discussion of the instrument was subsequently presented by Wills, et al. (1974) in which they described the relationship between various SOC summary scores and daily measures of marital satisfaction. By 1976, the SOC had been revised and expanded to a checklist of over 400 items.

2. Variables Assessed

As of 1976, the SOC assessed the frequency of occurrence of *pleasing* and *displeasing* spouse behavior in terms of the following 12 categories: affection, companionship, consideration, sex, communication process, coupling activities, child care and parenting, household management, financial decision-making, employment and education, personal habits and appearance, and self and spouse independence.

3. Description of the Instrument

Each SOC item describes a relevant relationship behavior which a spouse may perform. For example, "Spouse said something unkind to me" is a displeasing consideration item. In addition, some of the SOC items describe shared activities engaged in by both partners in the relationship. For example, "We took the children on a family outing" is a pleasing child care and parenting behavior item. The items are grouped together into the 12 content areas noted above. For 10 of these content areas, items are divided into pleases and displeases, whereas the two content areas of affection (e.g., "Spouse hugged or kissed me") and companionship (e.g., "We played cards") contain only pleasing behaviors. Other investigators (e.g., Jacobson, Follette, & McDonald, 1982), using the same SOC items, have alternated pleases and displeases and have dropped the observer feeling labels. Although all SOC items have been identified on an *a priori* basis as being pleasing or displeasing, many investigators also ask spouses to rate the level of affective impact for each behavior that occurs (e.g., Volkin & Jacob, 1981; Wills *et al.*, 1974). These subjective weightings have then been used to personalize the summary pleasing and displeasing daily spouse scores. Because particular behaviors may vary in their perceived affective impact across spouses and/or occasions, the use of these hedonic measures allows for a more accurate description of the impact of daily spouse behavior to specific couples.

Spouses complete the SOC independently but at the same, agreed-upon time every day. Due to the number of items contained in the SOC, time to complete the form usually requires 20 to 30 minutes. Many factors can affect this rate, however, including repeated experience with the materials, reading ability, and spouses' concern/motivation for reporting accurately.

After the SOC is completed, the investigator sums the total number of pleases and displeases within each behavioral category. These subtotals can be used if behavior in specific content areas is of interest or they can all be summed to obtain for each spouse a total daily pleases and displeases score. If hedonic ratings have also been obtained, then personally weighted summary scores can also be made.

4. Psychometric Properties and Applications

Reliability. As a quasi-observational instrument, the appropriate method for determining the reliability of the SOC is less clear than for self-report or nonparticipant observational procedures. The most common approach has been to calculate interrater agreement between spouses. For example, Jacobson and Moore (1981) had one spouse complete the regular SOC while his or her partner completed a self-monitoring (SM) version of the same instrument. Within the SM version, all of the "spouse" items were reworded to become "I" items (e.g., "I worked on the budget"). By comparing the SOC completed by one spouse ("My spouse worked on the budget today") and the SM version completed by the partner ("I worked on the budget today"), interrater agreements (IRA) can be determined.

Reported IRA's have not been as high as those considered acceptable with nonparticipant observational procedures. Jacobson and Moore (1981), for example, reported an overall IRA of 48% in a sample of couples recruited through the newspaper. Further examination of these data indicated that less inferential items were most reliably recorded and that level of marital satisfaction was directly related to the IRA or couples. In a related study by Christensen, average agreement levels across all couples were also relatively low (IRA = 46%; κ = .51) (Christensen & Nies, 1980; Christensen, Sullaway, & King, 1983). Further analyses indicated that IRA was correlated with global marital satisfaction, daily ratings of marital satisfaction, and the social desirability of items. Most recently, Tennenbaum (1984) evaluated agreement level in relation to a 20-item and a 100-item SOC. As expected, the brief 20-item version produced higher levels of agreement than did the longer version (62% versus 53%).

Validity and Applications. The value of the SOC has been supported by its usefulness in addressing a number of substantive marital issues. First, the relationship between daily spouse behaviors and daily ratings of marital satisfaction has been assessed (Barnett & Nietzel, 1979; Jacobson *et al.*, 1982; Wills *et al.*, 1974). Although the strength of association has varied, SOC reports have generally accounted for significant amounts of variance on daily marital satisfaction ratings—findings which certainly support the instrument's construct validity.

The discriminant validity of the SOC has been demonstrated in studies involving various types of group comparisons. In particular, nondistressed couples consistently engage in more pleasing and fewer displeasing behaviors than do distressed couples (Barnett & Nietzel, 1979; Birchler, Weiss, & Vincent, 1975; Jacobson *et al.*, 1982; Margolin, 1981; Weiss, *et al.*, 1973). Additionally, distressed couples in therapy exhibit expected changes over time in their enactment of pleasing and displeasing behaviors (Jacobson, 1979).

Overall, the SOC has proven to be a useful quasi-observational assessment tool, although interpretive issues raised by relatively low levels of interspouse agreement need further exploration. In addition, comparable instruments which assess other family dyads are required. Two such procedures have recently been developed—the Parent–Child Observation Schedule (Grounds, 1985) and the Sibling Observation Schedule (Seilhamer, 1983).

C. Parent–Adolescent Observation Schedule (PCOS)

The parent–adolescent relationship affords the same opportunity for utilizing quasi-observational approaches as does the marital relationship. Building on this common characteristic, the Parent–Child Observation Schedule (PCOS; Grounds, 1985) was developed to describe daily relational behaviors engaged in by parents and their adolescent children. Patterned after the Spouse Observation Checklist (SOC; Weiss & Perry, 1979), the PCOS assesses pleasing and displeasing behaviors in parent–adolescent child dyads. Again, behavioral and social exchange theories provide the primary theoretical underpinnings for this approach; in particular, the contention that rates of positive and negative behaviors engaged in by partners in a relationship should affect their perception of the quality of the relationship.

Due to differences in the role behaviors of parents and children, two forms of the PCOS were developed—one to be completed by the adolescent regarding his or her parent, and the other to be completed by the parent regarding his or her teenager. Currently, the teenager form consists of 118 items, whereas the parent form contains 114 items.

Although only preliminary data are available, initial findings suggest that the reliability and validity of the PCOS follows a similar pattern to that of the SOC. Agreement rates are again quite low, although the relationship between daily PCOS data and global measures of relationship satisfaction confirm expectations. That is, both global and daily measures of relationship satisfaction are associated with higher rates of pleasing and lower rates of displeasing behavior. Consistent with these results, parents reports of child behavior problems using the Behavior Problem Checklist (Quay, 1977) were significantly correlated with the observed rates of teenagers' displeasing behaviors.

D. Sibling Observation Schedule (SOS)

Of all family subsystems, sibling relationships have been the least studied and as a consequence, are the most poorly understood. To address this topic, the Sibling Observation Schedule (SOS; Seilhamer, 1983) was developed to facilitate the description of important, day-to-day interactions within adolescent sibling dyads. Items relevant to all possible gender pairs (i.e., brother–brother, brother–sister, sister–sister) and levels of family distress were included in the SOS. Together with the previously described SOC (Weiss & Perry, 1979) and PCOS (Grounds, 1985), the SOS completes the assessable dyads in families with adolescent children.

The 165-item SOS, like the SOC and the PCOS, is a quasi-observational instrument which requires members of a sibling dyad to record the occurrence of each other's pleasing and displeasing behaviors on a daily basis. It is closely patterned after the SOC and the PCOS, and as such, the variables derived from it are daily pleasing and displeasing behaviors. These variables can then be related to concurrently obtained daily measures of relationship satisfaction and other global or specific measures of interest.

Comparable to the PCOS, the interrater agreements obtained

with the SOS were lower than for similar investigations of the SOC. Even with these low agreement levels, the daily frequencies of pleasing and displeasing behaviors were significantly correlated with the daily measures of relationship satisfaction. In addition, preliminary discriminant validity data indicated that distressed and nondistressed sibling pairs could be differentiated on their SOS responses, with distressed pairs engaging in fewer pleasing and more displeasing behaviors.

Further clarification concerning the meaning of quasi-observational data is certainly needed given the low levels of interrater agreement found on all three instruments. Evidence for concurrent and discriminant validity of these procedures, however, encourages consideration of these instruments for evaluating dyadic relationships within the family. From our vantage point, the SOC, PCOS, and SOS provide a potentially important set of instruments for examining key family subsystems.

IX. Laboratory Observational Procedures: Outcome Measures

The assessment of interaction can emphasize one of two foci—the process of interchange as it unfolds over time, and the outcome of this process as reflected in some performance or solution variable. Although process and outcome assessments are not always entirely independent, the distinction can serve a useful organizing function in our attempt to group family strategies.

Derived most directly from laboratory studies of small group behavior, outcome measures involving families typically engage members in a laboratory game or structured task, that, when performed by the participants, yields measures of the family's success and style in negotiating the task. The common characteristic among the various outcome assessments is that the family's performance is assessed in a highly objective and reliable manner, requiring little if any judgment regarding the behavior that is to be described. Additional strengths of such procedures are that they minimize verbal interaction requirements, and as a result, can be used with relatively young children or with families from different ethnic and/or cultural groups. Furthermore, the game quality of these procedures can serve to increase comfort and reduce defensiveness of participating families.

In survey of laboratory outcome measures used with families, a wide range of procedures can be identified. In most cases, use has been limited to only one or two studies, psychometric properties have been woefully inadequate, and a compelling case for validity has not been demonstrated. The major exception to this conclusion concerns the Reiss Card Sort Procedure (CSP), an instrument that has been the methodological core of a long term, programmatic, and highly influential research program exploring the nature of family life, and the theoretical linkages between individually defined psychopathology and the complexities of the family matrix. In addition, the Revealed Difference Technique (RDT) and the Felt Figure Technique (FFT) are reviewed, the former having a long history in sociological and clinical research and the latter reflecting promise as a rather unique addition to the domain of outcome measures.

A. Card Sort Procedure

1. Background

The Card Sort procedure was devised by Shipstone in 1960, based upon earlier work of Miller (1967), Chomsky (1957), and Reiss (1958). The scoring procedure and its rationale, however, were developed by Reiss, and the current version was first utilized in 1971. Reiss's early interests involved the relationship between family interaction and individual thinking with a particular focus on schizophrenia—an interest stimulated by the work of Wynne and Lidz. Each of these investigators suggested that family interaction played an etiological role in the development of schizophrenia and discussed the possible interaction between parental cognitive processes and children's psychopathology. At that point in time, however, compelling empirical support for such a relationship was lacking.

As Reiss used the task, he became aware of its utility for studying a family's approach, not only to problem-solving situations, but novel social encounters as well, that is, "how a family searches and explores new experiences and how it interprets what it learns" (Reiss & Klein, 1987, p. 207). The family members' set of shared assumptions about the nature of the social environment and their place within it are collectively termed the *family paradigm*. (As defined, a family paradigm represents "shared, unspoken and unquestioned assumptions family members hold in common about their social environment" [Reiss & Klein, 1987, p. 206].) This paradigm influences the family's approach to its environment, problem-solving, and relationships across a variety of contexts, although Reiss acknowledges that the paradigm–behavior relationship is a subtle and complex one that can only be indirectly observed. Three major parameters or dimensions of paradigms have been proposed: configuration, coordination, and closure. These key variables are assessed using the Card Sort procedure. Although Reiss originally used these variables to assess differences between pathological and normal families, his recent emphasis has shifted to a more general interest in social process and the relationship between a family's paradigm and the wider social environment (Reiss, 1981; Reiss & Klein, 1987).

2. Variables Assessed

1. Configuration. "A perception of the social world as essentially ordered, with discoverable principles of organization and masterable by the family" (Oliveri & Reiss, 1981a, p. 411). More specifically, configuration refers to "the degree of patterning and lawfulness that the family perceives in its environment" (Reiss & Klein, 1987, p. 207).
2. Coordination. "A view that the environment perceives and treats the family as a unitary group; that is, that the environment regards family members' individual behavior as a reflection and product of the family" (Oliveri & Reiss, 1981a, p. 411).
3. Closure. This characteristic of paradigm refers to variation along a temporal dimension. In families with early closure, all events seem familiar, in families with delayed closure, the environment is seen as novel. Closure has also been defined as "openness to new information" (Reiss & Oliveri, 1980).

Originally, Reiss found differences between healthy and

pathological families on these three dimensions. Currently, he emphasizes the wide variability among normal groups and contends that no one paradigm, without taking other variables into account, is more adaptive or health-promoting than another. Rather than labeling either extreme as unhealthy, he is more interested in finding out how different positions effect a family's wider social interactions.

The family's position on the dimensions of configuration and coordination has been used to generate a family typology:

Environment sensitive families (high coordination/high configuration). "In our laboratory they carefully synchronize and integrate their behavior in such a way as to optimize their grasp on the overall environment of the laboratory, the problem, and its situation." (Costell, Reiss, Berkman, & Jones, 1981, p. 570)

Consensus-sensitive families (high coordination/low configuration). "Their primary focus is on careful agreement and consensus. They tolerate little divergence of views and, as a consequence, the quality of their problem-solving efforts is often poor. In other studies, they seemed ill at ease and mistrustful of the test solution." (p. 570)

Achievement-sensitive families (low coordination/high configuration). "seem to focus on energetic competitive achievement. In the laboratory they are careful to maintain disagreement, as if they equate agreement with surrender." (p. 571)

Distance-sensitive families (low coordination/low configuration). "In the laboratory they seem focused on maintaining great distance and isolation from one another. They seem pessimistic about their capacity to stick together as a group, or to gain anything of value by doing so." (p. 571)

3. Description of the Instrument

According to Reiss, the Card Sort procedure measures the subtlety and complexity of patterns that a family recognizes in the card symbols, the degree to which members work together as a group, and the extent to which individuals' schemas are affected by new evidence derived from the family (group) interaction.

Each family member sits in a booth facing a one-way mirror

wearing a microphone-earphone apparatus. Each member individually sorts a deck of 15 cards, each containing a sequences of letters or nonsense syllables. During this task, the family members have no contact with each other (Initial Individual Sort). Following the first sort, the individual family members sort a second deck of cards, separately but concurrently. Through the closed communication environment, they are encouraged to discuss the puzzle with each other as they go through the deck. At first, each member is given two cards and is asked to press a finish button when they have been sorted. When all three members have pressed the finish button, they are given the next card. They continue receiving one card at a time until there have been 14 trials (Family Sort). After the family task, each member works alone to sort another set of 15 cards (Final Individual Sort).

In both individual phases (Initial Individual Sort and Final Individual Sort) and the family phase (Family Sort), there are two basic strategies for sorting the deck of cards: by length (number of symbols per card), and by pattern (arrangement of symbols on the card). (The two individual sorts use cards with nonsense syllables whereas the Family Sort uses cards with different numbers and patterns of letters.) Scoring involves comparisons between obtained sorts and "ideal" sorts, comparisons between the obtained sorts of the different family members, and recording of time to complete the various trials. From these data, scores are derived that measure the key variables of configuration, coordination and closure.

Briefly, configuration measures the change in problem-solving strategy and sophistication from Initial Individual Sort to the Family Sort, indicating the degree to which the family improves upon or worsens the problem-solving behavior of the individual member. Coordination compares one member's sort with that of another, indicating the correspondence (similarity) between individual efforts. Closure measures correspondence between sorts on different trials and the trial time, data that relate to the family's degree of reflection/impulsivity and openness/rigidity.

4. *Psychometric Properties and Applications*

   Reliability. The scoring is highly objective, requires little if any judgment on the part of the examiner, and yields highly reliable indices. The temporal stability of the major variables was reported to be quite high over a 6- to 9-month interval: $r = .72$ for configuration, $r = .86$ for coordination, and $r = .43$ for closure (Reiss & Klein, 1987).

Validity and Applications. A wide range of validity studies and applications have been reported by Reiss and his associates during the past 15 years.

1. The three key variables—configuration, coordination, and closure—have been shown through factor analysis to be independent and to account for a large proportion of the test variance (Oliveri & Reiss, 1981a).

2. The procedure has differentiated schizophrenics, character disorders, and normal children's families (Reiss, 1981), as well as subtypes of alcoholic families (Steinglass, 1979; Davis, Stern, Jorgenson, & Steier, 1980).

3. Coordination and configuration measures are not effected when the participating child is administered secobarbital, suggesting that the procedure is measuring underlying, family-wide constructs rather than information processing deficits of individual members (Reiss & Salzman, 1973). In addition, scores are unrelated to intelligence, education, social class, and family size (Oliveri & Reiss, 1981a) and to a wide variety of individual measures of perceptual style (Reiss & Oliveri, 1983).

4. The family paradigm variables have been shown to be predictive of a family's view of other families (Reiss et al., 1980), a family's relationship with their extended family (Oliveri & Reiss, 1981b), and a family's relationship with hospital staff when their child is hospitalized (Reiss, Costell, Jones, & Berkman, 1980).

5. The procedure has effectively explained differences between identified patients and their siblings in distance-sensitive and consensus-sensitive families (Shulman & Klein, 1983).

6. Families who chose conventional family structure on the Madanes figure placement procedure were shown to have low configuration and coordination scores (Oliveri & Reiss, 1982).

7. Recently, the family paradigm was hypothesized to be indicative of a family's coping responses to stress (Reiss & Klein, 1987).

B. Revealed Difference Technique (RDT)

1. Background

The Revealed Difference Technique was developed by Strodtbeck (1951) to study group structures. It has been used extensively to study power in families and as a controlled situation for eliciting conversation. In this summary, only those studies that actually analyzed the families' outcome data (i.e., questionnaire answers) are reported.

Strodtbeck began developing the RDT in 1948, as a method for studying small group interaction. "An effort was made to determine some of the correlates of differential ability to persuade others in accordance with the actor's desires" (Strodtbeck, 1951, p. 468). He found the procedure had validity in studying small groups of strangers and decided to investigate whether marital-dyad decision-making was similar. Strodtbeck's technique of asking each member of a couple to fill out a questionnaire and then having the husband and wife come to a joint agreement is used frequently in family research. Many procedural variations have evolved since Strodtbeck first developed the technique, including different scoring systems, questionnaires contents, and questionnaire formats. Perhaps the most significant modification has been the development of the unrevealed difference technique (Ferreira, 1963; Ferreira & Winter, 1965), whereby the couple does not have their original answers during the joint task. This modification has been theorized to be a more realistic approximation of actual decision-making; the people involved usually do not begin with a clear, overt statement of their discrepancies. The UDT is hypothesized to allow for more subtle and complex modes of interaction.

2. Variables Assessed

1. Power—who wins the most decisions or whose individual choices are accepted as family choices (Ferreira, 1963; Hadley & Jacob, 1973, 1976; Jacob, 1974a; Olson, 1969; Strodtbeck, 1951, 1954).
2. Choice fulfillment—the family's ability to satisfy preference of all family members (Ferreira & Winter, 1966, 1968; Mead & Campbell, 1972; Murrell, 1971).

3. Failure to agree—number of times a mutual solution is not reached (Farina, 1960).
4. Spontaneous agreement—amount of agreement among individual questionnaire responses before joint discussion (Ferreira, 1963; Ferreira & Winter, 1966; Mead & Campbell, 1972; Murrell, 1971; Schuham, 1972). Initial disagreement, the inverse of SA, was used by Jacob (1974a).
5. Decision time—time spent completing the joint questionnaire (Ferreira & Winter, 1966; Mead & Campbell, 1972; Murrell, 1971; Stabenau, Tupin, Werner, & Pollin, 1965).
6. Ferreira (1963) classified the types of decisions families made: *unanimous decision* (wherein the family's choice corresponds with the individual choices of all members); *majority decisions* (wherein the family's choice corresponds with the individual choices of a majority of the members); *dictatorial decision* (wherein the family's decision corresponds with the individual choice of only one of its members); *chaotic decisions* (wherein the family's decision does not correspond with the individually established preference of any of the members).

Bodin (1966) has a particularly careful analysis of scoring procedures based upon differences in the rank orderings of choice preferences, the assumption being that the larger the absolute differences between any two rank orderings, the greater the disagreement. Comparison of the individual rankings by this means provides an index of agreement, whereas comparing individual and joint rankings provide information regarding relative influence; that is, the smaller the absolute difference between individual and joint rankings, the more influence the individual exhibited in having his preferences accepted as the group's preferences. Additional procedures are described for taking initial degree of similarity into account in calculating influence scores.

3. Description of the Instrument

Two or more family members each fill out a questionnaire individually. Then, they are brought into the same room and told to come to a joint decision on how to best answer each questionnaire item. One important variation on this procedure was introduced (Ferreira, 1963; Ferriera & Winter, 1965) in which subjects were not given information about other members' individual responses as the family began the joint discussion phase. This format was referred to as the *unrevealed difference technique*.

Different questionnaires have been used as the basis for discussion. Strodtbeck's (1951) original questionnaire asked couples to rank friends on attributes such as religion, ambition, and happiness. Bodin (1966) used a questionnaire which covered family strengths, problems, authority, communication, defensiveness, and discipline; questions that were "designed to tap attitudes toward emotionally charged family concerns" (Bodin, 1966, p. 34). Bodin's questionnaire was revised and used by Hadley and Jacob (1973, 1976), Jacob (1974a), Zuckerman and Jacob (1979). Ferreira and Winter developed a questionnaire consisting of seven situations chosen to be as neutral as possible (famous people they would like to meet, foods, films, travel, sports, magazines, and car colors). This questionnaire was used by Ferriera and Winter (1966, 1968, 1974); and Mead and Campbell (1972).

Different questionnaires have had different answer formats as well. For Strodtbeck's questions, the couple chose which one of three families best fit the question. Each of Ferreira and Winter's questions had 10 alternatives; the subjects were instructed to indicate the three alternatives they liked most and the three they liked least. Bodin's questions each had five alternatives, that the family was instructed to rank from "most like my family" to "least like my family." Obviously, scoring formulas would be affected by the format of the questionnaire used. Other investigators have used a list of family situations and alternatives developed by Jackson (1956: cited in Farina, 1960).

The technique has been used with children as young as 8 years of age (Titchner & Golden, 1963; Titchner, D'zmura, Golden, & Emerson, 1963). Haley (1967) reports using the procedure with 9 year olds, and Murrell (1971) used the RDT with 10 to 12 year olds.

4. Psychometric Properties and Applications

Reliability. Ferreira and Winter (1966) retested 13 couples after 6 months, and reported test–retest correlations of .71 for spontaneous agreement, .72 for decision time, and .57 for choice fulfillment. Bodin's RDT covered five content areas with two questions on each topic, and split-half reliability was calculated by comparing the items with the same content. Using rank difference scores, reliability coefficients were .84 for total dyadic disagreement, and .96 for total individual compromise.

Validity and Applications. 1. In the earliest use of the Revealed Difference Technique, Strodtbeck (1951) studied three communities in which the power of the wife is thought to differ: the Navaho Indians (wherein the woman is relatively powerful), dry farmers from Texas (wherein the husband and wife are fairly egalitarian), and active Mormon couples (wherein the husbands are very powerful). Results of his study provided strong evidence for differences in the marital power structures that had been predicted.

2. Ferreira (1963) found more initial (spontaneous) agreement in normal families than in families wherein a child was schizophrenic, a significant correlation between child age and degree of child's participation, greater influence of parent versus children, and greater coalition between children and the same sex parent than the opposite sex parent.

3. Bodin (1966) found significantly more spontaneous agreement in normal or problem families than synthetic triads, as well as more father–son disagreement in problem than normal families (Problem families had a delinquent adolescent son.)

4. Ferreira and Winter (1968) found spontaneous agreement and choice fulfillment to be significantly higher in normal families than families where one member had an emotional or criminal problem. They also found decision time to be significantly higher in abnormal than normal families. Murrell (1971) replicated these findings with a nonclinic sample categorized on the basis of sons' social acceptance and achievement. Mead and Campbell (1972), studying families with a drug abusing child, also attempted to replicate the Ferreira and Winter findings. Moderate support for the original finding was reported.

5. Schuham (1972) found more spontaneous agreement in a control group than in families wherein a child had been diagnosed as borderline psychotic. He also found that "every normal

family included in the analysis showed a majority of parent–parent over parent–child agreement, whereas parent–child agreement slightly outweighed parent–parent agreement in disturbed families" (p. 73).

6. Jacob (1974a) found differences in initial disagreement between lower- and middle-class families, and between families with children who were younger or older. He also found differences in power according to social class and child age.

7. Ferreira and Winter (1974) report a relationship between spontaneous agreement and the length of marriage for normal couples. For couples with criminal or emotional problems, spontaneous agreement was not higher in couples who had been married longer.

C. Family Hierarchy Test

1. Background

Madanes's Family Hierarchy Test is based upon the felt-figure methodology originally employed by Kuethe (1962) to investigate social schemas. As described, social schemas are learned cognitive structures that help people organize interpersonal relationships. Schemas determine how individuals categorize people and often determine what expectations are held of other people. From this perspective, it is assumed that schemas are learned from common cultural experiences, and if people manifest schemas differing from the norm, it is because of personality factors. Thus, Kuethe used the felt-figure test to predict personality characteristics and to investigate normative schemas.

Kuethe developed two ways of using felt figures. With the felt-figure technique, subjects were given different sets of figures and told to place them against the background in any way they wished. The figures included a man, a woman, children, a dog, and geometric figures. Using this technique, Kuethe found a tendency for people to organize figures horizontally with people closer to other people than to geometric figures (Kuethe, 1962). With the replacement technique, the figures were placed before the subject for five seconds and then removed. The subject is then instructed to replicate the experimenter's placement, and scoring is based on the accuracy of replacement (Kuethe & Weingarten, 1964). Weinstein (1967) reported that the distance between figures in the replacement technique was related to children's reports of parental acceptance, whereas Thornton and Gottheil (1971) found that schizophrenics placed the figures significantly further apart than normals.

Although used in various studies, the replacement technique was not as popular as the figure placement task, the latter viewed as more relevant to familial schemas. Weinstein (1968) used Kuethe's figure placement task, and interpreted the placements as representative of the index's relationship to his mother and father. Subsequent researchers informed the subject that they were placing members of a family (Guardo & Meisel, 1971; Higgins, Peterson, & Dolby, 1969). In the early 1970s, researchers began asking siblings (Duhamel & Jarmon, 1971) or the whole family (Gerber & Kaswan, 1971; Gerber, 1977; Klopper, Tittler, Friedman, & Hughes, 1978; Oliveri & Reiss, 1982; Tittler, Friedman, Blotcky, & Stedrak, 1982) to arrange the felt figures.

Madanes's contribution to this task was to have the family complete the task jointly after the individual members had completed the task. Madanes also labeled the figures as representing the subject's family rather than any family.

The Madanes Family Hierarchy (a similar version is referred to as the Family Structure Task) test was first used by Madanes in 1978 to study relationships in a family with a child who was a heroin addict. The investigator's objective was to develop a methodology that was compatible with a therapeutic approach focused on family interaction rather than individual family members, although the underlying theory was not specified beyond that of a general systems approach. The specific variables considered were chosen on the basis of clinical observations. The original case study used the task to study variables such as incongruity, pseudo-agreement, inappropriate hierarchical relations, self-centralization, and irresponsibility (Madanes, 1978). In this preliminary effort, the task outcome and associated conversations were interpreted clinically, whereas two later studies utilized fairly precise scoring rules to determine the hierarchy and attachment within the family.

2. Description of the Instrument

> In the first stage of the Family Structure task, each family member is shown diagrams of eight different family structures and is asked to choose the one that most resembles the family relations of the four people who have come to the interview. After he has done so, the subject is asked to write down by each stick figure the name of the family member it represents and finally to move the figures to show how close and how distant family members are from each other." (Madanes, 1978, p. 375)

After each family member completes the task individually, the task is done by the marital dyad and then the entire family.

In the Madanes and Harbin (1983) and Madanes (1978) studies, three people were involved, while in the Madanes, Dukes, and Harbin study (1980), four people were involved. No estimate of the amount of time is given, but this would be expected to vary with families, particularly in the joint decision. Administration is straightforward and requires no additional training. Subjects are read standardized instructions. Scoring procedures in the two later studies are well-defined and fairly simple.

3. Variables Assessed

In the Madanes *et al.* (1980) study three variables were assessed:

1. Hierarchical reversal—a parent was placed below a child, or a younger sibling was placed above an older sibling
2. Same generation attachments—two parent figures touching or overlapping or two siblings touching or overlapping
3. Cross-generational attachments—each incidence of a parent figure touching a child figure.

The Madanes and Harbin (1983) study used similar variables with the exception that a sibling was included. This study measured hierarchical reversals and cross-generational attachments, although no measure of same generation attachments was made. Hierarchical reversals were scored if a parent was placed below or on the same level as the child. Hierarchical reversals were not scored if all family members were seen as equal. Cross-generational attachments were measured and analyzed in two different ways: if a parental and child stick figure were touching or if the distance between a parent and child stick figure was less than the distance between the two parental figures.

4. Psychometric Properties and Applications

Reliability. Madanes and Harbin (1983) report no need to consider reliability because their scoring procedure is operationalized down to mathematical rules. Consistent with this view, Madanes et al. (1980) reported 100% reliability in scoring hierarchical reversals by two judges and 95% reliability in scoring attachment by three judges.

Validity and Applications. 1. Madanes (1978) used the MFHT as pretreatment assessment of a case study. Although no information is given regarding the actual treatment or results, the author concluded that the test was a clinically useful addition to a pretreatment assessment battery.
  2. Madanes et al. (1980) used the test to differentiate families with children who are heroin addicts, schizophrenics, or high-achieving normals. The families containing heroin addicts had significantly more hierarchical reversals. (The children in this study ranged in age from 18 to 35 years and were accepted regardless of marital status.)
  3. Madanes & Harbin (1983) found differences on the MFHT between families with children who were assaultive versus non-assaultive adolescents. Like Madanes et al. (1980), this study demonstrated significantly more hierarchical reversals in disturbed families.
  4. Although a joint task was not included, several other studies are relevant to evaluation of Madanes' procedure. Duhamel and Jarmon (1971), reported that emotionally disturbed children, as well as their siblings, placed figures further apart than normal children. Gerber (1977) found parents of emotionally disturbed boys to show distance and close doll placement more often than normal families, suggesting that distance is a curvilinear function with the midpoint being healthier than either endpoint. Relevant

to concurrent validity, Klopper *et al.* (1978) found that prominence (as measured by who was placed higher or more to the left) was correlated with other measures of prominence, whereas Reiss and Oliveri (1983) found a significant relationship between social schema as measured by the Card Sort procedure and the figure placement procedure. Finally, Tittler *et al.* (1982) found a significant correlation between mother–child distance in the figure placement task and several posttreatment measures.

X. Laboratory Observational Procedures: Coding Systems

To the extent that problem behaviors of children are often displayed in family contexts, systematic observations of disturbed children and their families can provide the researcher with a rich, intimate, and direct view into this very complex process. According to Lytton (1971), the systematic study of parent–child interaction has a relatively short history, beginning during the 1940s with the work of Baldwin, Kalhorn, and Breese (1945, 1949) at the Fels Research Institute. During the next 40 years, however, the field produced a large and impressive body of data and theories relevant to the family's role in childhood disorders. Although the central dimensions of family interaction—affect expression and control—have been germane to parent–child relationships at all stages of development, studies focused on young children have assessed different behaviors and have employed different tasks than have investigations of families with adolescents.

Parent–child interactions with young children have frequently involved the assessment of mother–child behavior during "free-play" situations or during tasks structured so as to elicit a sample of the mothers' control strategies and their children's responses to them. Codes developed to describe these sessions have therefore included rather discrete, behavioral events emitted by parents and children, in particular, mothers' requests for change in child behavior (e.g., command) and children's responses to such directives (e.g., comply, noncomply).

With studies of adolescent-age children, the experimental paradigm has typically involved problem-solving or conflict-resolution tasks with a strong emphasis on the verbal interactions

DETAILED REVIEW OF METHODS

transpiring between parents and children. Although certain relatively clear aspects of these interactions have been assessed (for example, who-speaks-to-whom), the subtlety of observed communication sequences has generally required the development of more inferential coding systems.

Early family studies of psychopathology included families with adolescent-age children because schizophrenia (Mishler & Waxler, 1968) and delinquency (Hetherington, Stouwie, & Ridberg, 1971) were the disorders of major interest at that time. Both systems theory and small group theory were particularly influential in determining the content of these early coding systems. Most importantly, the coding system developed by Bales, Interaction Process Analysis (IPA), had a major impact on the structure and content of later approaches that were more specifically targeted for families. The most direct extensions of IPA to studies of family interaction and psychopathology were Mishler and Waxler's (1968) classic study of schizophrenia and the Bells more recent work on adolescent development (Bell & Bell, 1982; Bell, Bell, & Cornwell, 1982).

Subsequently, social learning theory became a dominant influence in the field, encouraging both an interest in the creation of new coding systems and suggesting the types of behaviors to observe. The development of the Family Interaction Coding System (FICS; Patterson, Ray, Shaw, & Cobb, 1969) was of particular importance to further developments in observational coding systems. Most importantly, the FICS led to the development of coding systems for studying marital interactions (Hops, Wills, Weiss, & Patterson, 1972) in laboratory settings and the multiple extensions of those procedures that followed (e.g., Robinson & Eyberg, 1981). A parallel trend involved a developing interest in assessing families of adolescents from a more systems/communications framework. The seminal work of James Alexander (1973) in the development and application of a coding system based on the theoretical writings of Gibb (1961) was of particular importance to subsequently developed systems for assessing marital interaction (Hawkins, Weisberg, & Ray, 1977) and family interactions involving adolescent-age children (Hauser, Powers, Noam, Jacobson, Weiss, & Follansbee, 1984). Continued interest in systems theory has also led to new coding systems such as the Family Alliances

Coding System (Gilbert, Saltar, Deskin, Karagozian, Severance, & Christensen, 1981), which attempts to operationalize and describe alliances in families, a concept that has frequently been used in the family therapy literature (Minuchin, 1974). The system's influence can also be seen in the Relational Communication Coding System (Ericson & Rogers, 1973), another approach that focuses on the marital dyad. Finally, as a logical outcome of the importance placed on the role of affective expression for family interactions, the Specific Affect Coding System has been developed to more precisely describe this dimension.

In terms of the development of laboratory coding systems focused on younger children, a somewhat different route has been followed. Specifically, investigations of parent–child interactions are often characterized by the development of unique sets of observation codes that are not part of a formal system bearing a distinguishable name. Another characteristic of these investigations is the use of well-differentiated negative codes and minimal, poorly differentiated positive codes. Several of these systems have received at least moderate use, however, and therefore will be briefly mentioned in this section.

A. Marital Interaction Coding System (MICS)

1. Background

The Marital Interaction Coding System (Hops et al., 1972; Weiss & Summers, 1983) was developed to describe the behavior of couples as they engaged in problem-solving discussions in a laboratory setting as recorded on videotape. As one of several behaviorally oriented assessment procedures developed by Weiss and his colleagues, the MICS resulted in a less inferential description of couples communication than could be obtained using more traditional self-report procedures. Measures of interaction derived from the MICS could then be used for identifying couples' behaviors that in turn, could provide a focus for therapy and for evaluation of therapy outcome. By far, the MICS has been the most frequently used coding system found within the marital interaction research literature. Additionally, the applicability of the MICS to family subgroups other than the marital dyad make it a viable instrument for studying the family context of child psychopathology, particularly for older, adolescent-age children. This general utility has increasingly been exploited by researchers who use the MICS to describe interactions of parent–child dyads, triads, and tetrads (Blechman & Olson, 1976; Jacob et al., 1981; Baer, Vincent, William, Bourianoff, & Bartlett, 1980).

The behavioral theories that Weiss and his colleagues were guided by, encouraged a focus on discrete, relatively well-defined behaviors. As noted, the instrument's format and style were influenced by the Family Interaction Coding System (Patterson et al., 1969) that had been developed within the same theoretical framework to perform the related function of describing family interactions in the home.

The originally published MICS has been revised three times, leading to the currently used MICS-III (Weiss & Summers, 1983). Although advances have been incorporated in succeeding versions of the MICS, the general framework has remained the same. Therefore, although the description of the instrument focuses on MICS-III, studies using other versions is included in this review.

2. Description of the Instrument

The MICS includes about 30 codes that are used to describe all behavior observed in the problem-solving discussions of married couples. Behavior is coded sequentially so that the patterns of interaction can be described. One advance incorporated in MICS-III, building on the work of John Gottman (1979), is that a simultaneous record is maintained of both speaker and listener behavior. The complexity of the MICS requires that raters be extensively trained and have their work regularly monitored to ensure adequate levels of reliability.

The MICS is applied to videotapes of interactions, rather than being coded live, so that the tapes can be replayed until all of the behaviors that occurred can be described. In this way a more complete description of the observed interaction is obtained than is possible using coding systems that are applied in real time. To help coders keep track of the location of behavior on the tape, a beep is dubbed on every 30 seconds. Raters then switch to a new rating line after they hear the beep. The addition of a time code to the tape is another feature that facilitates the rater's job. Because no transcripts of interactions are utilized in the application of the MICS, these practical aids are very important.

Each interaction is coded by a pair of coders so that their reliability can be determined (Weiss & Summers, 1983). After identifying all agreements and disagreements on a code-by-code basis, the two coders discuss and reach consensus on those behaviors about which they had disagreed. Interrater agreement is then recorded and the corrected MICS data is entered into the computer.

After the data are entered, a series of software programs are applied to each interaction. These programs result in summaries of various codes and code groups as well as the creation of "dyadic behavior units" (to be described later), and the statistical description of the pattern of interaction exhibited by a couple. These reports offer the opportunity for quickly obtaining a rich description of particular interactions. Similar types of approaches to summarizing and analyzing data can later be applied to larger sets of group data.

3. Variables Assessed

When using the MICS, codes are applied to each new behavioral unit defined as "behavior of homogeneous content, irrespective of duration or formal grammatical accuracy emitted by a single partner" (Weiss & Summers, 1983, p. 89). Although homogeneity is required because of the complexity of verbal interactions, more than one code may be needed to fully describe a particular behavioral unit. When the behavioral unit changes, a new code or codes are applied. The codes are recorded sequentially with interruptions also being indicated. Additionally, a description of listener behaviors is maintained indicating at a minimum whether the listener is "attending" or "not tracking."

The MICS codes include positive verbal and nonverbal behavior (e.g., approve, comply, smile–laugh), negative verbal and nonverbal behavior (e.g., complain, put down, turn off), problem-solving behaviors (e.g., positive solution and compromise), and the two codes, attend and not tracking, that describe the listener state rather than a discrete behavior.

Investigators using the MICS usually have grouped MICS codes together into summary categories prior to conducting their analyses. This greatly simplifies the investigator's task of interpreting obtained outcomes across 30 different behaviors, as well as increasing the power of the analysis and stability of the results. However, though the summary code names are often similar, the component codes are frequently different. For example, accept responsibility has been included in various summary scores including verbal problem solving (Birchler et al., 1975), positive (Margolin & Weiss, 1978), problem-solving positive (Vincent, Friedman, Nugent, & Messerly, 1979), and problem solving (Margolin & Wampold, 1981). This use of different summary scores makes comparisons across studies more difficult.

The MICS-III attempts to remedy this by providing summary code categories in addition to individual codes. The development of categories based on code function was also necessitated by creation of the dyadic behavior units. The seven categories are problem description, blame, proposal for change, validation, invalidation, facilitation, and irrelevant. Although the presentation of summary categories is helpful, the strategy used to decide on these categories has not been reported. Support for some of these categories, however, can be found in a recent study by Jacob and Krahn (1987) that reports on three methods for empirically grouping MICS codes: multidimensional scaling (MDS), principle components analysis (PCA), and transitional probability analyses (TPA).

One reason for developing summary codes is to facilitate the creation of dyadic behavior units (DBU). Each DBU contains the behavior of the speaker, described by one of the seven functional category codes, and the concurrent behavior of the listener. This simultaneous description of dyadic behavior serves to clarify the sequence of coded behavior and to give a context to the speaker's words. It also allows for the statistical evaluation of the contribution of both speaker and listener behavior to the occurrence of subsequent behavior. Software developed within the Oregon Marital Studies program automatically converts raw MICS data into DBU's that can then be analyzed. The availability of this process should greatly facilitate sophisticated analysis of MICS-III data.

Training. The training of MICS raters, similar to the training required when using other complex coding systems, involves trainees memorizing the coding manual, being shown examples of the behaviors described by all of the codes, and engaging in extended practice with training tapes. When their skills improve, trainees are evaluated against precoded criterion tapes. After they reach acceptable levels of ability and start to code real data, raters continue to attend regularly scheduled meetings to maintain their high levels of performance.

4. Psychometric Properties and Applications

The reliability of MICS raters is assessed by determining interrater agreement (IRA) on a point-by-point basis. Because raters are maintained at better than a 70% IRA level, the mean IRA for a particular study is greater than 70% (e.g., 82% IRA reported by Stein *et al.*, 1982). Because MICS codes usually are grouped prior to analysis, and because rater disagreements often involve disagreements among codes from the same group, the reported IRA is actually an underestimate of the reliability that would be obtained if it were assessed at the unit of analysis.

Another way to address the issue of the reliability of MICS raters is to conduct a generalizability study as was done by Wieder and Weiss (1980). They determined the amount of variance accounted for by coders, couples, and occasions. Among other findings, they reported that the majority of variance in their results was attributable to differences between couples and the interactions of couples by occasions, whereas differences between coders did not contribute to significant amounts of variance. This again suggests that coders can reliably use the MICS.

Validity and Applications. During the relatively lengthy history of the MICS, many studies have served to demonstrate its validity for assessing marital interactions and its multiple applications. First, it was used in several methodological studies which have contributed to the understanding of factors, such as demand characteristics (Cohen & Christensen, 1980; Vincent & Friedman, 1979), that affect direct observation procedures. Next, it was useful as an outcome measure for marital therapy (Jacobson & Anderson, 1980) and for discriminating between distressed and nondistressed groups (Birchler et al., 1975). Additionally, it was used to address theoretical issues regarding marital interaction (Margolin & Wampold, 1981).

Because MICS use has expanded to include parent–child dyads and larger family groups, it again has been found to differentiate in interesting ways between the interactions observed in different family groups. For example, the MICS was used to compare interactions of normal families and families with an alcoholic father (Jacob et al., 1981), families where the father was normotensive versus hypertensive (Baer et al., 1980), and families where a child was delinquent versus normal (Jacob, 1974b). Additionally, projects are currently underway that assess dyadic and triadic interactions in families with a blind or physically handicapped adolescent (Van Hasselt & Hersen, 1987). The sensitivity of the MICS to affective and problem-solving behaviors encourages its expanded use with other family types when these interactional variables are of interest.

B. Specific Affect Coding System (SPAFF)

1. Background

As a primary dimension in interpersonal behavior, the assessment of affect has played a key role in research regarding marital and family interaction. The majority of coding systems used to assess interactions in such relationships included codes that describe the positive and negative behaviors in which spouses and their children engage. Investigators using such coding systems have already greatly contributed to our understanding of intimate relationships by describing, for example, differences between nondistressed and distressed couples regarding their use of negative behaviors and their cycles of negative affect reciprocity. The value of these initial attempts at describing family behavior has encouraged the development of more refined approaches for coding emotional expression, because it is these types of behaviors that appear to be responsible for most of the substantive findings to date.

The SPAFF (Gottman, 1983; Gottman & Levenson, 1985, 1986) is an extremely promising coding system that has evolved out of Gottman's (1979) programmatic efforts aimed at understanding and describing marital interaction in distressed and nondistressed couples. Gottman first began describing marital interaction using the Couples Interaction Scoring System (CISS) which involved two separate coding procedures, one that described the content of each spouse message and another that described the associated affect. Instructions for the affect ratings were guided by principles developed by Ekman and Friesen (Ekman, Friesen, & Ellsworth, 1972) in their work on nonverbal expression of facial affect. Subsequently, Ekman and Friesen distilled their work into the Facial Action Coding System (FACS; Ekman & Friesen, 1978) which was designed to describe observable muscle movements in the face that investigators could then use to infer the expression of particular emotions.

Gottman's work with the CISS suggested that more relevant relationship information was contained in the affect ratings than in the content codes. Starting with this premise, he refined his coding of affect by integrating the CISS affect rating procedure with advances found in the FACS. This endeavor led to the development of a new coding system focused solely on the expression of emotion during dyadic communication. Rather than a simple extension of the FACS, he found that a new approach was required for adequately capturing affective expression in this complex interactional situation.

His experience in observing marital behavior led Gottman to conceptualize two forms of coding systems—the "physical specimen" and "cultural informant" approaches. Traditional behavioral coding systems, such as the MICS, fall into the physical specimen variety, because they attempt to carefully define the exact behavior described by each code. Gottman found that as he expanded his affect coding system to include rules to describe how every spouse expressed a particular emotion, his code definitions became increasingly complex and burdensome. As a solution, he adopted an alternative approach which was to focus on using coders who were naturally good and experienced at recognizing emotional expression. He then guided their natural ability with systematic knowledge derived from the FACS and other standard criteria for interpreting emotional expression so that coding could still be conducted in a reliable manner. Because it ultimately relies on the expert knowledge of coders, the SPAFF is an example of what he would call a cultural informant coding system.

Accompanying his decision to use this approach was the observation that what we see as emotional expression is really often a person's attempt at controlling the emotion. For example, we see people try to fight back tears when they are sad or clench their fist in attempt to control their feelings of anger. Based on this observation, he reasoned that the people who were best trained at controlling their behavior so as to express emotion to others were actors, because these were the skills they needed to portray characters in a play. Because of their experience and training with these skills he decided to use actors as raters for the SPAFF.

2. Description of the Instrument

The SPAFF contains 10 codes that describe the specific affect associated with particular spouse behaviors. Coders work with a videotape of the marital interaction and a verbatim transcript when applying SPAFF codes. Originally, the unit of behavior coded was the floor switch, which is all speaker behavior bounded by the speech of the other spouse. More recently, the coding system was modified so that the unit of behavior reflects a continuous emotional expression rather than a floor switch. This approach is analogous to the thought unit used in the MICS compared to the floor switch used in the CISS. For each speaker behavior that is coded, a simultaneous description of listener behavior is made as well. This allows for the subsequent application of more sophisticated statistical approaches for understanding the sequential relationships in the data.

3. Variables Assessed

The SPAFF was developed to describe the various emotions that spouses may exhibit in a laboratory interaction task. As such, the variables it contains cover 10 affect categories including 4 positive codes, 5 negative codes, and 1 neutral code. As with other systems, an investigator can decide to analyze codes separately, or to collapse them into summary codes. One possible summarizing scheme for this system is to collapse the 10 codes into positive, negative, and neutral categories. It should be pointed out that although the same words are used to describe these summary categories as would be used for describing summary categories within other coding systems, the categories so named are probably different because they are comprised of very different molecular codes.

The four positive codes are broadly suggested by the following category names:

- P1—humor
- P2—affection, caring
- P3—interest, curiosity
- P4—anticipation, surprise, excitement, enjoyment, joy

The five negative codes are broadly suggested by the following category names:

- N1—anger
- N2—disgust, scorn, contempt
- N3—whining
- N4—sadness
- N5—anxiety, stress, worry, fear

The tenth code is B—neutral.

Training. Although a cultural informant system is dependent on the prior skills of coders, extensive training experiences are still needed to learn the more technical material found in the manual. The SPAFF manual begins with an excellent section on the general topic of "watching" people, which introduces new raters to the idea of systematic observation and which is intended to make them more comfortable with engaging in the coding process. This section would be valuable reading for most coders using any system for observing subjects. Additional features of the training process include exercises that are designed to help coders act out what they see couples doing so that they can try to experience what a spouse may have been feeling during particular moments of an interaction. Following training, as with other coding systems, the investigator needs to continuously monitor raters to assure the reliability of the coding procedure.

4. Psychometric Properties and Applications

Reliability. Using a generalizability calculation described in Gottman (1979), Gottman and Levenson (1985) have reported Cronbach's alpha's for the summary categories of positive, negative, and neutral, for husbands and wives separately, ranging from .89, for wife negative affect, to .99, for wife neutral affect.

Validity and Applications. The SPAFF has been used to compare the ratings of husbands' and wives' reports of their own feelings to those of outside observers (Gottman & Levenson, 1985). In this study, spouses were asked to return to the laboratory to rate their own tapes using a dial ranging from 1 (very negative) to 9 (very positive) that they could manipulate in a continuous fashion. Among other interesting findings, they found a significant relationship between spouses ratings of their feelings and SPAFF raters coding of their emotional expression.

As a new instrument that is very time-consuming to use, a substantial number of reliability and validity studies have not yet been conducted. Nevertheless, the SPAFF present offers many conceptual advances to coding approaches for marital interaction. As investigators become concerned with breaking down summary codes into more specific emotional descriptions, the SPAFF will offer many important building blocks. The advantage of the smaller coding units is that spouses probably respond in a different manner to the various specific affects. For example, within the negative-emotion summary category, whether a spouse expresses anger or sadness probably leads to a different response by his or her partner. Our knowledge of interaction will be greatly enhanced by having coding systems available, like the SPAFF, that can capture these distinctions.

C. Relational Communication Coding System (RELCOM)

1. Background

Stimulated by the work of Bateson (1936, 1972) and the development of general systems theory, new ways of conceptualizing communication have been developed. These early influences led to further theoretical elaborations, as can be seen in the discussions of pragmatic communication by Waztlawick, Beavin, and Jackson (1967), and to various coding systems developed to describe the relational aspects of communication emphasized by these theorists. Bateson observed that within conversations, individual messages serve at least two functions which he labelled *report* and *command*. While the report component indicates the actual information that was sent, the command component reflects the type of relational control that is exerted by the message. Bateson suggested that it was the command aspect of a communication which served as a stimulus for the listener's response. Relational communication, therefore, is based on transactions that occur between two people, and at the simplest level its assessment requires comparisons of two consecutive messages.

Following from this theoretical perspective, the types of transactions of interest refer to whether partners compete for control in the relationship or whether one accepts or submits to control by the other. A competitive style, where for example both parties disagree with each other, has been referred to as a symmetrical relationship, while the submissive style, wherein one party gives in to the other, has been referred to as a complementary relationship. Within a specific conversation it is possible to observe individual transactions of various types. A premise of this approach, however, is that interpersonal control in the relationship is conveyed by the overall pattern of observed transactions.

The Relational Communication Coding System (RELCOM; Ericson & Rogers, 1973; Rogers & Bagarozzi, 1983) is an attempt to operationalize these concepts so that empirical investigations of marital communications can be conducted. It is a refinement of a previous coding system developed by Mark (1971). Although it has not been applied in clinical research, the RELCOM offers an interesting method for assessing the control dimension in dyadic communication, a variable which family reseachers have often focused on in attempting to understand the relationship between family interaction and the development or maintenance of psychopathology.

2. Description of the Instrument

When using the RELCOM, trained coders assign a code to each message found in verbatim transcripts of audiotaped marital interactions. For every message, three single digit codes are applied which describe the speaker, grammatical form of the message, and the "metacommunication" contained in the message. The authors cite Sluzki and Beavin (1965) as the source for this strategy. The five codes covering grammatical form include assertion, question, talk-over, noncomplete, and other. The third digit indicates one of the following nine categories of metacommunication: support, nonsupport, extension, answer, instruction, order, disconfirmation, topic change, initiation-termination, and other. When messages can be described by more than one code a hierarchy of importance determines which is used. The type of control demonstrated by each message is then determined from combinations of the second and third digit as will be described in the next section.

3. Variables Assessed

The RELCOM was developed to describe the types of control observed in dyadic transactions. To this end, each message is coded as described above. Subsequently each code combination is assigned one of three control descriptors called *one-up* ("a movement toward dominance of the exchange"); *one-down* ("movement toward being controlled by seeking or accepting dominance from the other"); and *one-across* ("a move toward neutralizing control, which has a leveling effect, since it is neither a move toward control nor being controlled") (Ericson & Rogers, 1973, p. 253). All support messages, for example, regardless of their form are coded as one-down communications while all nonsupport messages are coded as one-up.

Each transaction, a sequence of two messages, is then assigned a label based on the combination of control codes that were recorded. For example, a transaction which contained a one-down message followed by another one-down message would be a symmetrical transaction, and specifically a submissive, symmetrical transaction. Because each message can be described by one of three control codes, for a combination of two messages there are nine possible transactional types.

The primary variables available in the RELCOM are the nine transaction types just described. This data can be analyzed so that couples or groups of couples can be characterized and differentiated by the frequency with which they engage in particular types of transactions. Additionally, the patterns of symmetrical, complementary, and transitory transactions could be determined using sequential analytic strategies. Although of less interest to the developers of the coding system, aggregate and sequential analysis of the response codes themselves could also be conducted.

Examples of variables that have been derived from the RELCOM include:

1. Dominance—derived by calculating for each spouse the percentage of their one-up messages that are followed by one-down messages. A "dominance ratio" can then be formed by dividing the husbands dominance score by the wife's score.
2. Submission—in a parallel fashion to the dominance score, submission can be derived by calculating for each spouse the percentage of one-down messages that are followed in a complementary fashion by a one-up message.
3. Transactional redundancy—describes how rigid couples are in the transactional type that they use. It has been operationalized as the couples deviation from random use of the nine transactional types and more elaborately as a "coefficient of variation" which is described more fully in Courtright, Millar, and Rogers (1980).

Training. Ericson and Rogers (1973) report that they trained coders during three sessions lasting 2 hours each. This is a relatively brief training period compared to many other marital coding systems.

4. Psychometric Properties and Applications

Reliability. Reliability for the RELCOM has been reported as averaging 86% using percent agreement as the measure (Ericson & Rogers, 1973). It should be noted that this is for agreement on all three digits. Percent agreement was higher for each of the digits when they were assessed separately.

Applications. Initial reports using the RELCOM (Courtright, Millar, & Rogers, 1979, 1980; Ericson & Rogers, 1973) have evaluated the relationship of dominance to role strain and found that more dissatisfied couples had more symmetrical transactions in general and, in particular, the difference occurred for competitive symmetrical transactions and transitional symmetrical transactions. These latter styles occur when both messages in the transaction are one-across messages. They also found greater husband dominance in couples with less role strain. Finally, couples with greater role strain were more rigid in the pattern of transactions they displayed. Although the couples studied varied on questionaire assessments of role strain, the samples used so far have been normal ones. The potential for using this procedure with more distressed couples or wherein psychopathology is present has yet to be realized.

The approach to relational communication represented by the RELCOM has also been extended or modified to allow for investigations of similar phenomena in other contexts. Ellis (1979), for example, investigated relational communication in small groups. Watson (1982a,b), whose interests are in understanding organizational behavior, assessed interactions between managers and subordinates. Finally, Glauser and Tullar (1985) developed a variation of relational coding to identify determinants of citizen satisfaction during telephone conversations with police officers. Although the coding systems used by these investigators vary to some extent, the broad interest in this general approach supports the potential usefulness for this type of coding in marital and family research.

D. Constraining and Enabling Coding System (CECS)

1. Background

The Constraining and Enabling Coding System (CECS; Hauser, Powers, Weiss, Follansbee, & Bernstein, 1983; Hauser *et al.*, 1984) describes triadic interactions involving parents and an adolescent engaging in a problem-solving discussion. It was designed to assess important family transactions related to adolescent ego development. The theoretical position utilized by these investigators is an extension of the work of Stierlin (1974) who proposed that parents within disturbed families interfere with the development of autonomy in their children. Such behaviors are characterized as *constraining*. Additionally, Hauser et al. (1984) suggest that certain family interactions can encourage differentiation and autonomy of members. These behaviors are classified as *enabling*.

Although derived from a different theoretical source, the constraining and enabling dimensions appear related to the defensive and supportive dimensions suggested by Gibb (1961) and later incorporated into a coding system by Alexander (1973). The two parts of the CECS that capture these dimensions also appear to be a thoughtful elaboration of the Alexander coding system with a major advance being the division of each dimension into cognitive and affective domains.

The CECS also contains two additional dimensions, *adolescent change*, and *adolescent response*. The adolescent change dimensions assess the impact of parental comments on the adolescent's contributions to the continuation of the discussion. Are parents' speeches followed by the adolescent increasing the complexity of his or her expressions? Or, is there a decrease, no change or a topic shift in the adolescent's subsequent behaviors? The adolescent response dimension reflects whether he or she responds in an enabling or constraining manner to speeches made by his or her parents.

2. Description of the Instrument

The CECS is applied to transcripts of audiotapes made from family discussions. Families, which for this system include parents and an adolescent child, are audiotaped while they discuss topics presented to them by the experimenter. The topics of discussion have been generated using the revealed difference (Strodtbeck, 1951) approach with family members' responses to a Kohlberg Moral Judgment Interview (Colby, Kohlberg, Candee, Gibbs, Hewer, Kaufman, Power, & Speicher-Dubin, 1987). As with other coding systems, the CECS could also be applied to problem-solving discussions around issues generated in other ways.

The audiotapes are then transcribed, following a clear set of rules developed by the authors. These rules require that, in addition to all spoken words, nonverbal sounds are also described so that the rater is aware of the emotional tone of statements. Pauses, laughs, interruptions, and other relevant information are also included in transcripts. Each speech is then numbered for easy identification. A final step in the preparation of transcripts is that a unitizer goes through the transcript and identifies each occasion where codable adolescent speeches are separated by parental speeches. These adolescent speech pairs are marked for use in the determination of the adolescent change and adolescent response dimensions.

Finally, raters apply the constraining and enabling codes to all speeches and apply the two specific adolescent speech dimensions to the second of each pair of previously unitized adolescent speeches. Although only the second speech is coded, the entire unit is needed so the necessary comparisons between the second adolescent speech and previous speeches can be made.

3. Variables Assessed

As previously mentioned, the four major dimensions assessed by the CECS are constraining behaviors, enabling behaviors, adolescent change, and adolescent response. The coding unit for the first two dimensions is the speech, which is everything spoken by one family member until another family member's speech begins. For the latter two dimensions, the coding unit is the second of each previously unitized pair of adolescent speeches, given the context presented by the previous adolescent and parent behaviors.

The enabling dimension is divided into two categories, *cog-*

nitive codes (explanation, focusing, and problem solving) and *affective* codes (acceptance and empathy). The constraining dimension is divided into the same two categories with different codes, cognitive codes (distracting, withholding, and judgmental) and affective codes (indifference, affective excess, and devaluing). Each speech can be described by one of these 12 codes. If more than one code within a category applies to a particular speech, the coding manual contains rules for deciding which code to choose. In addition to choosing the appropriate code, whether or not the speech is an example of a high or low level of this code is indicated by following the explicit rules and examples found in the manual.

Parent's speeches only receive the enabling and constraining codes while the unitized adolescent speeches also receive the change and response dimensions. The adolescent change dimension contains four codes: regression, progression, foreclosure, and topic change. Progression refers to the adolescent giving a further elaboration or a speech with increasing complexity compared to his or her previous one. Foreclosure refers to maintaining the same level of communication while regression suggests a decrease in the quality of the adolescent speech. Topic change refers to a shift in the direction of the conversation. The last dimension, adolescent response, refers to the change that occurs between two adolescent speeches that is related to the parental speeches. If the parent's speech is constraining, the adolescent can engage in submission or opposition. If the parent's speech is enabling, the adolescent can engage in shifting, opposition, or collaboration.

Training. No information on training has been provided.

4. Psychometric Properties and Applications

Reliability. In Hauser *et al.* (1984), rater reliability based on interrater agreement, calculated using occurrence percent agreement and κ, is very good. For the 12 individual enabling and constraining codes, they reported percent agreements varying from 81% to 99%, and κ's ranging from .46 to .82, all of which were at least significant at $p < .05$. These are certainly within the traditionally acceptable range. The reliability of the unitizers was also adequate ranging from 75% to 85% agreement. The adolescent change codes were reliably coded with percent agreement varying between 81% and 88%, and κ's varying between .46 and .68, again all significant at $p < .05$. The reliability of the adolescent response dimension has not been reported.

Validity and Applications. The CECS was developed and used by Hauser to determine the relationship between specific family interactions and ego development. They confirmed that the CECS was able to identify family behaviors that varied with regard to their relationship to ego development, even when the status of the adolescent (psychiatric patient or normal high-school student) and adolescent's age were controlled. Among other results, they found that cognitive enabling interactions were used more frequently by adolescents at higher levels of ego development.

In a related study (Hauser, Powers, Jacobson, Schwartz, & Noam, 1982), preliminary results from the application of the CECS to interactions of families with a diabetic adolescent were reported. Again, they found that CECS variables were sensitive to the adolescent's level of ego development. Furthermore, they suggested that the relationship of family interaction to adolescent ego development decreased the likelihood of finding a general pattern of family behavior for all diabetic families.

Because the CECS contains an elaboration of the supportive and defensive dimensions coded by Alexander (1973), one can reasonably expect that it would successfully and interestingly differentiate groups of families with various child problems as well.

E. Other Laboratory Coding Systems

1. Family Alliances Coding System (FACS)

A recently reported procedure, the Family Alliances Coding System (FACS; Gilbert, Christensen, & Margolin, 1984; Gilbert *et al.*, 1981), offers the innovation of directly describing alliances in families on a speech by speech basis. The FACS, therefore, allows for direct tests of hypotheses generated by structural systems theory (Minuchin, 1974) regarding the patterns of alliances in distressed and nondistressed families. This attempt at operationalizing structural systems variables is an important step toward introducing empirical procedures for evaluating this rich but minimally researched domain of concepts.

The FACS has been applied to audiotaped problem-solving and negotiation interactions engaged in by families with children between 5 and 13 years of age. Each interaction is first transcribed and then coded. For each speech, which includes all words until there is a change in speaker, the coder records to whom the speech was directed, the content (alliance code) and a rating of affect (positive, neutral, negative). In addition, if a speech refers to another person, the about whom target, content, and affect are also recorded.

The 17 content codes each define a specific type of speech act. Some, such as agree-approve, are similar to MICS codes (Weiss & Summers, 1983) in that they describe a speech most directly relevant to the particular dyad involved. Other codes more specifically capture the nature of family alliances. For example, the code negative appeal is used to describe "a statement by A attempting to elicit opposition from B against a third person . . . e.g., He's the bad guy not me, blame him" (Gilbert et al., 1981, p. 167). Each content code has a weighted alliance value that was previously established by averaging the ratings of 20 clinical psychology graduate students. For example, the code attack was assigned an alliance value of −9 on a scale ranging from −10 to +10. For every interaction, the sum of all weighted content codes for a particular speaker and target combination results in their alliance score. The relative strength and affective tone of all dyadic alliances within the family can therefore be determined. Although further developmental work is needed, the instruments acceptable reliability together with initial findings would certainly encourage further utilization of the FACS for investigating this important feature of family systems.

2. *Adolescent Individuation and Family Interaction*

Another recently created coding system has as its primary interest the relationship between family interactions and the social development and individuation of adolescents (Condon, Cooper, & Grotevant, 1981; Cooper, Grotevant, & Condon, 1983; Grotevant & Cooper, 1985). The decision to gather observational data was influenced by their conceptualization of individuation as a relationship property rather than as a characteristic of the individual. The selection of behaviors for their coding system was influenced by family systems theorists (e.g., Minuchin, 1974) who emphasized the related concept of family cohesion and suggest that in healthy families a balance exists between the need for separateness and togetherness. As part of their assessment, Grotevant and his colleagues had families engaged in a "plan a trip together" discussion. Transcripts of the audiotapes of these discussions were then made and subsequently coded.

Their observation that communications can serve both stimulus functions (i.e., to move discussions in a particular direction) and response functions (that is, as reactions to previous speeches by other family members) influenced the design of their coding system. Specifically, each "utterence" in their system (roughly a sentence) receives two codes—one of six move codes (e.g., suggests action) and one of eight response codes (e.g., agrees, disagrees). Additionally, the speaker and target are identified. Consistent with their hypothesis, factor analyses suggested that their coding system includes two factors reflecting individuality (self-assertion and separateness) and two factors reflecting aspects of connectedness (permeability and mutuality). These dimensions of communication which were designed to assess behavioral indices of individuation, were then used in comparison with other measures of adolescent development; specifically, those for identity-formation and role-taking ability. Given the acceptable reliabilities and initial findings that have recently been obtained, the coding system appears to have considerable promise for investigating important aspects of family interaction. Further validation of this system and efforts aimed at extending its use to assessment of families with problem children are therefore warranted.

3. Couples Interaction Scoring System (CISS)

The Couples Interaction Scoring System (CISS; Gottman, 1979), developed by Gottman and his colleagues, has at this time only been used for assessing marital interaction. Because of its innovative approaches to issues faced in the creation of many family coding systems, a brief description of the procedure is warranted.

Like the MICS, the CISS was developed to describe problem-solving interactions in distressed and nondistressed marital dyads. Building on the work of Raush (Raush et al., 1974), and Weiss (Hops et al., 1972), Gottman attempted to define behavioral codes which captured the sequential patterning of marital discussions. Additionally, he simultaneously coded the speaker's and listener's behavior—data that enriched our understanding of the context of interaction and prepared the way for the application of sophisticated sequential analytic statistical approaches. The subsequent inclusion in the MICS-III of the continuous description of the listener's behavior demonstrates the immediate impact this system has had on the field.

Another factor which influenced the form of the CISS was the work of Eckman and Freisen on coding nonverbal expressions of emotion (Eckman, et al., 1972). In addition to content codes (e.g., agree, disagree), every speech in the CISS is given an affect rating based on nonverbal cues. In this way, greater differentiation of marital behavior is afforded. For example, when Gottman grouped codes he was able to separate "disagrees" that occurred with negative affect from those that were spoken in a neutral tone of voice. This probably led to the creation of a more homogeneous negativity code group than otherwise would have been possible if the content and affect of behavior had not both been coded.

As the CISS is reliably codable and contains some innovative features for describing marital interactions, it merits consideration for application to parent–adolescent discussions and, with some modifications, to describing triadic and tetradic family behavior.

F. Coding of Family Interactions with Younger Children

As noted on p. 183, parent–child interactions with younger children have often been recorded in laboratory settings, and as such, some mention of the frequently used instruments in this domain is warranted.

Children with conduct disorders or hyperactivity have been

the most frequent subjects in such studies, whereas the specific behaviors of interest have been parental attempts to influence child behavior (i.e., commands) and children's responses to parental commands (i.e., compliance and noncompliance). Additionally, negative child behaviors such as yell, whine, hit, and high rate, have often been included as behaviors of interest. For example, the system developed by Forehand (Atkeson & Forehand, 1981) was used to differentiate between clinic and nonclinic families (Forehand, King, Peed, & Yoder, 1975), and was found to be a sensitive measure of treatment outcome (Peed, Roberts, & Forehand, 1977). The system contains only three child codes: child compliance, child noncompliance, and child inappropriate behavior.

Although negative behaviors are frequently coded, prosocial behaviors such as "comforts and shares" (which have been included in coding systems in the literature on normal development [e.g., Bryant & Crockenberg, 1980]), have not often been well-differentiated in studies of clinical populations. Given the importance of negative behaviors in families with troubled children, this omission may be understandable, but nevertheless compromises the completeness of family descriptions.

The general format for coding parent–child dyads has been to choose a limited group of parent and child behaviors and to record at least the antecedent–consequent relationship. For example, the Response Class Matrix (RCM; Mash, Terdal, & Anderson, 1973) requires two observers, one of whom records a tally mark for the appropriate child–mother sequence of behaviors, while the other records a tally mark for the appropriate mother–child sequence. In this way, sequential relationships are captured by the system as well as more traditional frequency of occurrence data. Given the strong influence of learning theory in the development of these assessment strategies, this emphasis on antecedent–consequent relationships is to be expected. However, to evaluate the importance of longer behavioral chains, other coding systems beside the RCM are required (Lobitz & Johnson, 1975).

Laboratory interactions have played an important role in attempts to develop comprehensive therapy approaches for difficult children (e.g., Forehand, Sturgis, McMahon, Aguar, Green, Wells, & Breiner, 1979; Wahler, House, & Stambaugh, 1976). In these programs, the laboratory codings have served to identify problematic interactions and to measure treatment outcome. Additionally, such data have successfully differentiated family functioning across groups that have varied in terms of type of child disorder. The RCM, for example, was used to describe mother–child interactions with hyperactive boys (e.g., Mash & Johnston, 1982; Tarver-Behring, Barkley, & Karlsson, 1985) and with retarded children (e.g., Cunningham, Reuler, Blackwell & Deck, 1981). Another system, the Dyadic Parent–Child Interaction Coding System (DPICS; Robinson & Eyberg, 1981) was used to discriminate mother–child interactions with neglected and behavior-problem children (Aragona & Eyberg, 1981).

In summary, many systems have been used to describe parent–young child interactions exhibited in laboratory settings. These systems have emphasized antecedent–consequent relationships, and have focused on parental commands and negative child behaviors. The great commonality across these procedures, however, makes it difficult to strongly recommend a specific coding system within this set of instruments.

XI. Laboratory Observational Procedures: Rating Scales

Rating scales offer many advantages for describing important attributes of actual family behavior. As global measures, they can allow for the complete gestalt of an interaction to be captured. Given the limited number of major dimensions along which families can be characterized, it would appear that observers should be able to describe families using rating scales, given a sufficient sample of family behavior and carefully described scale anchors. These ratings could then be used to differentiate groups and to serve as criterion measures for related process or report measures. As yet, however, this approach has been an underutilized and poorly developed form of assessment. Therefore, only two good examples, both of which assess communication, are presented—Communication Rapid Assessment Scale (CRAS; Joanning, Brewster, & Koval, 1984) and the Marital Communication Rating Scale (MCRaS; Borkin, Thomas, & Walter, 1980).

In general, rating scales for other dimensions of family behavior have not been fully developed or constructed in a psychometrically sound manner. The most ambitious attempt at developing an integrated set of rating scales has been performed by Lewis, Beavers, Gossett, and Phillips (1976) who proposed 13 scales for assessing the many aspects of their model of family functioning. Even utilizing a somewhat weak measure of interrater agreement, however, they still obtained inadequate rater reliability for the majority of their scales. Therefore, these scales cannot be recommended at this time, although they would certainly be of potential interest in studies of family interaction and psychopathology.

Another set of scales, developed by Henggeler and his colleagues (Hanson, Henggeler, Haefele, & Rodick, 1984; Henggeler & Tavormina, 1980), attempt to assess key family dimensions that have been identified in the relevant literature. Similar to those variables we judged as important, Henggeler and Tavormina (1980) chose to assess affect, conflict, and dominance in marital and parent–adolescent dyads. Although adequate interrater reliabilities were obtained for each of the three scales, published descriptions leave the reader with considerable uncertainty regarding the meaning and independence of the three scales. Nevertheless, these dimensions of family behaviors warrant continued developmental efforts.

A. The Marital Communication Rating Scale (MCRaS)

1. Background

The Marital Communication Rating Scale (MCRaS) is an observational coding system designed to be used as a pretreatment measure to specify couples' communicative faults (Borkin et al., 1980). The 37 codes are largely based on the 49 codes used in an earlier version, the Verbal Problem Checklist (VPC; Thomas et al., 1974). The goals of the authors were to provide a clear, concise, efficient assessment of communication problems that could be amenable to therapeutic interventions.

Although designed with a clinical emphasis, the scale was developed so as to be psychometrically sound and appropriate for treatment-outcome research. The results of the ratings should clarify greatly the specific areas of communication on which clinicians should focus and be directly implemented in treatment planning. The authors place an emphasis on concrete, detailed specification of therapeutic goals.

2. Variables Assessed

The 37 MCRaS codes are grouped into four general categories: "content of the conversation, vocal characteristics, control or focus responses, referent representation" (Borkin et al., 1980, p. 290). Content of the conversation includes codes for 16 types of statements, such as positive statement, opinion given, or information. The dimension of vocal characteristics includes eight tonal or paralinguistic codes such as rate of speech, loudness, or aversive tone. The third dimension, conversational control statements, classifies messages which overtly influence the direction of the conversation, such as requests for opinions or information and includes four codes. The fourth dimension, referent representation, includes seven codes for statements which indicate some confusion or distortion of the topic being discussed (e.g., overgeneralization or presumptive attribution).

3. Description of the Instrument

After watching an interaction, the rater rates each member of the dyad in each of the 37 categories. The first 12 categories of behavior are rated along 7-point scales where 0 is "appropriate" and 7 is "inappropriate" (e.g., positive statements and opinions). The next seven categories are also 7-point scales, but 0 is "appropriate" and -3 or $+3$ are "inappropriate;" for example, talking either too slow or too fast would be considered detrimental to conversation. The other items are on a 4-point scale from nonoccurrence to frequent occurrence; for example, quibbling or incorrect autoclitic would be rated on a scale from not present to frequently present. Borkin et al. (1980) indicate that rater training requires approximately 20 hours, whereas rating itself requires 5 to 10 minutes per discussion.

4. Psychometric Properties and Applications

Reliability. Reliability was calculated on data from three raters' judgments across 35 discussions. The mean percent exact agreement ranged from 58% to 66%. When agreement was calculated within 1 point, the means ranged from 89% to 93%. Some items were more reliable than others. Exact agreement by item ranged from 19% to 97%; agreements within 1-point agreement ranged from 73% to 100% (Borkin et al., 1980).

Validity and Applications. One category from each of the four response types was chosen for analysis of concurrent validity.

1. Ratings of the "amount of talk" were compared with results from an electronic timer which measured the amount of talk time. The results from the two measures of amount of talk were significantly related ($p < .001$).

2. Ratings of statement negativity were compared with a frequency count of negative statements that were verbalized. Here, again, the ratings were significantly related to a frequency count ($p < .001$ for the total negative rate, $p < .004$ for the individual negative rate).

3. Ratings of the frequency of overgeneralization were significantly related to a frequency count of the number of overgeneralizations made.

4. Ratings of the appropriateness of the amount of information and opinions requested were compared with a count of the number of requests made. Results were in the predicted direction, but not significant.

B. The Communication Rapid Assessment Scale (CRAS)

1. Background

The Communication Rapid Assessment Scale (CRAS) is a behavioral rating scale for observing and categorizing dyadic communication. The goals of the developers were to provide a scale that

(a) is simple to use and to rate, (b) widely applicable in research and intervention settings, (c) scorable in real or clock time, (d) applicable to live or recorded sessions, (e) sensitive to verbal and/or nonverbal factors, (f) applicable to any dyadic verbal interaction regardless of format, (g), inexpensive, (h) useful as a guide to training or therapy, and (i) sensitive to change in communication quality over time. (Joanning et al., 1984, p. 410)

Over a 5-year period, the authors combined rational and empirical approaches to develop first a verbal, and then a nonverbal scale. Initially, communication descriptors were culled from literature reviews. These components were then rated for communicative relevance by two experts, both professors of communication. The components were edited and placed on the scale by the experts. Final revisions were made to support literature findings in the placement of the components.

2. Variables Assessed

There are two forms of the CRAS: verbal and nonverbal. Each form yields one rating, an overall 5-point rating of dyadic communication. The scale ranges from "highly conducive to communication or relationship maintenance" to "highly destructive to communication or relationship maintenance" (Joanning et al., 1984, p. 410).

3. Description of the Instrument

Ratings are based on 3 to 5 minutes of live or recorded dyadic conversation of an issue relevant to the couple's relationship. The verbal form requires more subjective judgment; nonverbal behaviors are based on frequency or presence of behaviors. Examples of constructive verbal communication include staying with an issue, equal speaking time, or sharing a personal point of view; destructive verbal communication includes many interruptions, attacking the other's point of view, or lack of sharing personal information. Nonverbal constructive behaviors include good eye contact, positive head nods or relaxed hand movements whereas fidgeting, gaze avoidance or backward trunk lean would be considered negative nonverbal behaviors (Joanning et al., 1984).

The amount of training required for raters is unspecified. In one study (Koval, 1979), rating was done by two experts in communications, two undergraduate home economics majors, and two graduate students in family studies. No appreciable difference was found for level of expertise. The rating is done in real time.

4. Psychometric Properties and Applications

Reliability. Estimates of interrater reliability for the verbal form have ranged from .84 to .97. Brewster (1983) found nonverbal form interrater reliability to be .86 and combined form interrater reliability to be .96. Brewster also computed test–retest reliability for 26 couples. His data were based on two, 3-minute discussions with 20 minutes intervening. Verbal test–retest reliability was .68, nonverbal was .65, and combined was .70 (Joanning et al., 1984).

Validity and Applications. 1. Joanning (1982) used the CRAS in a treatment outcome study of the Couple Communication Program. Mean CRAS scores at posttest and follow-up were significantly higher than pretest CRAS scores. MCI and MAT scores were also higher at posttest and follow-up than at pretests.

2. Brock and Joanning (1983) used the CRAS in a comparison of the Relationship Enhancement (RE) Program and the Minnesota Couples Communication Program. The CRAS scores were significantly higher for RE.

3. Two studies have compared the Marital Communication Inventory (Bienvenu, 1970) and the Marital Adjustment Test (Locke & Wallace, 1959) with the CRAS. Brewster found the MCI to correlate .54 with the combined form, .48 with the verbal only, and .53 with the nonverbal. Over several administrations, Joanning (1982) found correlations ranging from .18 to .58 between the MCI and the verbal form of the CRAS (Joanning et al., 1984). Brewster found the MAT correlated .48 with the combined CRAS, .44 with the verbal CRAS, and .42 with the nonverbal form. Joanning found correlations ranging from .05 to .27 between the MAT and the verbal CRAS.

XII. Naturalistic Observational Procedures

Observations of families in their own homes offers the clearest view of naturally occurring family processes. Although observations in the laboratory provide a direct view of family behavior and allow the investigator to select relevant interactional tasks for families to negotiate, the home setting gives the investigator the opportunity to observe routine, day-to-day interactions in a more natural setting. The appeal of studying naturally occurring family behavior has led investigators to go to the home and attempt to systematically record their observations.

Work in this area has been most influenced by Patterson and his associates and their development of the Family Interaction Coding System (FICS; Patterson *et al.*, 1969). Both their theory-driven focus on clearly defined, molecular behaviors, and the many methodological issues they have addressed, have generated a broader interest in naturalistic assessment procedures. Even with their intuitive appeal, however, the cost and complexity of these approaches probably continues to limit the extent of their use.

Aside from cost, a major concern with observational procedures has been whether their use influences the behavior of families while they are being observed. This issue of reactivity to observation is frequently raised when direct observation procedures are used, particularly in very private settings like the home. However, the apparent difficulty of demonstrating reliable reactivity effects (Christensen & Hazzard, 1983; Johnson & Bolstad, 1975; Tennenbaum, 1980) suggests that they are probably less ubiquitous than has previously been believed. Although continued evaluation of these effects is warranted, given the small number of studies conducted in this area, the current state of knowledge encourages greater confidence in the ability of investigators to observe naturally occurring family behavior without significantly influencing it.

Three coding systems are described further in this chapter. The first coding system, the FICS, has played a very important role in the field of naturalistic observation of families both historically and currently. The second instrument, the Home Observation Assessment Measure (HOAM; Steinglass, 1979), in addition to its excellent psychometric properties, is one of the few attempts to assess family systems concepts in the home. The last system, the Home Interaction Scoring System (HISS; Tennenbaum, Jacob, Bargiel, & Rushe, 1984), is a recent attempt to describe naturally occurring behavior in the home that is recorded on audiotape. As opposed to the FICS and HOAM, which require live coders who record in real time, the HISS was developed to be applied to a permanent record of naturally occurring behavior so that the obtained descriptions would capture in greater detail the subtleties and complexity of family behavior.

A. Family Interaction Coding System (FICS)

1. Background

The Family Interaction Coding System (FICS; Patterson et al., 1969; Reid, 1978) was developed as part of a broad attempt on the part of Patterson and his colleagues to develop better treatments for families with aggressive children. Their theoretical approach, social learning theory, suggested that continuous feedback to therapists about how client families were actually interacting would be valuable for guiding treatment, evaluating outcome, and facilitating hypothesis testing about the relationship of family interaction and the expression of aggression in children. Beginning with unstructured observations of families with aggressive children, family behaviors were carefully observed and described—descriptions that subsequently became the behavioral codes used in the FICS. Following a 3-year development period, the sixth version was published in 1969. Subsequently, the 29-code system has been extensively investigated for its psychometric properties. Additionally, methodological problems such as observer drift and the influence of observer presence on behavior have been addressed (Patterson, Reid, & Maerov, 1978a,b).

Other investigators, such as Bernal (1974), Forehand (Peed, Roberts, & Forehand, 1977), and Wahler (Wahler, House, & Stambaugh, 1976), have also developed coding systems for describing behavior of conduct disordered children. Although each coding system has been of value to its developer, the FICS has been the most widely investigated and utilized approach.

The home was chosen as the site of observations to capture as natural a sample of behavior as was possible in the temporal order in which it occurred. Social learning theory's emphasis on the antecedents and consequences of behavior guided the decision to focus on the sequential pattern of behavior. Additionally, the authors attempted to build on Wright's (1960) observations that previous observational studies based on frequency data "had not allowed for precise hypothesis testing" (Patterson, 1982, p. 42). Patterson also cites the work of Barker (1951), which emphasized the interaction of children and their environments, as influencing this approach.

2. Description of the Instrument

The FICS is a 29-code system, designed to describe sequentially the interactions of a target subject and any family member with whom the target subject interacts. Well-trained, nonparticipant observers perform the observations. During an observation, all family members are chosen as the target for specific time periods. In a randomly determined order, observers first focus on one family member for 5 minutes and then shift to another. Each family member is usually observed twice during a session. The observations are primarily conducted prior to or during dinner. Their own hunches and the diary data collected by Florence Goodenough (1931) suggested that this would be a good time for observing a high level of problem behavior.

The Patterson group developed a series of rules for families to follow during observations to facilitate their success. Although they originally intended to perform completely unstructured observations, they soon found that family members often would avoid the observers by leaving the room. To circumvent this problem, they developed a set of rules to be followed by families while observations were being conducted:

> (1) Everyone in the family must be present, (2) No guests, (3) The family is limited to two rooms, (4) The observers will wait only ten minutes for all to be present in the two rooms, (5) Telephone: No calls out; briefly answer incoming calls, (6) No TV, (7) No talking to observers while they are coding, and (8) Do not discuss anything with observers that relates to your problems or the procedures you are using to deal with them. (Patterson, Reid, & Maerov, 1978a, p. 8)

The actual coding process involves an observer recording a behavioral sequence, including the current target and another family member's behavior, approximately every 6 seconds. When a behavior continues, it is recorded again for all 6-second blocks in which it occurs. An observation session lasts for approximately 45 minutes.

3. Variables Assessed

The FICS is made up of 29 codes which exhaustively describe all behaviors in which family members may engage. The focus on aggressive children led to the inclusion of 14 codes which made fine discriminations between negative behaviors. These included behaviors such as noncompliance (NC), destructiveness (DS), and yell (YE). The remaining codes describe positive behaviors, such as approval (AP), and physical positive (PS); behaviors engaged in to influence others, such as command (CM); and routine activities like talk and play. The Patterson group primarily reports the rate-per-minute of the occurrence of these behaviors.

Depending on the question being addressed, data from the 29 codes can be reported for each code or they can be lumped together into relatively homogeneous groups. They have found that the most effective group of codes for differentiating families, named "Total Aversive Behavior (TAB)," is comprised of all 14 negative codes summed together.

In addition to assessing group differences using single codes or groups of codes, the Patterson group has also emphasized assessing the sequential patterning of observed behaviors. These temporal descriptions led to the development of their theory concerning coercive family interactions in the homes of aggressive children. The FICS data also allows for testing hypotheses generated by this theory. Again, either codes or code groups can be used for this purpose.

Although the TAB grouping was developed using a rational decision procedure, other strategies can also be used for deriving code groups. Carlson, Williams, and Davol (1984), for example, applied factor analytic procedures to FICS data gathered by the Oregon group to statistically identify which codes covary, and therefore represent similar aspects of family behavior. They included in their analysis the baseline FICS data gathered between 1968 and 1977 from 139 families which contained as a focus 27 normal, 31 stealers, and 81 children referred for control problems in the home. They concluded that the FICS codes could be reduced to five factors which they labeled: (a) verbal emotionality, (b) physical dependency, (c) social involvement, (d) hostile controlling, and (e) hostile impulsive. Using these factors, the three groups were discriminated from one another. In fact, the verbal emotionality factor, which contained only a subset of TAB codes (cry, yell, disapproval, command, whine, and noncompliance), appeared to explain most of the group differences identified by the entire TAB score.

Training. Observers need thorough training to use this coding system reliably. Maerov, Brumett, and Reid (1978) describe three phases of training. First, an overview of the field of naturalistic observation is offered followed by the trainees memorizing the code definitions and practicing the mechanics of using them. Then trainees practice approximately 15 to 20 hours until they reach acceptable levels of reliability on training tapes. Lastly, trainees go into homes with experienced coders and practice until they become "reliable," which they define as obtaining an "interobserver agreement rate of at least 75% on two consecutive observations" (p. 38) with different experienced coders. After raters have reached a satisfactory level of ability, regular meetings are scheduled to maintain their reliability and to prevent observer drift. Additionally, their subsequent home observations are regularly scheduled to be simultaneously coded by others so that rater reliability can be assessed. Materials required for this procedure are the coding manual (see Reid, 1978), training tapes (available from the OSLC, Maerov *et al.*, 1978), and experienced coders to conduct the in-home criterion observations. Additional costs include data entry and the software required to format the data prior to analysis.

4. Psychometric Properties and Applications

Reliability. The reliability of FICS data has been addressed in various ways. One method is that from 25% to 33% of home observations are conducted by two observers so that interobserver agreement can be calculated. The formula they use is the number of frames of agreement divided by agreements plus disagreements. An agreement for a 6-second frame occurs when the observers identify the same antecedant and consequent behavior by the same subject and respondent. They average approximately 75% agreement.

Another way they have assessed rater reliability is by conducting a generalizability study. Jones, Reid, and Patterson (1975) identified several facets that may influence the results of an observational study: rater, setting, and group status. They found that the variance in the data explained by differences due to raters was extremely small. This result strongly supports the ability of raters to reliably use the FICS.

Validity and Applications. The FICS has been utilized in a variety of studies. First, it has been used for assessing general methodological issues relating to naturalistic observations such as observer drift and the relationship of interrater agreement to the complexity of the interaction. Second, it has been used to assess differences between groups of normal and deviant children, with an emphasis on aggressive children and children who steal. Third, it has been used in treatment to suggest intervention goals for therapists and to evaluate outcome. Lastly, it has been used to generate and evaluate hypotheses regarding the etiology and maintenance of problem behaviors in children. (For an excellent description of this body of work, see Patterson, 1982).

B. *Home Observation Assessment Method (HOAM)*

1. Background

The Home Observation Assessment Method (HOAM) coding system, developed by Steinglass (1976, 1979, 1980, 1981) for the purpose of describing family interaction in the home, has unique features which both distinguish it from other coding systems and argue for its broader use. Guided by systems theory, the HOAM focuses on the structure and style of family behavior rather than on the antecedent–consequent relationships emphasized by behavioral theories. With the HOAM, objective events—location within the home, how much they move around, and with whom they interact—are recorded by live observers.

The HOAM was developed in the context of Steinglass's attempts to better understand families with an alcoholic parent. However, the descriptions of behavior that derive from the HOAM are more broadly applicable to understanding the structure and style of other types of families containing either nondistressed or distressed family members. Although the HOAM assesses different types of behavior, the practical aspects of its implementation were influenced by the FICS (Patterson et al., 1969). In both systems, project staff code observable behavior of families in their homes using operational definitions found in their coding manual. Steinglass, however, decided to focus on more concrete behaviors—a decision which was influenced by previous, successful use of such measures (e.g., who speaks to whom) for describing important features of families (e.g., Rebelsky & Hanks, 1971).

Another factor in deciding to use this approach was the desire to observe family behavior over relatively long periods of time. For this reason, raters needed to be able to continue coding without experiencing excessive fatigue and an accompanying decline in reliability. By 1979, Steinglass reported that the HOAM had been in use for approximately 20 months with more than 250 observations conducted on 31 families.

2. Description of the Instrument

The HOAM requires two observers for every observation session. Each observer is assigned to follow and record the behavior of a particular parent. The behavior of children is described as they interact with or are present in the same room with a parent. Observations usually take place over a 4-hour time period divided into 40 minutes of observation followed by 15 minutes of rest.

During observations family members are unrestricted in their movements about their home. As a result, their use of space and traffic patterns can be described. Although observers are instructed to move as little as possible, they follow their assigned parent throughout the home unless the parent moves into locations that previously had been designated as off limits for observers. Each 40 minute observation period is divided into 20, 2-minute blocks. During each block the observer records certain features of the first "interactional sequence" engaged in by the target parent. First, the observer records the task orientation, which can be one of three types: problem solving, work, or information exchange. Next, the affective level of the interaction is rated on a 7-point scale ranging from anger to warmth. Finally, using the perspective of the target subject, the coder decides whether the outcome of the interaction was positive, unclear, or negative.

Following the coding of the first "interactional sequence," observers record the location of their target parent and the path taken by them when they change rooms. They also identify other people who are present in the room with the target, and in what activity the target is engaged (e.g., conversation or physical contact—positive).

Following the completion of a home observation, the data are entered into a computer. Various software programs, developed for the HOAM, can then be applied. First, rater reliability is assessed where appropriate data have been collected. Second, several programs were developed to plot the temporal occurrence of particular behaviors in individual families. These tools facilitate the idiographic assessment of families as a compliment to group analysis.

3. Variables Assessed

From the raw HOAM data, 25 indices of family behavior were derived (e.g., location shifts per hour, mean distance between interactors, and mean affect level for verbal exchanges). Approximately half of these codes are activity measures and half are variability measures. To reduce this large number of dependent measures, a principal components analysis was conducted, resulting in five identified factors:

1. Intrafamily engagement—reflecting the extent to which family members interacted with each other and during

those interactions, the variability of the distance they maintained between themselves.
2. Distance regulation—indicating whether family members tended to stay close together or remain far apart from each other.
3. Extrafamily engagement—relating to family's acceptance of nonfamily members in their home.
4. Structural variability—the degree of variability in patterns of family behavior across sessions.
5. Content variability—the type of problem solving engaged in by families and the variability in affect associated with these exchanges. For example, families high on this variable had more frequent and longer decision-making discussions.

Although observers code the interactions for only one target parent, Steinglass was interested in measures of family, rather than individual behavior. His solution was to analyze the mean of mother and father behavior for each family rather than analyze their individual data. Additionally, observers do not specifically target children, although they are included in the interactional record whenever they are in close proximity to either parent. Therefore, the resulting descriptions of behavior describe the level and variability of the entire family's behavior.

Training. Observers for the HOAM have been trained using what Steinglass called a "practicum" method. He reported that they achieved "acceptable reliability levels with ease." The more objective behaviors that the HOAM focuses on undoubtedly facilitates the training of new raters.

4. Psychometric Properties and Applications

Reliability. Acceptable levels of rater reliability have been reported for the HOAM. Based on percent agreement, the levels reported varied from 63% to 95% with only the who-to-whom ratings being below 70%. The levels of κ reported for the same behaviors were also respectable with the vast majority being greater than .40 and significant at $p < .05$.

Validity and Applications. To date, the HOAM has only been applied to families with an alcoholic member. Within this group, use of the HOAM identified important behavioral characteristics which distinguished subgroups of families. For example, distance regulation was sensitive to the extent that alcohol had been a problem for a family member (Steinglass, 1980). Families with a greater history of alcohol related problems remained in much closer proximity to each other. In another report (Steinglass, 1981), three types of alcoholic families were identified: stable wet (SW—currently drinking), stable dry (SD—currently not drinking), and transitional (TR—changed from wet or dry state during the 6-month observation period). Again, distance regulation differentiated subgroups with SW families remaining in each other's presence much more so than TR families, and SD families being in the middle. The content variability factor also differentiated the three subgroups (SD > SW > TR).

C. Home Interaction Scoring System (HISS)

1. Background

The Home Interaction Scoring System (HISS; Tennenbaum, Jacob, Bargiel, & Rushe, 1984) was developed to objectively describe minimally structured family interaction in the home as recorded on audiotape. The demands presented by the density, intensity, and spontaneity of family members interacting with minimal external structure required the development of a new coding system able to richly describe these family events. An integration of behavioral and systems theory guided the decisions made in the development of this system. As such, the HISS captures the pattern of whole family interactions while minutely describing the individual behaviors of all family members. Additionally, the HISS emphasizes affective communications and instrumental behaviors so that important questions relating to the family socialization process can be answered.

Although not required by the HISS, recordings have always been made during dinner time so as to minimize the need to impose any external structure on family behaviors. This period was chosen because it is an active interactional period with well-established routines where affective and problem-solving behaviors are likely to be expressed. Additionally, more family members naturally gather at this time than at any other. This increased the likelihood of obtaining more representative samples of family behavior because it decreased the number of rules families had to follow while recordings were made.

The form and content of the HISS was heavily influenced by previous coding systems. In particular the MICS (Hops et al., 1972) and CISS (Gottman, 1979) coding systems for laboratory interactions and the work of Christensen (Royce, Christensen, Johnson, & Bolstad, 1976) in coding audiotape records of families were strongly relied on predecessors to the HISS. Additionally, previous experience by the same group in the development of a simpler audiotape coding system, the Family Affect–Content Coding System (FACCS, Tennenbaum, 1980) was important in the creation of the HISS.

HISS-I was first used in 1982 following 3 years of extensive developmental work. Continued experience with new raters and families led to the currently used version, HISS-II, in 1984. More than 100 dinnertime interactions have now been coded using HISS-II.

2. Description of the Instrument

The HISS is applied to audiotaped records of dinnertime family interactions. Recordings can be made in several ways. One method is to use reel-to-reel recorders set to activate automatically every day around dinnertime. Another is to have family members turn on a tape recorder themselves just prior to dinner. As previously mentioned, the HISS can be applied regardless of the recording procedure. After the tapes are collected, they are dubbed onto cassettes during which time nonvocal frequencies are filtered out and an audible signal is added to identify locations on the tape. The identification includes a segment number every 20 seconds and a "beep" 10 seconds after every number. The prepared tapes are then transcribed. Who is speaking and the temporal order of their behavior is visually captured on the transcript. Although time consuming, taking approximately 18 minutes to transcribe 1 minute of tape, the complexity of interactions, due to their density and spontaneous nature, necessitates giving the rater as much concrete information as possible. Additionally, the use of transcripts allows raters to record how they unitized family communications so that reliability coders can rate the exact behavior as the original rater did.

The HISS is then applied by highly trained raters who simultaneously use the prepared audiotape and transcript. This also is time consuming, taking 20 minutes to rate 1 minute of tape. Approximately 25% of all dinners are then rerated to both assess and facilitate the maintenance of acceptable levels of rater reliability.

Following rating, the data are entered and subsequently run through a series of software programs that serve to edit the data for obvious errors, calculate rater reliability if appropriate, and format the data in preparation for further analysis. Although a lengthy process, the description of family behavior that results is extremely rich in detail and compatible with both frequency and sequential approaches to analysis.

3. Variables Assessed

The HISS describes all family behaviors in the temporal order in which they occur. As many family members as are present are coded. However, at this time only dinners with a minimum of three people, including the mother, father, and at least one child have been coded. Other people present, such as relatives living in the home or friends, are also coded. Through the use of speaker and target symbols, the HISS captures all streams of communication whether they occur sequentially or simultaneously. In this way, a complete record of all family behavior is developed.

The unit of behavior utilized by the HISS is the *thought unit*, which is a continuous, homogeneous communication. A new code is applied when any of the components of a *coding unit* changes. A complete coding unit contains multiple information including the speaker and target of the communication, up to three content codes, the context of the message, and whether one of several types of overlapping speech occurred.

At the core of the HISS are 27 behavioral content codes which describe the affective and instrumental behaviors family members may engage in while interacting with each other. The major groupings of HISS codes are as follows: direct positive, direct negative, nondirect positive, nondirect negative, and instrumental behaviors, which include influence, sharing knowledge and problem solving. Of primary importance are the behaviors which directly communicate positive or negative affect to another person present. The direct positive behaviors include positive evaluation (PE), agree (AG), attend (AT) and Comply (CO). The direct negative behaviors include direct negative (DN), general negative (GN), disagree (DG), and noncomply (NC). The next grouping of codes contains those behaviors which are positive or negative but where the affect is not necessarily directed at a target who is present. Although these behaviors do not directly reflect personal evaluations by family members of other dinner participants, they do importantly contribute to the general character or tone of a family's interactions. The nondirect positive codes include positive self-statement (PS), evaluate other positive (EP), subjective talk positive (SP), humor (HM) and laugh (LA). The nondirect negative codes include negative self-statement (NS), evaluate other negative (EN) and subjective talk negative (SN).

The next group of codes describes instrumental behaviors. They include command (CM), command repeat (CR) and command stop (CS). In addition, two instrumental behaviors that indicate a sharing of knowledge, teach (TE) and instruct (IN), are included here. Codes that describe problem-solving behaviors include solution (SO), question (QT), and planning permission (PP) complete this group of instrumental codes.

The last group of codes contains talk (TA), nonverbal (NV), and unintelligible (UN). NV is used in those instances where clear indications exist for a family member having complied or noncomplied with a command. Therefore, it is always double coded with CO or NC. TA and UN are used when none of the other codes are applicable and when the rater cannot understand a particular speech.

A coding hierarchy was developed to clarify which codes to use when more than one applied to a particular behavior. However, rather than lose information offered by additional codes, a rater can include up to three content codes for each behavior. Subsequently, these codes are collapsed in different ways depending on the focus of analysis.

DETAILED REVIEW OF METHODS 157

Additionally, several HISS codes, including AG, DG, CO, NC, CM, CR, CS, and QT, are required to be multiply coded. The codes in this category all describe a communication process. As such, they may contain content of interest as well. For example, "He sure is" following a statement like "Johnny is a real nice guy" is coded agree/evaluate other positive (AG/EP) because the speaker's communication includes the process, AG, and the content, EP. Depending on the question asked during a particular analysis, this code unit would be analyzed whole or collapsed into AG or EP.

Training. The complexity of the HISS requires that extensive training be given to raters. New raters are trained in small group meetings for 2 hours, three times a week. After approximately 10 weeks of training, new raters reach acceptable levels of reliability.

The training itself begins with an overview of observational research and the reading and discussion of the coding manual. Subsequently, a weekly pattern is followed wherein a group of related codes is introduced at the beginning of the week and then is practiced for the next two sessions. This pattern continues until all codes have been presented. Before being judged reliable, raters must code three dinners at above 70% interrater agreement levels with precoded criterion tapes.

4. Psychometric Properties and Applications

The reliability of HISS raters is strictly maintained so as to assure high quality data. Reliability assessments need to be conducted for all of the multiple pieces of information available in each code unit. Therefore, the following series of calculations are conducted, making use of software developed for the HISS (Coffman, Jacob, Tennenbaum, & Schmidhammer, 1985).

First, the reliability of the content codes is calculated. This is done on a point-by-point basis, using the Kappa statistic and occurrence-percent agreement, so that the data has the accuracy required both for frequency based and sequential analysis. The primary calculations use the stringent criteria that the entire coding unit, including up to three content codes, be identical for an agreement to be counted. Additionally, although less stringent, reliability is also calculated on an individual code basis, to conform to the traditional assessments performed by others using similar systems.

In addition to the content codes, rater reliability is assessed for the target of the communication, the type of behavior, and for the overlapping speech symbols. Dispersion charts are printed for each of these parts of the coding unit. Having all of this information facilitates the rater supervisor's job of maintaining rater quality.

As previously mentioned, raters reach at least a 70% IRA level for content codes based on the most stringent IRA formula, before beginning rating. They are expected to maintain this level throughout their career. Weekly rater meetings and individual feedback facilitate maintaining this level of agreement.

Currently, IRA based on the stringent formula averages approximately 75%. IRA based on single codes as the unit of agreement averages approximately 82%. The remaining parts of the coding unit, the target type, and overlapping speech codes, are all rated at better than a 90% level of IRA, which indicates the relatively straightforward nature of these decisions.

4

CONCLUSIONS AND FUTURE DIRECTIONS

From the foregoing review of family measurement procedures, one conclusion should be clear—the domain is characterized by a great diversity of instruments that span a range of constructs, assessment foci, data sources, target populations, and applications. At the same time, it must be acknowledged that for most measures found in the extant literature, limitations regarding psychometric strength or frequency of use argue against a clear endorsement of their application. A relatively small set of instruments, however, can be identified and recommended to the interested researcher, given the more-than-adequate reliability and validity characteristics associated with these procedures and/or the considerable promise they possess as useful measures. On this basis, our evaluation of the field is generally positive and optimistic, yet tempered by the recognition that much work needs to be conducted before the field's potential contributions can be realized. In this chapter, future research needs are presented with the aim of encouraging rigorous and programmatic research concerned with the development, refinement, and validation of family assessment procedures of relevance to studies of child psychopathology.

I. General Limitations of Report and Observational Methods

In our analysis of family assessment methods, we suggested that both report and observational methods have attributes aplenty and that each approach can make significant and unique contributions to understanding the family/psychopathology relationship.

As noted, report procedures are not only convenient and relatively inexpensive, but allow for the possibility of large-sample, normative data to which individual protocols can be related. Most importantly, only report procedures can capture members' cognitions and attributions about relationships and events—data that are increasingly viewed as essential to the goals of understanding and predicting family processes and outcomes (Robinson & Jacobson, 1987). On the other hand, report procedures are in the end, an individual's perceptions of self and other—perceptions that can be inaccurate, biased, and at times serious distortions of what other observers might conclude about the individuals and relationships in question. Furthermore, the researcher must reconcile the inevitable inconsistencies that are seen in the reports from different family members. Finally, most report data provide little in the way of the fine-grained details of moment to moment, day-to-day interactions between family members—data that are of great importance to researchers interested in the analysis of actual family processes.

In contrast with report procedures, observational procedures inform us most directly about actual interchanges among family members. If recorded, coded, and analyzed carefully and creatively, such data provide a critical foundation for an empirically-based theory of family interaction and its links with disorders of children and adults. Notwithstanding these attributes, direct observation strategies involving the use of complex coding procedures are costly and labor intensive, requiring a significant commitment of time and resources in order to collect, collate, and analyze the "prized" interaction data. Furthermore, there are methodological issues of continuing concern involving this approach, including subject reactivity and the meaningfulness of highly specific behavioral codes as indices of the larger dimensions and constructs of relevance to family theory and therapy.

The unique features and methodological limitations of report and observational procedures have been the subjects of various publications in the family research literature. Although the field includes respected family scholars who are primarily identified with either report or observational approaches, it would be a mistake to conclude that one method is *generally* more valuable, useful, or defensible than the other in family studies of psychopathology. Instead, we would suggest that both strategies are necessary for a full understanding of so complex a process as family interaction and psychopathology. To question which approach is better does not seem very useful. Instead, determining what understanding of what problems can be achieved with what methodologies seems to be a more fruitful strategy.

Before one can begin to answer such questions, we need to know a great deal more about the characteristics and limitations of each methodology. In particular, we need to know how dependable and interpretable the information is that we obtain from a report procedure or an observational coding system. It is also critical to assess the issue of cross-method correspondence, and, in so doing, to identify and document those sources of variance that relate to low versus high degrees of association. Even with the insights resulting from investigations of within-method and between-method relationships, it is likely that additional research methodologies and strategies will have to be considered in order to fully appreciate the phenomena we seek to understand, that is the family matrix. Finally, one must acknowledge the developing nature of our guiding concepts, the impact of the field's theoretical immaturity on all of the above endeavors, and the need to develop stronger links between instrument and theory development. In the remaining pages of this chapter, each of these issues will be discussed in more detail.

II. *Within-Method Assessments*

Within each major assessment approach, there remains a need to examine basic issues of instrument reliability and validity. For many of the reviewed instruments, such data were adequate but certainly not compelling. For the procedures identified as promising, such support had only begun to appear. Beyond obvious psychometric weaknesses, which in time will hopefully be addressed, each major approach is associated with certain characteristics that raise important questions bearing on an instrument's interpretability, and, as a result, its usefulness. Several of these characteristics deserve special mention.

First, family assessment instruments often include a variety of subscales (codes, rating scales, outcome measures) purporting to assess particular concepts of general or specific relevance to the theoretical model on which the instrument is based. In many instances, however, a convincing case has not been made for the statistical independence of these component scales, a case that, in turn, requires one to question the conceptual differentiations initially proposed by the model. The Family Assessment Measure (Skinner *et al.*, 1983) and the Family Environment Scale (Moos & Moos, 1981) can be used to exemplify this point. The Family Assessment Measure (FAM) derived from Epstein's earlier clinical-theoretical model of family functioning (Epstein *et al.*, 1968), posits seven primary dimensions (processes) of family functioning: task accomplishment, role performance, communication, affective expression, involvement, control, and values and norms. Notwithstanding the careful and rigorous manner in which the FAM was developed and refined, Skinner reports that the intercorrelations among most scales are substantial, ranging from .39 to .70 for the general format, from .63 to .82 for the dyadic relationship format, and from .25 to .63 for the self-rating format. Similarly, recent factor analyses of the 10 scales from the Family Environment Scale identified two primary factors referred to as cohesion versus conflict and organization versus control (Fowler, 1981, 1982). Given substantial correlation among purportedly distinct concepts, researchers must question the ability of their methodology to capture hypothesized differences among concepts, the correctness of the underlying theory, or both. On the one hand, it may not be possible for individuals to differentiate relationships as clearly and subtly as theory suggests or as other methods, such as observational procedure, are able to do. The influence of general response styles and biases are simply too powerful to allow for reliable and differentiated perceptions from individuals, especially when those reports focus on intimate, emotionally charged relationships in which the respondent is a participant. On the other hand, the model may be overly complex or complex in the wrong way. In reality, relationships are most clearly and parsimoniously differentiated along only two or three dimensions—a conclusion that receives much support from a wide range of theory and research in the domain of interpersonal processes (Foa & Foa, 1974; Leary, 1957; Olson et al., 1980).

A parallel issue is relevant to various observational procedures, including multicode coding systems (Weiss & Summers, 1983), sets of rating scales along which observed interactions are assessed (Thomas, 1977), and multiple measures for indexing conflict and influence constructs from RDT outcome procedures (Bodin, 1966). Evaluating the dimensionality of any instrument, be it a report procedure or observational technique, is certainly of importance to the goals of both theory and instrument development. The specific strategy by which such efforts are pursued varies as a function of the investigator's theoretical, methodological, and statistical biases. In some cases, "sameness" is judged on the basis of similarity in score elevation (high scores on "involvement" occur with high scores on "affective expression") or frequency of occurrence (the observed frequency of "put-downs" covaries with the observed frequency of "negative response"). In these instances, statistical analyses involving some variant of a correlational strategy would probably be considered. In other cases, decisions to collapse or combine variables may involve reference to functional similarity, for example, both "put-down" and "negative response" follow instances of "criticize." (See Jacob & Krahn, 1985, for an example of alternative strategies involved in reducing observational coding systems to a smaller number of composites.)

A second issue, of particular relevance to report procedures, concerns the investigator's interpretation and use of test data obtained from different family members, specifically, differences in the responses of two or more members completing the same questionnaire. With observational methods, the researcher usually provides raters (coders) with a great deal of training in the assessment of relatively specific behaviors or behavioral dimensions. Assuming that high interrater agreement can be achieved, the investigator can be reasonably confident that different observers generally perceive things in the same way and that one set of observations can be interchanged with another. Similarly, the problem of discrepancies among the perceptions of family members is not an issue with laboratory outcome measures, because very objective performance variables (scores) are used to characterize the family as a totality or specific relationships within the family. With questionnaires, tests, quasi-observational procedures, or structured interviews, however, it is almost certain that the correspondence between different members' reports and perceptions will be far from perfect and most often will only be moderate.

Within a single family, assessed and treated within a clinical setting, such discrepancies are not problematic at all, may even enlighten the therapist and family and may suggest likely treatment goals. For the clinical researcher, confronted with an already large matrix of independent and dependent variables distributed across several samples and/or points in time, the issue of intermember discrepancy is likely to complicate an already complex undertaking. Unfortunately, there are no quick answers to this problem or simple strategies by which further clarification can necessarily be achieved. Systematic examination of the issue requires time and effort. Potentially fruitful approaches would include (a) the careful assessment of the reports of different family members (husbands versus wives, parents versus children, sibling versus sibling) plus other appropriate measures (e.g., a Social Desirability Scale) (Crowne & Marlowe, 1967) in order to identify sources of variance accounting for such disparities—for example, differential sensitivity to interpersonal meanings; differences in motivation to report carefully and accurately; differences in "person" variables, such as defensiveness and denial, that may influence and distort responses; and differences in how items/questions are interpreted; (b) the development of composite or complex scores from individual reports (e.g., mean scores, difference scores, extreme scores), followed by the systematic comparison of individual and complex scores regarding their relationship with key methodological and theoretical variables; and (c) the application of multivariate analytic procedures whereby all individual reports are retained within a family profile that, in turn, can be the basis on which families are grouped and subsequently analyzed; for example, families reflecting high agreement among all members versus families reflecting high agreement between parents and low agreement between parents and children versus families reflecting low agreement among all members (Fisher, Kokes, Ransom, Phillips, & Rudd, 1985).

III. Correspondence between Methods

Discrepancies that occur when different members' reports are compared on the same instrument actually represents probably the least complex, example of correspondence. That is, for such comparisons, there is only one instrument (e.g., scores on the FAM) and one method (report procedure). To the extent that other evidence is available (e.g., factor analyses of data from different members yielding the same factors) one can also assume that the same concept (trait, construct) is being measured; for example, marital conflict as determined by wives' test scores and from husbands' test scores. As one begins to introduce other "differences," however, comparisons become increasingly complicated; for example, when comparisons are made within methods but across instruments (e.g., mothers' responses on the FACES versus the FAM) or between two instruments based on different methods (e.g., mothers' reports on the FAM versus laboratory observations coded with the MICS). In considering the latter continuum, it is clear that some comparisons are more different than others because of variations in the specific instrument (e.g., FAM versus FACES), general type of instrument (report versus observation), member providing data (e.g., mother versus father or mother versus ratings of the whole family's participation in a laboratory interaction task), and concepts assessed (e.g., cohesiveness versus coordination). Stated otherwise, comparisons involving two family assessment procedures can reflect differences between data sources, between instruments, between methods, between concepts, or any combination of these conditions. Given such complexity, it is clear that cross-method comparisons can involve a lot more than differences in general method and that interpretation of low correspondence becomes increasingly difficult as the number of differences between the two assessment procedures increases.

In general, empirical studies of cross-method correspondence among family assessment procedures have been limited and nonsystematic in design. One partial exception to this conclusion involved a study of *family power* carried out between 1960 and 1980, although even this literature cannot be considered entirely adequate. (For reviews, see Hadley & Jacob, 1973, 1976.) More recently, two studies examined the correspondence between marital assessment procedures based on report, observational, and quasi-observational methods, with one analysis yielding little evidence for cross-method correspondence (Margolin, 1978), and the other providing substantial support for correspondence across methods (Stein *et al.*, 1982). With work that is most relevant to family (versus marital) assessment procedures, Reiss and his colleagues recently published two studies comparing the correspondence between the Card Sort Procedure and two report instruments: the FES (Oliveri & Reiss, 1984) and the FACES (Sigafoos, Reiss, Rich, & Douglas, 1985). In both analyses, there was little, if any, support for correspondence across methods.

At this time, it is necessary to begin rigorous and programmatic efforts aimed at determining the degree of correspondence within and across important subsets of family measurement procedures. Four guidelines for such an effort are: (a) Within each major subset of measures, correspondence between different members' reports on the same construct as well as the independence of the different constructs should be determined and, if necessary, instrument modification considered. (b) A series of precise comparisons that systematically varies the number and nature of differences between assessment procedures should be initiated. In this effort, care must be taken to manipulate one variable at a time in determining the level of correspondence. Subsequently, a second variable (difference) can be introduced and the resulting level of correspondence compared with the simpler assessment. Such research most certainly involves a considerable number of time-consuming substudies before firm conclusions can be reached. (c) Measures selected for more systematic study should span the several major domains described in this paper—report, observational-laboratory outcome, observational-laboratory process, observational-naturalistic, and quasi-observational instruments should be selected on the basis of this psychometric strengths and theoretical richness (d) Throughout this enterprise, methodological and statistical considerations is obviously of critical importance, coming into play in the investigator's selection of specific research designs, power estimates, correlational versus noncorrelational measures of association, desirable sample characteristics, and so on. At the same time, theoretical considerations, as much as possible, should help guide the investigator to choose the best questions and to sift through the various explanations that will be available upon completion of data collection and analyses. Reiss's recent analyses of report versus observational methodologies—in terms of the type of relationship the subject attempts to create with the experimenter and the impact of instrument ambiguity on the subject's ability to communicate a particular relationship—represents an unusually insightful conceptualization of a most complicated issue (Oliveri & Reiss, 1984; Sigafoos et al., 1985).

IV. Underdeveloped Assessment Targets and Concepts

In our survey of family assessment procedures relevant to studies of psychopathology, several subsets of measures appeared to be largely underdeveloped. Given the multicomponent nature of family structure and the importance and impact of each subsystem on one another, on particular individuals, and on the family as a totality, it is only reasonable to develop reliable and valid procedures for the description of all significant family components (individual, dyadic, triadic, or whole family units). Several areas are noteworthy because of the relative abundance of potentially useful procedures (e.g., assessment of the whole family through report procedures), whereas other subgroups of instruments are only now beginning to develop. Several of these subsets of needed measures deserve additional comment.

First, the assessment of sibling relationships (especially among preadolescent and adolescent age children) is an area of both great concern and relative neglect (Bank & Kahn, 1982; Lamb & Sutton-Smith, 1982). Within the domain of report procedures, only one, Furman's Sibling Relationship Questionnaire (SRQ), was sufficiently developed to warrant a detailed review within this chapter (Furman & Buhrmester, 1985a,b). The SRQ is part of a larger set of instruments tapping children's relationships with various individuals and support structures and, not surprisingly, yields interpersonal dimensions found across a range of family and nonfamily assessment procedures (namely, warmth/closeness, relative status/power, conflict). Whether their final factor, rivalry, will stand up to future psychometric probing remains to be seen. Based upon a very different methodology, a quasi-observational procedure, Seilhamer's (1983) recent modification of the Spouse Observation Checklist (SOC, Weiss et al., 1973) for the assessment of sibling relationships (Sibling Observation Schedule [SOS]) shows considerable promise as a relatively objective, behaviorally specific cataloguing procedure, whereby important day-to-day events (both negative and positive) transpiring in sibling relationships can be collected. Both the SRQ and the SOS have only negotiated the early stages of test development, and their ultimate value as useful instruments depends upon the considerable amount of psychometric and application experiences that lie ahead.

Aside from these two procedures, assessment of child–sibling relationships has only been attempted with quite young children using observation procedures as the major assessment procedure (Dunn & Kendrick, 1981, 1982) or using familywide assessment procedures that include information on various subsystems, including the child–sibling relationship. For example, the dyadic format section of the FAM allows the respondant (child) to assess his or her relationship with each of his or her siblings in terms of the instrument's seven key dimensions, whereas several of the laboratory or naturalistic observation procedures at least allow for specific emphasis on child–sibling relationship (e.g., in interactions with parents, index child, and sibling, rate and sequential analyses can be conducted with a specific focus on child–sibling interactions). Finally, it is possible that various instruments, although not developed for specific assessments of child–sibling relationships, can be modified and/or recaste to provide just such data should the investigator find this subsystem to be of particular interest to his or her research objectives; for example, the relative amount of EE transmitted between index case and sibling (versus index case and parent); the inclusion of the index child and one sibling in laboratory interactions so that the child–sibling dyad (as well as the marital and parent–child dyads) are subjected to careful scrutiny; and the modification of outcome measures such as the CSP to include different combinations of family members (e.g., two siblings) in order to assess differences in performance outcomes.

A second area in which there is a surprising scarcity of psychometrically sound, well-researched instruments involves reports of parent–child relationships. The measures selected for detailed review represent an interesting but rather small set of procedures varying considerably in terms of established psychometric foundations, range of applications, and concepts assessed. Only four instruments seemed worthy of detailed review, clearly indicating the absence of programmatic empirical and theoretical effort directed toward such developments, notwithstanding the key role that parent–child relationships have played in theories of the etiology, course, outcome and treatment of childhood disorders. Tempering this conclusion, however, it must be recognized that a plethora of laboratory and naturalistic observation coding systems for describing family, and more particularly, parent–child interaction have been carefully developed and widely applied since the mid-1960s. Furthermore, other sets of procedures allow for assessment of parent–child relationships as part of a more general family assessment goal (e.g., the dyadic format section of the FAM), whereas several newly developed instruments within other domains (e.g., the Parent–Child Observation Schedule [PCOS] as a quasi-observational procedure) offer considerable promise for the future.

Finally, instruments specifically designed for the assessment of systems properties, although sometimes found within the literature, are relatively few in number, still at an early stage of development, and do not include various key constructs and relationships relevant to this focus. An important exception is the recent effort by Steinglass (1979, 1980, 1981) in the development of the HOAM coding system that is relevant to the family's regulation of its internal environment. With respect to other systems variables, attempts to operationalize concepts from Structural Family Theory (Minuchin, 1974) can be found in the Philadelphia Child Guidance Clinic Family Task and Scoring Procedure (Rosman, 1985) (an observational coding system attempting to operationalize and assess such key concepts as enmeshment, alliance, homeostatic shifts and generational boundaries) as well as Perosa's (Perosa, Hansen, & Persosa, 1981) attempt to assess similar concepts with a self-report procedure (e.g., enmeshment, disengagement, rigidity, flexibility, triangulation, and detouring). Given these instrument's relatively limited use and yet-to-be determined psychometric foundations, an endorsement regarding their application seemed premature. Other instruments, similar in objective and design, can also be identified (Barbarin & Tirardo, 1985; Gilbert *et al.*, 1984), although again, test development efforts thus far remain quite limited. Finally, various systems properties or systems concepts positing links between the family and extrafamilial systems are not yet given serious and sustained attention by family researchers, notwithstanding the obvious need to operationalize such potentially key processes. A recent effort worth noting, however, is Wahler's attempt to understand the *insular* family, an effort to describe and assess relationships between community institutions (systems) and the parent that in turn, exert significant influences on the ongoing nature of parent–child relationships (Wahler, 1980; Wahler & Dumas, 1987). Other efforts such as this one would certainly be encouraged.

V. *The Need for Additional Assessment Methods*

Notwithstanding the considerable range of available family assessment procedures, each major grouping is, characterized by significant limitations; in particular, the underdeveloped status of various subsets of instruments and/or inherent limitations involved in operationalizing concepts and providing compelling demonstrations for reliability and validity. Our earlier discussion of the two major methods—report and observational approaches—indicated various threats to internal and external validity that characterize such techniques. By implication these observations encouraged the search for and development of strategies that reflected greater potential strength and promise in these areas of vulnerability than could be expected of the "parent" instruments themselves. Two relatively new and certainly promising methods—viewed as additions rather than replacements—are noted.

First, there is a developing set of quasi-observational techniques that were briefly described (the prototype being Weiss's Spouse Observation Checklist [SOC]). Although representing members' reports or perceptions of self, other, and associated interactions, the strength of these techniques resides in the potential for collecting objective information on contemporary patterns of interchange among family members. Weiss's term, *quasi-observational*, was intended to capture a point along the continuum ranging from global self-reports of a retrospective nature to detailed codings (observations) of current family interactions as rated by highly trained ("stranger") observers. In contrast with the former, quasi-observational procedures emphasize more molecular and contemporary behaviors of specific relevance to relationship processes, and differ from the latter in terms of utilizing a "participant observer" format which allows access to events and interactions that "outsiders" would not be able to "see." Beyond these characteristics, quasi-observational data methods are still relatively inexpensive to obtain, allowing for the collection of large data sets to which powerful multivariate data-analytic procedures can be applied. Although not without limitations and methodological difficulties of their own (e.g., potential reactivity effects and reconciliation of intermember differences in resultant observations) their uniqueness and potential significance would certainly encourage continued examination, refinement, and validation of these procedures.

A second measurement technique (thus far used only within strictly research contexts) involves the use of physical and physiological data believed to be compelling predictors, concomitants, and/or consequences of family communication processes. Minuchin (1974), for example, developed a technique for measuring physiological responses to family stress in his provocative work with psychosomatic children and their families. In the context of the interaction laboratory, blood samples (unobtrusively drawn from individual family members) were analyzed for level of plasma-free fatty acid (FFA)—a biochemical indicator of emotional arousal that reportedly increases within a short time after emotional stress. Results from these studies were particularly important observations indicating that even when the index children were not directly involved in the marital interaction—they are observing from behind a one-way mirror—their levels of FFA rose as they watched and listened to the parents' conflictual interactions. Most fascinating, however, was the finding that the parents' FFA levels decreased when the children entered into the interaction and the spouses assumed parental functions. That is, the children seemed to function as conflict-detouring mechanisms, although the price they paid may have been a steep one, that is, their own FFA levels increased and did not quickly return to baseline. As summarized by Minuchin,

> the interdependence between the individual and his or her family—the flow between "inside" and "outside"—is poignantly demonstrated in the experimental situation in which events among members can be measured in the bloodstream of other family members (p. 104)

An equally innovative and provocative assessment of "under-the-skin" indicators of emotional arousal was reported in a recent series of studies by Gottman and Levenson (Gottman & Levenson, 1985; Levenson & Gottman, 1983, 1985). In these efforts, physiological recordings of spouses were obtained during the couples' involvement in laboratory, conflict-resolution tasks. Several extremely important findings emerged from these studies which can only be briefly summarized at this point. First, Gottman and Levenson demonstrated a strong relationship between the couples' level of marital satisfaction and pattern of physiological response—namely, distressed couples reflected greater physiological interrelatedness, which, according to the investigators, "reflect the ebb and flow of negative affect, the escalation and deescalation of conflict, and the sense of being 'locked into' the interaction and being unable to 'step back'" (p. 35). Second, initially obtained patterns of physiological arousal predicted a decline in marital dissatisfaction 3 years later; that is, the more initial arousal the greater the decline in satisfaction. Third, spouses' ratings of their own affect as they watched their previously recorded interactions were reliably related to marital satisfaction and to observers' codings of the couples' affect. Of particular interest, physiological recordings obtained during these recall sessions were significantly related to the physiological recordings when the sessions were first conducted.

The wealth of insights resulting from these pioneering efforts is impressive indeed, bearing on such fundamental problems as cross method relationships, the examination of affect and arousal within intimate relationships and their causal and consequent relationships with self-reported distress; and most importantly, the development of reliable and illuminating new assessment methods for probing further the relationship between family interaction and psychopathology. A whole range of "next steps" can be identified from these seminal efforts, many of which, if focused on issues of relevance to parent-child interaction and child outcomes, could provide major insights into this area of inquiry.

VI. The Interplay between Theory and Instrument Development

Although referred to throughout this chapter, it is necessary to make explicit our belief that theory and instrument development must proceed simultaneously and in an integrated fashion. Although by now it must certainly sound like an old saw, research cannot take place in a theoretical vacuum. In like manner, the development, refinement, and validation of any family assessment instrument must ultimately arise from and be relatable to some theoretical matrix, whether loosely construed as a conceptual model, or tightly and systematically organized around a set of testable propositions and axioms. The elegance of the latter is abundantly clear when one refers to the current status of family sociology and the truly landmark offering of Burr, Hill, Nye, and Reiss (1979) in which various family-relevant research topics are reviewed, critiqued, and organized around sets of propositions based upon available empirical and theoretical literature. For clinical theory relevant to the family's role in psychopathology, however, the theories themselves have not always been completely delineated, terribly compelling, or easily testable. There are many problems resulting from such imprecision and ambiguity, including the difficulty in appreciating a family variable's role in a particular aspect of a specific psychopathology; the relationships (primary–secondary, antecedent–consequent, direct–indirect, etc.) among the several family variables that comprise the working model; and the ability to clearly operationalize the concept in order to develop some instrument—be it a questionnaire or observation code—necessary for more systematic study of the theory in which the concept is embedded. Ultimately, some instrument must be developed so that theories can be empirically tested. If hypotheses are not confirmed, one may need to revise an incorrect theory, determine more carefully the basic psychometric foundations of the instrument, or question the validity of the instrument in describing and measuring the construct in question. In the world of science, where our emotions and intellects are intensely challenged, it is often the case that more than one of these explanations may be operating; hence, the need to explore several of these explanations (and their interrelationships) at the same time.

To conclude that the field is "theory-barren" is certainly not our intention. Quite to the contrary, the influences of sociological, systems/communications, developmental, and learning theories are clearly evident in many of family models and concepts found within this literature. Although formal theories of the family's role in psychopathology are not easily identified, the past several decades have witnessed the development and refinement of several "minitheories" focused on a limited sector of the family–psychopathology matrix. Furthermore, several of these research programs have been characterized by a clear and continued commitment to integrate theoretical and instrument development efforts. Most notably, the influential work of such investigators as Patterson, Weiss, Wahler, and Jacobson—beginning with a rather unadorned social learning theory and gradually incorporating constructs from other theoretical perspectives—has not only made significant contributions to family theory but has clearly demonstrated the intimate and necessary interplay among concepts, assessment techniques, and theory development. The efforts of other family researchers have also involved important theoretical components, as well as the development and refinement of instruments that are clearly and systematically related to key theoretical concepts. The contributions of David Reiss and Harvey Skinner, for example, certainly reflect these characteristics and, in addition, provide unusually articulate analyses of the relationship between theory and instrument development.

In a particularly elegant analysis of the scientific enterprise, Reiss and Wyatt (1975) discuss the study of family variables related to schizophrenia, indicating both limitations of the field and remedies that promise greater future yield. Of special relevance to the present context, and germane to family studies of any type of psychopathology is the need to identify "substantial" variables—

variables which depend upon a rigorous and systematic process of definition.

> This definition has, at a minimum, three components: (1) It must have an operational component so that the manner in which the variable is to be measured or inferred is precisely described; (2) It must have a contrast component so that the variable is clearly distinguished from other similar variables with which it might be confused; and (3) It must have a theoretical component so that the functional relationship between the variable and others in the system or domain is spelled out, insofar as possible. (p. 71)

Reiss's own studies of family paradigms and their measurement certainly embody this guiding strategy (Reiss & Kline, 1987), whereas his studies of cross-method correspondence clearly emphasize the role that theory can play in reconciling discrepancies and in guiding future efforts (Oliveri & Reiss, 1984; Sigafoos et al., 1985).

Through a variety of publications, Skinner has also pushed the family field to consider the importance of "theory-driven" efforts at instrument development (Skinner, 1981a, 1984). Skinner used such an approach to test development, which he described as a "construct validation paradigm," in the development of the Family Assessment Measure (Skinner et al., 1983). In an overview of his efforts, Skinner (1987) notes that

> the history of assessment has witnessed the progression from a simple rational approach with little or no empirical analyses, to an empirical strategy that largely set aside theoretical considerations until after the test was constructed, through the construct validation viewpoint which integrates theoretical formulations with empirical research. The construct validation paradigm, as the basis for the FAM, involved an active interplay between the specification of a theoretical model of family functioning, and the construction of an assessment instrument to measure central concepts of the model. In brief, the construct validation paradigm integrates theory formulation with test construction principles. This approach has dual advantages. The theoretical model may be evaluated empirically through studies using the assessment instrument. Also, since the assessment measure has a theoretical basis, this framework should facilitate interpretation of the instrument itself. (p. 425)

The development and validation of family assessment procedures relevant to psychopathology is an admittedly complex process. To pursue and achieve a reliable, valid, and useful set of procedures will require understanding various materials in the fields of epistemology and test theory and development. Each of these literatures will demand great effort and commitment of the investigator in order to acquire a working knowledge of key principles and methods. Without appreciating the role and need for both theory and methodology and their interdependencies, efforts to measure family influences in psychopathology are likely to be seriously compromised.

REFERENCES

Achenbach, T. M. (1978). The child behavior profile: I. Boys aged 6–11. *Journal of Consulting and Clinical Psychology, 46,* 478–488.
Achenbach, T. M. (1982). *Developmental psychopathology,* New York: Wiley.
Achenbach, T. M. & Edelbrock, C. (1979). The child behavior profile: II. Boys aged 12–16 and girls aged 6–11 and 12–16. *Journal of Consulting and Clinical Psychology, 47,* 223–233.
Ainsworth, M. D. S., Blehar, M. C., Waters, E., & Wall, S. (1978). *Patterns of attachment: A psychological study of the strange situation.* Hillsdale, NJ: Lawrence Erlbaum.
Alexander, J. F. (1973). Defensive and supportive communications in normal and deviant families. *Journal of Consulting and Clinical Psychology, 40,* 223–231.
Anderson, C. (1982). The community connection: The impact of social networks on family and individual functioning. In F. Walsh (Ed.), *Normal family process.* New York: Guilford.
Aragona, J. A., & Eyeberg, S. M. (1981). Neglected children: Mothers' report of child behavior problems and observed verbal behavior. *Child Development, 52,* 596–602.
Atkeson, B. M., & Forehand, R. (1981). Conduct disorders. In E. J. Mash & L. G. Terdal (Eds.), *Behavioral assessment of childhood disorders.* New York: Guilford.
Ayllon, T., & Azrin, N. (1968). *The token economy: A motivational system for therapy.* New York: Prentice-Hall.
Baer, P., Vincent, J., William, B., Bourianoff, G., & Bartlett, P. (1980). Behavioral response to induced conflict in families with a hypertensive father. *Hypertension, 2,* 170–177.
Bagarozzi, D. A. (1984). Family measurement techniques. *American Journal of Family Therapy, 12,* 59–62.
Baldwin, A. L., Kalhorn, J., & Breese, F. H. (1945). Patterns of parent behavior. *Psychological Monographs, 58,* (3, Whole No. 268).
Baldwin, A. L., Kalhorn, J., & Breese, F. H. (1949). The appraisal of parent behavior. *Psychological Monographs, 63,* (4, Whole No. 299).

Bales, R. F. (1950). *Interaction process analysis*. Cambridge, MA: Addison-Wesley.

Bandura, A. (1977). *Social learning theory*. Englewood Cliffs, NJ: Prentice-Hall.

Bandura, A., & Walters, R. H. (1963). *Social learning and personality development*. New York: Holt.

Bank, S., & Kahn, M. D. (1982). *The sibling bond*. New York: Basic Books.

Barbarin, O. A., & Tirado, M. (1985). Enmeshment, family processes, and successful treatment of obesity. *Family Relations, 34,* 115–121.

Barker, R. G. (1951). *One boy's day*. New York: Harper & Row.

Barnes, H. L., & Olson, D. H. (1982). Parent–adolescent communication. In D. H. Olson, H. I. McCubbin, H. Barnes, A. Larsen, M. Muxen, & M. Wilson (Eds.), *Family inventories: Inventories used in a national survey of families across the family life cycle*. St. Paul, MN: Family Social Science.

Barnes, H. L. & Olson, D. H. (1985). Parent–adolescent communication and the circumplex model. *Child Development, 56,* 438–447.

Barnett, L. R., & Nietzel, M. T. (1979). Relationship of instrumental and affectional behaviors and self-esteem to marital satisfaction in distressed and nondistressed couples. *Journal of Consulting and Clinical Psychology, 44,* 946–957.

Bateson, G. (1935). Culture contact and schismogenesis. *Man, 35,* 148–183.

Bateson, G. (1972). *Steps to an ecology of the mind*. New York: Ballantine.

Baucom, D. H. (1982). A comparison of behavioral contracting and problem-solving communication training in behavioral marital therapy. *Behavior Therapy, 13,* 162–174.

Beach, S. H., & Arias, I. (1983). Assessment of perceptual discrepancy: Utility of the Primary Communication Inventory. *Family Process, 22,* 309–316.

Becker, W. C. (1964). Consequences of different kinds of parental discipline. In M. L. Hoffman & L. Hoffman (Eds.), *Review of child development research* (Vol. 1). Chicago: University of Chicago Press.

Bell, D. C., & Bell, L. G. (1982). Family process and child development in unlabeled (normal) families. *Australian Journal of Family Therapy, 3,* 205–210.

Bell, D. C., Bell, L. G., & Cornwell, C. S. (1982). *Interaction process coding scheme*. Unpublished manuscript.

Benjamin, L. S. (1974). Structural analysis of social behavior. *Psychological Review, 81,* 392–425.

Benjamin, L. S. (1977). Structural analysis of a family in therapy. *Journal of Consulting and Clinical Psychology, 45,* 391–406.

Benjamin, L. S. (1985). Adding social and intrapsychic descriptors to axis 1 of DSM-III. In T. Milton & G. Klerman (Eds.), *Contemporary issues in psychopathology*. New York: Guilford.

Bentler, P. M. (1968). Heterosexual behavior assessment. *Behavior Research and Therapy, 6,* 21–30.

Berg, P., & Snyder, D. K. (1981). Differential diagnosis of marital and sexual distress: A multidimensional approach. *Journal of Sex and Marital Therapy, 7,* 290–295.

Berkowitz, R., Kuipers, L., Eberlein–Frief, R., & Leff, J. (1981). Lowering expressed emotion in relatives of schizophrenics. In M. J. Goldstein (Ed.), *New* developments in interventions with families of schizophrenics. London: Jossey-Bass.

Bernal, M. E. (1974). *Scoring system for home and school*. Unpublished manuscript.

Bienvenu, M. J. (1970). Measures of marital communication. *Family Coordinator, 19,* 26–31.

Billings, A. G., & Moos, R. H. (1982). Family environments and adaptation; A clinically applicable typology. *American Journal of Family Therapy, 10,* 26–38.

Birchler, G. R., & Webb, L. J. (1977). Discriminating interaction behaviors in happy and unhappy marriages. *Journal of Consulting and Clinical Psychology, 45,* 494–495.

Birchler, G. R., Weiss, R. L., & Vincent, J. P. (1975). Multimethod analysis of social reinforcement exchange between maritally distressed spouse and nondistressed spouse and stranger dyads. *Journal of Personality and Social Psychology, 31,* 349–360.

Blechman, E. A., & Olson, D. H. L. (1976). The family contract game: Description and effectiveness. In D. H. L. Olson (Ed.), *Treating relationships.* Lake Mills, IA: Graphic Publishing.

Bodin, A. (1966). *Family interaction, coalition, disagreement, and compromise in problem, normal and synthetic family triads.* Unpublished doctoral dissertation, University of New York at Buffalo. (University Microfilms No. 66-7960)

Borkin, J. Thomas, E. J., & Walter, C. L. (1980). The marital communication rating schedule: An instrument for clinical assessment. *Journal of Behavioral Assessment, 2*(4), 287–307.

Bowers, K. S. (1973). Situationism in psychology: An analysis and a critique. *Psychological Review, 80,* 307–336.

Brewster, J. R. (1983). *The development of a rapid measure to assess dyadic nonverbal communication.* Unpublished thesis, Texas Tech University.

Brock, G. W., & Joanning, H. (1983). A comparison of the relationship enhancement program and the Minnesota communication program. *Journal of Marital and Family Therapy, 9*(4), 413–421.

Brown, G. W., & Rutter, M. L. (1966). The measurement of family acitivites and relationships. *Human Relations, 19*(3), 241–243.

Brown, G. W., Carstairs, G. M., & Topping, G. (1958). Post-hospital adjustment of chronic mental patients. *Lancet, 2,* 685–689.

Brown, G. W., Monck, E. M., Carstairs, G. M., & Wing, J. K. (1962). The influence of family life on the course of schizophrenic illness. *British Journal of Preventive Social Medicine, 16,* 355–368.

Brown, G. W., Birley, J. L. T., & Wing, J. F. (1972). Influence of family life on the course of schizophrenic disorders: A replication. *British Journal of Psychiatry, 121,* 241–258.

Brutz, J. L., & Ingoldsby, B. B. (1984). Conflict resolution in Quaker families. *Journal of Marriage and the Family, 46,* 21–26.

Bryant, B. K., & Crockenberg, S. B. (1980). Correlates and dimensions of prosocial behavior: A study of female siblings with their mothers. *Child Development, 51,* 529–544.

Burgess, E. W. (1926). The family as a unit of interacting personalities. *Family, 7,* 3–9.

Burns, T. (1973). A structural theory of social exchange. *Acta Sociologica, 16,* 188–208.

Buros, O. K. (Ed.). (1978). *Eighth mental measurements yearbook.* Highland Park, NJ: Gryphon.

Burr, W. R., Hill, R., Nye, F. I., & Reiss, I. L. (Eds.). (1979). *Contemporary theories about the family: Vol. 1. Research-based theories.* New York: Free Press.

Campbell, S. B. (1984). Research issues in clinical child psychology. In A. S. Bellack & M. Hersen (Eds.), *Research methods in clinical psychology.* New York: Pergamon.

Carlson, W. J., Williams, W. B., & Davol, H. (1984). A factor structure of child home observation data. *Journal of Abnormal Child Psychology, 12,* 245–260.

Chamberlain, P. (1980). *A parent daily report measure.* Unpublished doctoral dissertation, University of Oregon.

Chomsky, N. (1957). *Syntactic structures.* Mouton: The Hague.

Christensen, A., & Hazzard, A. (1983). Reactive effects during naturalistic observation of families. *Behavioral Assessment, 5,* 349–362.

Christensen, A., & Nies, D. C. (1980). The spouse observation checklist: Empirical analysis and critique. *American Journal of Family Therapy, 8,* 69–79.

Christensen, A., Sullaway, M., & King, C. (1983). Systematic error in behavioral reports of dyadic interaction: Egocentric bias and content effects. *Behavioral Assessment, 5,* 129–140.

Coffman, G. A., Jacob, T., Tennenbaum, D. L., & Schmidhammer, J. (1985). *A general purpose FORTRAN program for the computation of weighted kappa.* Unpublished manuscript.

Cohen, R. S., & Christensen, A. (1980). A further examination of demand characteristics in marital interaction. *Journal of Consulting and Clinical Psychology, 48,* 121–123.

Colby, A., Kohlberg, L., Candee, D., Gibbs, J. C., Hewer, A., Kaufman, K., Power, C., & Speicher–Dubin, B. (1987). *Assessing moral judgments: A manual.* New York: Cambridge University Press.

Condon, S. M., Cooper, C. R., & Grotevant, H. D. (1981). *Manual for the analysis of family discourse.* Austin, TX: University of Texas Press.

Cooper, C. R., Grotevant, H. D., & Condon, S. M. (1983). Individuality and connectedness in the family as a context for adolescent identity formation and role-taking skill. In H. D. Grotevant & C. R. Cooper (Eds.), *Adolescent development in the family: New directions for child development.* San Francisco: Jossey-Bass.

Costell, R., Reiss, D. Berkman, H., & Jones, C. (1981). The family meets the hospital: Predicting the family's perception of the treatment program from its problem-solving style. *Archives of General Psychiatry, 38,* 569–578.

Courtright, J. A., Millar, F. E., & Rogers, L. E. (1979). Domineeringness and dominance: Replication and expansion. *Communication Monographs, 46,* 179–192.

Courtright, J. A., Millar, F. E., & Rogers, L. E. (1980). Message control intensity as a predictor of transactional redundancy. In D. Nimmo (Ed.), *Communication yearbook III*. New Brunswick, NJ: Transaction.

Cronbach, L. J. (1951). Coefficient alpha and the internal structure of tests. *Psychometrika, 16*, 297–334.

Crowne, D. P., & Marlowe, D. (1967). *The approval motive*. New York: Wiley.

Cunningham, C. E., Reuler, E., Blackwell, J., & Deck, J. (1981). Behavioral and linguistic developments in the interactions of normal and retarded children with their mothers. *Child Development, 52*, 62–70.

Davis, P., Stern, D., Jorgenson, J., & Steier, F. (1980). *Typologies of the alcoholic family: An integrated systems approach*. Unpublished manuscript, University of Pennsylvania, Wharton Applied Research Center.

De Amicis, L. A., Goldberg, D. C., LoPiccolo, J., Friedman, J., & Davies, L. (1985). Clinical follow-up of couples treated for sexual dysfunction. *Archives of Sexual Behavior, 14*, 467–489.

Dentch, G. E., O' Farrel, T. J., & Cutter, H. S. G. (1980). Readability of marital assessment measures used by behavioral marriage therapists. *Journal of Consulting and Clinical Psychology, 48*(6), 790–792.

Doane, G. W., West, K. L., Goldstein, M. J., Rodnick, E. H., & Jones, J. E. (1981). Parental communication deviance and affective style: Predictors of subsequent schizophrenia spectrum disorders in vulnerable adolescents. *Archives of General Psychiatry, 38*, 679–685.

Doane, J. & Singer, M. (1977). *Communication deviance scoring manual for use with the consensus Rorschach*. Unpublished manuscript, University of Rochester.

Doane, J., Jones, J. E., Fisher, L., Ritzler, B., Singer, M. T., & Wynne, L. C. (1982). Parental communication deviance as a predictor of competence in children at risk for adult psychiatric disorder. *Family Process, 21*, 211–223.

Doherty, W. J. (1981). Locus of control differences and marital dissatisfaction. *Journal of Marriage and the Family, 43*, 369–377.

Droppleman, L. F., & Schaefer, E. S. (1963). Boys' and girls' reports of maternal and paternal behavior. *Journal of Abnormal and Social Psychology, 67*, 648–654.

Dryden, W. (1981). The relationships of depressed persons. In S. Duck & R. Gilmour (Eds.), *Personal relationships: 3. Personal relationships in disorder*. New York: Academic.

Duhamel, T. R., & Jarmon, H. (1971). Social schemata of emotionally disturbed boys and their male siblings. *Journal of Consulting and Clinical Psychology, 36*(2), 281–285.

Dunn, J., & Kendrick, C. (1981). Social behavior of young siblings in the family context. Differences between same-sex and different-sex dyads. *Child Development, 52*, 1265–1273.

Dunn, J., & Kendrick, C. (1982). *Siblings: Love, envy, and understanding*. Cambridge, MA: Harvard University Press.

Eidelson, R. J., & Epstein, N. (1982). Cognition and relationship maladjustment: Development of a measure of dysfunctional relationship belief. *Journal of Consulting and Clinical Psychology, 50*, 715–720.

Ekman, P., & Friesen, W. V. (1978). *Facial Action Coding System*. Palo Alto, CA: Consulting Psychologist Press.

Ekman, P., Friesen, W. V., & Ellsworth, P. (1972). *Emotion in the human face: Guidelines for research and an integration of findings*. New York: Pergamon.

Ellis, D. G. (1979). Relational control in two group systems. *Communication Monographs, 46,* 153–166.

Ely, A. L., Guerney, B. G., & Stover, L. (1973). Efficacy of the training phase of conjugal therapy. *Psychotherapy: Theory, Research and Practice, 10,* 201–207.

Emery, R. E., & O'Leary, K. D. (1982). Children's perceptions of marital discord and behavior problems of boys and girls. *Journal of Abnormal Child Psychology, 10,* 11–24.

Endler, N. S., & Magnusson, D. (1976). Toward an interactional psychology of personality. *Psychological Bulletin, 83,* 956–974.

Epstein, N. (1982). Cognitive therapy with couples. *American Journal of Family Therapy, 10,* 5–16.

Epstein, N., & Eidelson, R. J. (1981). Unrealistic beliefs of clinical couples: Their relationship to expectations, goals, and satisfaction. *American Journal of Family Therapy, 9,* 13–22.

Epstein, N. B., Rakoff, V., & Sigal, J. J. (1968). *Family categories schema* Monograph prepared by the Family Research Group of the Department of Psychiatry, Jewish General Hostipal, Montreal in collaboration with the McGill University Human Development Study.

Epstein, N., Fleming, B., & Pretzer, J. (1985). *The role of multidimensional cognitive appraisal in self-reports of marital communication*. Paper presented at the annual convention of the Association for the Advancement of Behavior Therapy, Houston, TX.

Ericson, P. M., & Rogers, L. E. (1973). New procedures for analyzing relational communication. *Family Process, 12,* 245–267.

Farber, B. (1964). *Family organization and interaction*. San Francisco: Chandler.

Farina, A. (1960). Patterns of role dominance and conflict in parents of schizophrenic patients. *Journal of Abnormal and Social Psychology, 61*(1), 31–38.

Ferreira, A. J. (1963). Decision-making in normal and pathologic families. *Archives of General Psychiatry, 8,* 68–73.

Ferreira, A. J., & Winter, W. D. (1965). Family interaction and decision-making. *Archives of General Psychiatry, 13,* 214–223.

Ferreira, A. J., & Winter, W. D. (1966). Stability of interactional variables in family decision-making. *Archives of General Psychiatry, 14,* 352–355.

Ferreira, A. J., & Winter, W. D. (1968). Decision-making in normal and abnormal two-child families. *Family Process, 7,* 17–36.

Ferreira, A. J., & Winter, W. D. (1974). On the nature of marital relationships: Measurable differences in spontaneous agreement. *Family Process, 13,* 355–369.

Filsinger, E. E., & Wilson, M. R. (1984). Religiosity, socioeconomic rewards, and family development. Predictors of marital adjustment. *Journal of Marriage and the Family, 46,* 663–670.

Finney, J., Moos, R. & Newborn, R. (1980). Posttreatment experiences and treatment outcome of alcoholic patients six months and two years after hospitalization. *Journal of Consulting and Clinical Psychology, 48,* 17–29.

Finney, J. W., Moos, R. H., Cronkite, R. C., & Gamble, W. (1983). A conceptual model of the functioning of married persons with impaired partners: Spouses of alcoholic patients. *Journal of Marriage and the Family, 45,* 23–34.

Fisher, L., Kokes, R. F., Ransom, D. C., Phillips, S. L., & Rudd, P. (1985). Alternative strategies for creating "relational" data. *Family Process, 24,* 213–224.

Foa, V., & Foa, E. (1974). *Societal structures of the mind.* Springfield, IL: Charles C. Thomas.

Forehand, R., King, H. E., Peed, S., & Yoder, P. (1975). Mother–child interactions: Comparison of a noncompliant clinic group and a nonclinic group. *Behavior Research and Therapy, 13,* 79–84.

Forehand, R., Sturgis, E. T., McMahon, R., Aguar, D., Green, K., Wells, K. C., & Breiner, J. (1979). Parent behavioral training to modify child noncompliance: Treatment generalization across time and from home to school. *Behavior Modification, 3,* 3–25.

Forgatch, M. S., & Toobert, D. J. (1979). A cost-effective parent training program for use with normal preschool children. *Journal of Pediatric Psychology, 4,* 129–145.

Forman, B. D., & Hagan, B. J. (1983). A comparative review of total family functioning measures. *American Journal of Family Therapy, 11,* 25–40.

Forman, B. D., & Hagan, B. J. (1984). Measures for evaluating total family functioning. *Family Therapy, 11,* 1–36.

Fowler, P. C. (1981). Maximum likelihood factor structure of the Family Environment Scale. *Journal of Clinical Psychology, 37,* 160–164.

Fowler, P. C. (1982). Factor structure of the Family Environment Scale: Effects of social desirability. *Journal of Clinical Psychology, 38,* 285–292.

Fuhr, R. A., Moos, R. H., & Dishotsky, N. (1981). The use of family assessment and feedback in ongoing family therapy. *American Journal of Family Therapy, 9,* 24–36.

Furman, W., & Buhrmester, D. (1985a). Children's perceptions of the qualities of sibling relationships. *Child Development, 56,* 448–461.

Furman, W., & Buhrmester, D. (1985b). Children's perceptions of the personal relationships in their social networks. *Developmental Psychology, 21,* 1016–1024.

Furman, W., Adler, T., & Buhrmester, D. (1984, July). *Structural aspects of relationships: A search for a common framework.* Paper presented at the Second International Conference of Personal Relationships, Madison WI.

Gerber, G. L. (1977). Family schemata in families of symptomatic and normal. children. *Journal of Clinical Psychology, 33,* 43–48.

Gerber, G. L., & Kaswan, J. (1971). Expression of emotion through family grouping: Schemata, distance and interpersonal focus. *Journal of Consulting and Clinical Psychology, 36*(3), 370–377.

Gibb, J. R. (1961). Defensive communications. *Journal of Communication, 3,* 141–148.

Gilbert, R., Saltar, K., Deskin, T., Karagozian, A., Severance, G., & Christensen, A. (1981). *The Family Alliances Coding System (FACS) manual.* Unpublished manuscript, University of California, Los Angeles, CA.

Gilbert, R., Christensen, A., & Margolin, G. (1984). Patterns of alliances in nondistressed and multiproblem families. *Family Process, 23,* 75–87.

Glauser, M. J., & Tullar, W. L. (1985). Citizen satisfaction with police officer/citizen interaction: Implications for the changing role of police organizations. *Journal of Applied Psychology, 70,* 514–527.

Goldstein, M. J., & Stracham, A. M. (1987). The family and schizophrenia. In T. Jacob (Ed.), *Family interaction and psychopathology: Theory methods, and findings.* New York: Plenum Press.

Goldstein, M. J., Rodnick, E. H., Jones, J. E., McPherson, S. R., & West, K. (1978). Familial precursors of schizophrenia spectrum disorders. In L. C. Wynne, R. L. Cromwell, & S. Matthysse (Eds.), *The nature of schizophrenia: New approaches to research and treatment* (pp. 487–498). New York: Wiley.

Goodenough, F. L. (1931). *Anger in young children.* Minneapolis, MN: University of Minnesota Press.

Gottman, J. M. (1979). *Marital interaction: Experimental investigations.* New York: Academic.

Gottman, J. M. (1982). *Time-series analysis: A comprehensive introduction for social scientists.* New York: Cambridge University Press.

Gottman, J. M. (1983). *Rapid coding of specific affects.* Unpublished manuscript, University of Illinois, Urbana–Champagne, IL.

Gottman, J. M., & Levenson, R. W. (1985). A valid procedure for obtaining self-report of affect in marital interaction. *Journal of Consulting and Clinical Psychology, 53,* 151–160.

Gottman, J. M., & Levenson, R. W. (1986). Assessing the role of emotion in marriage. *Behavioral Assessment, 8,* 31–48.

Gottman, J., Notarius, C., Gonson, J., & Markman, H. (1976). *A couple's guide to communication.* Champaign, IL: Research Press.

Grotevant, H. D., & Cooper, C. R. (1985). Patterns of interaction in family relationships and the development of identity exploration in adolescence. *Child Development, 56,* 415–428.

Grounds, L. M. (1985). *The Parent–Child Observation Schedule: An instrument for the assessment of parent–adolescent relationships.* Unpublished doctoral dissertation, University of Pittsburgh, Pittsburgh, PA.

Guardo, C. J., & Meisels, M. (1971). Child–parent spatial patterns under praise and reproof. *Developmental Psychology, 5*(2), 365.

Hadley, T. R., & Jacob, T. (1973). Relationship among measure of family power. *Journal of Personality and Social Psychology, 27*(1), 6–12.

Hadley, T. R. & Jacob, T. (1976). The measurement of family power: A methodological study. *Sociometry, 39*(4), 384–395.

Hafner, R. J. (1986). *Marriage and mental illness: A sex roles perspective.* New York: Guilford.

Hahlweg, K., & Jacobson, N. N. (1984). *Marital interaction: Analysis and modification.* New York: Guilford.

Haley, J. (1967). Experiment with abnormal families: Testing done in a restricted communication setting. *Archives of General Psychiatry, 17,* 53–63.

Hamilton, G. V. (1929). *A research in marriage.* New York: Alber & Charles Boni.

Handel, G. (1965). Psychological study of whole families. *Psychological Bulletin, 63,* 19–41.

Hansen, G. L. (1981). Marital adjustment and conventionalization. A reexamination. *Journal of Marriage and the Family, 43,* 855–863.

Hanson, C. L., Henggeler, S. W., Haefele, W. F., & Rodick, J. D. (1984). Demographic, individual, and family relationship correlates of serious and repeated crime among adolescents and their siblings. *Journal of Consulting and Clinical Psychology, 52,* 528–538.

Hartup, W. W. (1977). Perspectives on child and family interaction: Past, present, and future. In R. M. Lerner & G. B. Spanier (Eds.), *Child influences on marital and family interaction.* New York: Academic.

Hathaway, S. R., & McKinley, J. C. (1951). *MMPI manual.* New York: Psychological Corporation.

Hauser, S., Powers, S., Jacobson, A. M., Schwartz, J., & Noam, G. (1982). Family interactions and ego development in diabetic adolescents. *Pediatric adolescent endocrinology* (Vol. 10, pp. 69–76). Basel: Karger.

Hauser, S., Powers, S., Weiss, B., Follansbee, D., & Bernstein, E. (1983). *Family Constraining and Enabling Coding System (CECS) manual.* Unpublished manuscript, Boston, MA.

Hauser, S. T., Powers, S. I., Noam, G. G., Jacobson, A. M., Weiss, B., & Follansbee, D. J. (1984). Familial contexts of adolescents ego development. *Child Development, 55,* 195–213.

Hawkins, J. L., Weisberg, C., & Ray, D. L. (1977). Marital communication and social class. *Journal of Marriage and the Family, 39,* 479–490.

Hazzard, A., Christensen, A., & Margolin, G. (1983). Children's perceptions of parental behaviors. *Journal of Abnormal Child Psychology, 11,* 49–59.

Henggeler, S. W., & Tavormina, J. S. (1980). Social class and race differences in family interaction: Pathological, normative, or confounding, methodological factors? *Journal of Genetic Psychology, 137,* 211–222.

Henry, J. (1967). My life with the families of psychotic children. In G. Handel (Ed.), *The psychosocial interior of the family.* Chicago: Aldine.

Herman, B. F., & Jones, J. E. (1976). Lack of acknowledgement in the family Rorschachs of families with a child at risk for schizophrenia. *Family Process, 15,* 289–302.

Hersen, M., Kazdin, A. E., & Bellack, A. S. (Eds.). (1983). *The clinical psychology handbook.* New York: Pergamon.

Hetherington, E. M., & Martin, B. (1979). Family interaction. In H. C. Quay & J. S. Werry (Eds.), *Psychopathological disorders of childhood* (2nd ed.). New York: Wiley.

Hetherington, E. M., Stouwie, R. J., & Ridberg, E. H. (1971). Patterns of family interaction and child rearing attitudes related to three dimensions of juvenile delinquency. *Journal of Abnormal Psychology, 78,* 160–176.

Higgins, J. Peterson, J. C., & Dolby, L. L. (1969). Social adjustment and familial schema. *Journal of Abnormal Psychology, 74*(3), 296–299.

Hilgard, E. R., & Bowers, G. H. (1966). *Theories of learning*. New York: Appleton-Century.

Hill, R. (1949). *Families under stress*. New York: Harper.

Hill, R. (1958). Generic features of families under stress. *Social Casework, 49,* 139–150.

Hirsch, S. R., & Leff, J. P. (1975). *Abnormalities in parents of schizophrenics*. London: Oxford University Press.

Hops, H., Wills, T. A., Weiss, R. L., & Patterson, G. R. (1972). *Marital Interaction Coding System*. Eugene, OR: University of Oregon Press.

Hughes, H. M., & Haynes, S. N. (1978). Structured laboratory observation in the behavioral assessment of parent–child interactions. A methodological critique. *Behavior Therapy, 9,* 428–447.

Humphrey, L. L. (1986). Structural analysis of parent–child relationships in eating disorders. *Journal of Abnormal Psychology, 95,* 395–402.

Humphrey, L. L., Apple, R., & Kirschenbaum, D. S. (1985). *Differentiating bulimic-anorexic from normal families using an interpersonal and a behavioral observation system*. Unpublished manuscript, University of Wisconsin, Madison, WI.

Jacob, T. (1974a). Patterns of family conflict and dominance as a function of child age and social class. *Developmental Psychology, 10*(101), 1–12.

Jacob, T. (1974b). *Family interaction, child age, and diagnostic status* (NIMH Grant No. 2R01MH2502). Unpublished manuscript.

Jacob, T. (1975). Family interaction in disturbed and normal families: A methodological and substantive review. *Psychological Bulletin, 82,* 33–65.

Jacob, T. (1976). Behavioral assessment of marital dysfunction. In M. Hersen & A. Bellack (Eds.), *Behavioral assessment: A practical handbook*. New York: Pergamon Press.

Jacob, T. (Ed.). (1987). *Family interaction and psychopathology: Theory, methods and findings*. New York: Plenum Press.

Jacob, T., & Krahn, G. (1987). The classification of behavioral observation codes in studies of family interaction. *Journal of Marriage and the Family, 49,* 677–687.

Jacob, T., & Lessin, S. (1982). Inconsistent communication in family interaction. *Clinical Psychology Reviews, 2,* 295–309.

Jacob, T., Rushe, R., & Seilhamer, R. A. (in press). Alcoholism and family interaction: A research paradigm. *American Journal of Drug and Alcohol Abuse*.

Jacob, T., & Seilhamer, R. A. (1985). Adaptation of the Areas of Change Questionnaire for parent–child relationship assessment. *American Journal of Family Therapy, 13,* 28–38.

Jacob, T., Ritchey, D., Cvitkovic, J., & Blane, H. (1981). Communication styles of alcoholic and nonalcoholic families when drinking and not drinking. *Journal of Studies on Alcohol, 42,* 466–482.

Jacobson, N. S. (1979). Increasing positive behavior in severely distressed marital relationships: The effects of problem-solving training. *Behavior Therapy, 10,* 311–326.

REFERENCES

Jacobson, N. S. (1984). A component analysis of behavioral marital therapy: The relative effectiveness of behavior exchange and communications/problem-solving training. *Journal of Consulting and Clinical Psychology, 52*(2), 295–305.

Jacobson, N. S., & Margolin, G. (1979). *Marital therapy: Strategies based on a social learning and behavior exchange principles.* New York: Brunner/Mazel.

Jacobson, N. S., & Moore, D. (1981a). The effects of behavior rehearal and feedback on the acquisition of problem-solving skills in distressed and nondistressed couples. *Behavior Research and Therapy, 18,* 25–36.

Jacobson, N. S., & Moore, D. (1981b). Spouses as observers of the events in their relationship. *Journal of Consulting and Clinical Psychology, 49,* 269–277.

Jacobson, N. S., Follette, W. C., & McDonald, D. W. (1982). Reactivity to positive and negative behavior in distressed and nondistressed married couples. *Journal of Consulting and Clinical Psychology, 50,* 706–714.

Janes, C., & Hesselbrock, V. (1976, August). *Perceived family environment and school adjustment of children of schizophrenics.* Paper presented at the American Psychological Association's Annual Convention, Washington, D.C.

Joanning, H. (1982). The long-term effects of the couple communication program. *Journal of Marital and Family Therapy, 8,* 463–468.

Joanning, H., Brewster, J., & Koval, J. (1984). The Communication Rapid Assessment Scale: Developments of a behavioral index of communication quality. *Journal of Marital and Family Therapy, 10*(4), 409–417.

Johnson, S. M., & Bolstad, O. D. (1975). Reactivity to home observation: A comparison of audio recorded behavior with observers present or absent. *Journal of Applied Behavior Analysis, 8,* 181–185.

Johnson, S. M., & Greenberg, L. S. (1985). Differential effects of experimential and problem-solving interventions in resolving marital conflict. *Journal of Consulting and Clinical Psychology, 53,* 175–184.

Jones, J. E. (1977). Patterns of transactional style deviance in the TAT's of parents of schizophrenics. *Family Process, 16,* 327–337.

Jones, R. G. A. (1968). *A factored measure of Ellis's irrational belief system with personality and maladjustment correlates.* Unpublished doctoral dissertation, Texas Technological College, Lubbock, TX.

Jones, R. R. (1974). "Observation" by telephone: An economical behavior sampling technique (Tech. Rep. No. 14, pt. 1). Oregon Research Institute, Eugene, OR.

Jones, R. R., Reid, J. B., & Patterson, G. R. (1975). Naturalistic observation in clinical assessment. In P. McReynolds (Ed.), *Advances in psychological assessment* (Vol. 3). San Francisco: Jossey-Bass.

Kalmuss, D. (1984). The intergenerational transmission of marital aggression. *Journal of Marriage and the Family, 46,* 11–19.

Kantor, D., & Lehr, W. (1975). *Inside the family.* San Francisco: Jossey-Bass.

Karoly, P., & Rosenthal, M. (1977). Training parents in behavior modification: Effects on perceptions of family interaction and deviant child behavior. *Behavior Therapy, 8,* 406–410.

Kelley, H., & Thibaut, J. W. (1978). *Interpersonal relations: A theory of interdependence.* New York: Wiley.

REFERENCES

Kerns, R. D., & Turk, D. C. (1984). Depression and chronic pain. *Journal of Marriage and the Family, 46,* 845–852.

Klein, D. M., & Hill, R. (1979). Determinants of family problem-solving effectiveness. In W. R. Burr, R. Hill, F. I. Nye, & I. L. Reiss (Eds.), *Contemporary theories about the family* (Vol. 1). New York: Free Press.

Klopper, E. J., Tittler, B. I., Friedman, S., & Hughes, S. J. (1978). A multimethod investigation of two family constructs. *Family Process, 17,* 83–93.

Kottgen, C., Sonnichsen, I., Mollenhauer, K., & Jurth, R. (1984). Families high-expressed emotions and relapses in young schizophrenic patients: Results of the Hamboz Camberwell-Family-Interview, Study II. *International Journal of Family Psychiatry, 5,* 71–82.

Koval, J. (1979). *Development of a rapid measure to assess dyadic communication.* Unpublished thesis, Texas Tech University, Lubbock, TX.

Kuethe, J. L. (1962). Social schemas. *Journal of Abnormal and Social Psychology, 64*(1), 31–38.

Kuethe, J. L., & Weingartner, H. (1964). Male–female schemata of homosexual and non-homosexual penitentiary inmates. *Journal of Personality, 32,* 23–31.

Kuipers, L., Sturgeon, D., Berkowitz, R., & Leff, J. P. (1983). Characteristics of expressed emotion: Its relationship to speech and looking in schizophrenic patients and their relatives. *British Journal of Clinical Psychology, 22,* 257–264.

Lamb, M. E., & Sutton–Smith, B. (1982). *Sibling relationships: Their nature and significance across the life span.* Hillsdale, NJ: Lawrence Erlbaum.

Leary, T. (1957). *Interpersonal diagnosis of personality.* New York: Ronald Press.

Levenson, R. W., & Gottman, J. M. (1983). Marital interaction: Physiological linkage and affective exchange. *Journal of Personality and Social Psychology, 45,* 587–597.

Levenson, R. W., & Gottman, J. M. (1985). Physiological and affective predictors of change in relationship satisfaction. *Journal of Personality and Social Psychology, 49,* 85–94.

Levinger, G. (1965). Marital cohesiveness and dissolution: An integrative review. *Journal of Marriage and the Family, 27,* 19–28.

Levinger, G. (1979). A social psychological perspective on marital dissolution. In G. Levinger, & O. C. Moles (Eds.), *Divorce and separation.* New York: Basic Books.

Lewis, J. M. Beavers, W. R., Gossett, J. T., & Phillips, V. A. (1976). *No single thread: Psychological health in family systems.* New York: Brunner/Mazel.

Lewis, J. M., Rodnick, E. H., & Goldstein, M. J. (1981). Intrafamilial interactive behavior, parental communication deviance and risk for schizophrenics. *Journal of Abnormal Behavior, 90,* 448–457.

Lewis, R. A., & Spanier, G. B. (1979). Theorizing about the quality and stability of marriage. In W. R. Burr, R. Hill, F. I. Nye, & I. L. Reiss (Eds.), *Contemporary theories about the family,* (Vol. 1). New York: Free Press.

Lieber, D. J. (1977). Parental focus of attention in a videotape feedback task as a function of hypothesized risk for offspring schizophrenics. *Family Process, 16,* 467–475.

Liem, J. H. (1980). Family studies of schizophrenia: An update and commentary. *Schizophrenia Bulletin, b,* 429–455.

Lobitz, W. C., & Johnson, S. M. (1975). Parental manipulation of the behavior of normal and deviant children. *Child Development, 46,* 719–726.

Locke, H. J. (1951). *Predicting adjustment in marriage: A comparison of a divorced and a happily married group.* New York: Holt.

Locke, H. J., & Wallace, K. M. (1959). Short marital-adjustment and prediction tests: Their reliability and validity. *Marriage and Family Living, 21,* 251–255.

Locke, H. J., & Williamson, R. C. (1958). Marital adjustment: A factor analysis study. *American Sociological Review, 26,* 368–380.

Locke, H. J., Sabagh, G., & Thomes, M. M. (1956). Correlates of primary communication and empathy. *Research Studies of the State College of Washington, 24,* 116–124.

LoPiccolo, J., & Steger, J. C. (1974). The Sexual Interaction Inventory: A new instrument for assessment of sexual dysfunction. *Archives of Sexual Behavior, 3,* 585–595.

Lytton, H. (1971). Observation studies of parent–child interaction: A methodological review. *Child Development, 42,* 651–684.

Maccoby, E. E., & Martin, J. A. (1983). Socialization in the context of the family: Parent–child interaction. In P. Mussen (Ed.), *Handbook of child psychology* (Vol. IV).

Madanes, C. (1978). Predicting behavior in an addict's family: A communicational approach. In L. Wurmser (Ed.), *The hidden dimension: Psychodynamics in compulsive drug use.* New York: Aronson.

Madanes, D. J., & Harbin, H. T. (1983). Family structure of assaultive adolescents. *Journal of Marital and Family Therapy, 9*(3), 311–316.

Madanes, C., Dukes, J., & Harbin, H. (1980). Family ties of heroin addicts. *Archives of General Psychiatry, 37,* 889–894.

Maerov, S. L., Brummett, B., & Reid, J. B. (1978). Procedures for training observors. In J. B. Reid (Ed.), *A social learning approach to family intervention: Vol. 2. Observation in home settings.* Eugene, OR: Castalia.

Margolies, P. J., & Weintraub, S. (1977). The revised 56-item CRPBI as a research instrument: Reliability and factor structure. *Journal of Clinical Psychology, 33,* 472–476.

Margolin, G. (1978). Relationships among marital assessment procedures: A correlational study. *Journal of Consulting and Clinical Psychology, 46*(6), 1556–1558.

Margolin, G. (1981a). Behavior exchange in distressed and non-distressed marriages: A family cycle perspective. *Behavior Therapy, 12,* 329–343.

Margolin, G. (1981b). The reciprocal relationship between marital and child problems. In J. P. Vincent (Ed.), *Advances in family intervention, assessment and theory* (Vol. II). Greenwich, CT: JAI Press.

Margolin, G. (1987). Participant observation procedures in marital and family assessment. In T. Jacob (Ed.), *Family interaction and psychopathology: Theory, methods and findings.* New York: Plenum Press.

Margolin, G., & Wampold, B. E. (1981). Sequential analysis of conflict and accord in distressed and nondistressed marital partners. *Journal of Consulting and Clinical Psychology, 49*(4), 554–567.

Margolin, G., & Weiss, R. (1978). A comparative evaluation of therapeutic components associated with behavioral marital treatment. *Journal of Consulting and Clinical Psychology, 46,* 1476–1486.

Margolin, G., Christensen, A., & Weiss, R. L. (1975). Contracts, cognition, and change: A behavioral approach to marriage therapy. *Counseling Psychologist, 5,* 115–125.

Margolin, G., Talovic, S., & Weinstein, C. D. (1983). Areas of Change Questionnaire: A practical approach to marital assessment. *Journal of Consulting and Clinical Psychology, 51*(6), 920–931.

Mark, R. (1971). Coding communication at the relationship level. *Journal of Communication, 21,* 221–232.

Mash, E. J., & Johnston, C. (1982). A comparison of the mother–child interactions of younger and older hyperactive and normal children. *Child Development, 53,* 1371–1381.

Mash, E. J. Terdal, L. G., & Anderson, K. (1973). The response-class matrix: A procedure for recording parent–child interactions. *Journal of Consulting and Clinical Psychology, 40,* 163–164.

Masters, W. H., & Johnson, V. E. (1970). *Human sexual inadequacy.* Boston: Little Brown.

McCubbin, H., & Patterson, J. (1981). *Systematic assessment of family stress, resources, and coping: Tools for research, education, and clinical intervention.* Department of Family Social Science, College of Home Economics, University of Minnesota, St. Paul, MN.

McCubbin, H., Larson, A., & Olsen, D. H. (1982). (F-Copes) Family coping strategies. In D. H. Olsen, H. I. McCubbin, H. Barnes, A. Larson, M. Muxen, & M. Wilson (Eds.), Family inventories: *Inventories used in a national survey of families across the family life cycle.* St. Paul, MN: Family Social Science, University of Minnesota, 101–119.

McGovern, K. B., Stewart, R. C., & LoPiccolo, J. (1975). Secondary orgasmic dysfunction: I. Analysis and strategies for treatment. *Archives of Sexual Behavior, 4,* 265–283.

Mead, D. E., & Campbell, S. S. (1972). Decision-making and interaction by families with and without a drug-abusing child. *Family Process, 11,* 487–498.

Medling, J. M. & McCarrey, M. (1981). Marital adjustment over segments of the family life cycle. The issue of spouses' value similarity. *Journal of Marriage and the Family, 43,* 195–203.

Miller, G. A. (1967). Project grammarama. In *The psychology of communication.* New York: Basic Books.

Minuchin, S. (1974). *Families and family therapy.* Cambridge, MA: Harvard University Press.

Mischel, W. (1973). Toward a cognitive social learning reconceptualization of personality. *Psychological Review, 80,* 252–283.

Mishler, E. G., & Waxler, N. E. (1965). Family interaction processes and schizophrenia: A review of current theories. *Merrill-Palmer Quarterly of Behavior and Development, 11,* 269–315.

Montemayor, R. (1982). The relationship between parent–adolescent conflict

REFERENCES

and the amount of time adolescents spend alone with parents and peers. *Child Development, 53,* 1512–1519.

Moos, R. (1974). *Combined preliminary manual for the family, work, and group environment scales.* Palo Alto, CA: Consulting Psychologists Press.

Moos, R., & Fuhr, R. (1982). The clinical use of social-ecological concepts: The case of an adolescent girl. *American Journal of Orthopsychiatry, 52,* 111–122.

Moos, R. H., & Moos, B. S. (1976). A typology of family social environments. *Family Process, 15,* 357–371.

Moos, R., & Moos, B. S. (1981). *Family Environment Scale: Manual.* Palo Alto, CA: Consulting Psychologists Press.

Moos, R., & Moos, B. S. (1984). The process of recovery from alcoholism: III. Comparing functioning in families of alcoholics and matched control families. *Journal of Studies on Alcohol, 45,* 111–118.

Moos, R., Bromet, E., Tsu, V., & Moos, B. (1979). Family characteristics and the outcome of treatment for alcoholism. *Journal of Studies on Alcoholism, 40,* 78–88.

Moos, R., Finney, J. & Chan, D. A. (1981). The process of recovery from alcoholism: I. Comparing alcoholic patients and matched community controls. *Journal of Studies on Alcohol, 42,* 383–402.

Moos, R., Finney, J. & Gamble, W. (1982). The process of recovery from alcoholism: II. Comparing spouses of alcoholic patients and matched community controls. *Journal of Studies on Alcohol, 43,* 888–909.

Morokoff, P. J., & LoPiccolo, J. (1986). A comparative evaluation of minimal therapist contact and 15-session treatment for female orgasmic dysfunction. *Journal of Consulting and Clinical Psychology, 54,* 294–300.

Mugana, A. B., Goldstein, M. J., Karno, M., Miklowitz, D. J., Jenkins, J. & Falloon, I. R. H. (1986). A brief method for assessing expressed emotions in relatives of psychiatric patients. *Psychiatry Research, 17,* 203–212.

Murrell, S. A. (1971). Family interaction variables and adjustment of nonclinic boys. *Child Development, 42,* 1485–1494.

Navran, L. (1967). Communication and adjustment in marriage. *Family Process, 6,* 173–184.

Nowinski, J. K., & LoPiccolo, J. (1979). Assessing sexual behavior in couples. *Journal of Sex and Marital Therapy, 5,* 225–243.

O'Farrell, T. J., Harrison, R. H., Schulmeister, C. A., & Cutter, H. S. G. (1981). A closeness to divorce scale for wives of alcoholics. *Drug and Alcohol Dependence, 7,* 319–324.

Oliveri, M. E., & Reiss, D. (1981a). A theory-based empirical classification of family problem-solving behavior. *Family Process, 20,* 409–418.

Oliveri, M. E., & Reiss, D. (1981b). The structure of families' ties to their kin: The shaping role of social constructions. *Journal of Marriage and the Family, 43,* 391–407.

Oliveri, M. E., & Reiss, D. (1982). Families' schemata of social relationships. *Family Process, 21,* 295–311.

Oliveri, M. E., & Reiss, D. (1984). Family concepts and their measurement: Things are seldom what they seem. *Family Process, 23,* 33–48.

Ollendick, D. G., LaBerteaux, P. J., & Howe, A.M. (1978). Relationships among maternal attitudes, perceived family environments, and preschoolers' behavior. *Perceptual and Motor Skills, 46,* 1092–1094.

Ollendick, T. H., & Hersen, M. (1983). A historical overview of child psychopathology. In T. H. Ollendick & M. Hersen (Eds.), *Handbook of child psychopathology.* New York: Plenum Press.

Olson, D. H. (1969). The measurement of family power by self-report and behavioral methods. *Journal of Marriage and the Family, 31,* 545–550.

Olson, D. H. L. (1976). Treating relationships: Trends and overview. In D. H. L. Olson (Ed.), *Treating relationships.* Lake Mills, IA: Graphic.

Olson, D. H., & Portner, J. (1983). Family adaptability and cohension evaluation scales. In E. E. Filsinger (Ed.), *Marriage and family assessment.* Beverly Hills, CA: Sage.

Olson, D. H., Sprenkel, D. H., & Russell, C. S. (1979). Circumplex model of marital and family systems: I. Cohesion and adaptability dimensions, family types, and clinical applications. *Family Process, 18,* 3–28.

Olson, D. H., Russell, C. S., & Sprenkle, D. H. (1980). Circumplex model of marital and family systems: II. Empirical studies and clinical intervention. In J. Vincent (Ed.), *Advances in family intervention assessment and theory* (Vol. I). Greenwich, CT: JAI Press.

Olson, D. H. L., McCubbin, H. I., Barnes, H. Larsen, A. Muxen, M., & Wilson, M. (1982). *Family inventories: Inventories used in a national survey of families across the family life cycle.* St. Paul, MN: Family Social Science.

Parke, R. (Ed.). (1984). *Review of child development research: Vol. VII. The family.* Chicago: University of Chicago Press.

Parsons, T., & Bales, R. E. (1955). *Family, socialization and interaction process.* New York: Free Press.

Patterson, G. R. (1974). Interventions for boys with conduct problems: Multiple settings, treatments and criteria. *Journal of Consulting and Clinical Psychology, 42*(4), 471–481.

Patterson, G. R. (1982). *A social learning approach: Vol. 3. Coercive family process.* Eugene, OR: Castalia.

Patterson, G. R., & Hops, H. (1972). Coercion, a game for two: Intervention techniques for marital conflict. In R. E. Ulrich & P. Mountjoy (Eds.), *The experimental analysis of social behavior* (pp. 424–440). New York: Appleton-Century-Crofts.

Patterson, G. R., & Reid, J. B. (1973). Intervention for families of aggressive boys: A replication study. *Behavior Research and Therapy, 11,* 383–399.

Patterson, G. R., Ray, R. S., Shaw, D. A., & Cobb, J. A. (1969). *Manual for coding of family interaction* (rev. ed.). New York: Microfiche Publications.

Patterson, G. R., Reid, J. B., Jones, R. R., & Conger, R. E. (1975). *A social learning approach to family intervention: I. Families with aggressive children.* Eugene, OR: Castalia.

Patterson, G. R., Reid, J. B., & Maerov, S. L. (1978a). Development of the Family Interaction Coding System (FICS). In J. B. Reid (Ed.), *A social learning approach to family intervention: Vol. 2. Observation in home settings.* Eugene, OR: Castalia.

REFERENCES

Patterson, G. R., Reid, J. B., & Maerov, S. L. (1978b). The observation system: Methodological issues and psychometric properties. In J. B. Reid (Ed.), *A social learning approach to family intervention: Vol. II. Observation in home settings.* Eugene, OR: Castalia.

Peed, S., Roberts, M., & Forehand, R. (1977). Evaluation of the effectiveness of a standardized parent training program in altering the interaction of mothers and their noncompliant children. *Behavior Modification 1,* 323–350.

Penk, W., Robinowitz, R., Kidd, R., & Nisle, A. (1979). Perceived family environment among ethnic groups of compulsive heroin users. *Addictive Behavior, 4,* 297–309.

Perosa, L., Hansen, J., & Perosa, S. (1981). Development of the structural family interaction scale. *Family Therapy, 8,* 77–90.

Piaget, J. (1970). Piaget's theory. In P. H. Mussen (Ed.), *Carmichael's manual of child psychology* (Vol. I). New York: Wiley.

Quay, H. C. (1977). Measuring dimensions of deviant behavior: The Behavior Problem Checklist. *Journal of Abnormal Child Psychology, 5,* 277–289.

Raush, H. L., Barry, W. A., Hertel, R. K., & Swain, M. A. (1974). *Communication, conflict, and marriage.* San Francisco: Jossey-Bass.

Rebelsky, F., & Hanks, C. (1971). Fathers' verbal interaction with infants in the first three months of life. *Child Development, 42,* 63–68.

Reid, J. B. (Ed.). (1978). *A social learning approach to family intervention: Vol. II. Observation in home settings.* Eugene, OR: Castalia.

Reiss, D. (1958). *Subjective models of finite state grammars.* Honor's thesis, Harvard College.

Reiss, D. (1981). *The family's construction of reality.* Cambridge, MA: Harvard University Press.

Reiss, D., & Klein, D. (1987). Paradigm and pathogenesis: A family-centered approach to problems of etiology and treatment of psychiatric disorders. In T. Jacob (Ed.), *Family interaction and psychopathology: Theory, methods, and findings.* New York: Plenum Press.

Reiss, D., & Oliveri, M. E. (1980). Family paradigm and family coping: A proposal for linking the family's intrinsic adaptive capacities to its responses to stress. *Family Relations, 29,* 431–444.

Reiss, D., & Oliveri, M. E. (1983). Sensory experience and family process: Perceptual styles tend to run in but not necessarily run families. *Family Process, 22,* 289–308.

Reiss, D., & Salzman, C. (1973). Resilience of family process: Effect of secobarbital. *Archives of General Psychiatry, 28,* 425–433.

Reiss, D., & Wyatt, R. J. (1975). Family and biological variables in the same etiologic studies of schizophrenia: A proposal. *Schizophrenia Bulletin, 14,* 64–81.

Reiss, D., Costell, R., Jones, C., & Berkman, H. (1980). The family meets the hospital: A laboratory forecast of the encounter. *Archives of General Psychiatry, 37,* 141–154.

Renson, G. J., Schaefer, E. S., & Levy, B. I. (1968). Cross-national validity of a spherical conceptual model for parent behavior. *Child Development, 39,* 1229–1235.

Roach, A. J., Frazier, L. P., & Bowden, S. P. (1981). The Marital Satisfaction Scale: Development of a measure for intervention research. *Journal of Marriage and the Family, 43*, 537–546.

Robinson, E. A., & Eyberg, S. M. (1981). The Dyadic Parent–Child Coding System: Standardization and validation. *Journal of Consulting and Clinical Psychology, 49*, 245–250.

Robinson, E. A., & Jacobson, N. S. (1987). Social learning theory and family psychopathology: A Kantian model in behaviorism? In T. Jacob (Ed.), *Family interaction and psychopathology: Theory, methods, and findings.* New York: Plenum Press.

Rogers, L. E., & Bagarozzi, D. A. (1983). An overview of relational communication and implications for therapy. In D. A. Bagarozzi, A. P. Jurich, & R. W. Jackson (Eds.), *Marital and family therapy: New perspectives in theory, research and practice.* New York: Human Sciences.

Rollins, B. C., & Thomas, D. L. (1979). Parental support, power, and control techniques in the socialization of children. In W. R. Burr, R. Hill, F. I. Nye, & I. L. Reiss (Eds.), *Contemporary theories about the family* (pp. 317–364). New York: Free Press.

Rosman, B. L. (1985). *The Philadelphia child guidance clinic family task and scoring manual.* Unpublished manuscript.

Royce, K., Christensen, A., Johnson, S., & Bolstad, O. (1976). *A manual for coding family interactions obtained from audio tape recordings.* Unpublished manuscript.

Sabatelli, R. M. (1984). The marital comparison level index: A measure for assessing outcomes relative to expectations. *Journal of Marriage and the Family, 46*, 651–662.

Sass, L. A., Sunderson, J. L., Singer, M. T., & Wynne, L. L. (1984). Parental communication deviance and forms of thinking in male schizophrenic offspring. *Journal of Nervous and Mental Disease, 172*, 513–520.

Satir, V. (1967). *Conjoint family therapy.* Palo Alto, CA: Science and Behavior Books.

Schaefer, E. S. (1959). The circumplex model for maternal behavior. *Journal of Abnormal and Social Psychology, 59*, 226–235.

Schaefer, E. S. (1961). Multivariate measurement and factorial structure of children's perceptions of maternal and paternal behavior. *American Psychologist, 16*, 345–346.

Schaefer, E. S. (1965a). Children's reports of parental behavior: An inventory. *Child Development, 36*, 413–424.

Schaefer, E. S. (1965b). A configurational analysis of children's reports of parent behavior. *Journal of Consulting Psychology, 29*, 552–557.

Schaefer, E. S., & Bell, R. Q. (1958). Development of a parental attitude research instrument. *Child Development, 29*, 339–361.

Schuham, A. I. (1972). Activity, talking time, and spontaneous agreement in disturbed and normal family interaction. *Journal of Abnormal Psychology, 79*(1), 68–75.

Scoresby, A. & Christensen, B. (1976). Differences in interaction and environmental conditions of clinic and non-clinic families: Implications for counselors. *Journal of Marriage and Family Counseling, 2*, 63–71.

REFERENCES

Seilhamer, R. (1983). *The Sibling Observation Schedule: An instrument for the assessment of sibling relationships.* Unpublished master's thesis, University of Pittsburgh, Pittsburgh, PA.

Shapiro, L. N., & Wild, C. M. (1976). The product of the consensus Rorschach in families of male schizophrenics. *Family Process, 15,* 211–224.

Sharpley, C. F., & Cross, D. G. (1982). A psychometric evaluation of the Spanier Dyadic Adjustment Scale. *Journal of Marriage and the Family, 34,* 739–741.

Shulman, S., & Klein, M. M. (1983). Distance-sensitive and consensus-sensitive families: The effect on adolescent referral for psychotherapy. *American Journal of Family Therapy, 11*(2), 45–58.

Seigelman, M. (1965a). College student personality correlates of early parent-child relationships. *Journal of Consulting Psychology, 29,* 558–564.

Seigelman, M. (1965b). Evaluation of Bronfenbrenner's questionnaire for children concerning parental behavior. *Child Development, 45,* 269–281.

Sigafoos, A., Reiss, D., Rich, J., & Douglas, E. (1985). Pragmatics in the measurement of family functioning. *Family Process, 24,* 189–203.

Singer, M. T. (1973). *Scoring manual for communication deviances seen in individually administered Rorschach.* Unpublished manuscript, University of California, Berkeley, CA.

Singer, M. T., & Wynne, L. (1966). Principles for scoring communication defects and deviances in parents of schizophrenics: Rorschach and TAT scoring manuals. *Psychiatry, 25,* 260–288.

Skinner, H. A., (Ed.). (1981b). *FAM III administration and interpretation guide.* (Available from Addiction Research Foundation, 33 Russell St., Toronto, Ontario, Canada M5S251.)

Skinner, H. A. (1984). Models for the description of abnormal behavior. In H. E. Adams & P. B. Sutker (Eds.), *Comprehensive handbook of psychopathology.* New York: Plenum Press.

Skinner, H. A. (1987). Self-report instruments for family assessment. In T. Jacob (Ed.), *Family interaction and psychopathology: Theories, methods, findings.* New York: Plenum Press.

Skinner, H. A., Steinhauer, P. D., & Santa-Barbara, J. (1983). The family assessment measure. *Canadian Journal of Community Mental Health, 2,* 91–105.

Skinner, H. A., Steinhauer, P. D., & Santa-Barbara, F. (1984). Toward the integration of classification theory and methods. *Journal of Abnormal Psychology, 90,* 68–87.

Sluzki, G. E., & Beavin, J. (1965). Simetria y complementaridad: Una definicion operacional y una tipologia de parejas. *Acta Psiquiatricia y Psiquiatrica y Psicologica de America Latina, 11,* 321–330.

Snyder, D. K. (1979). Multidimensional assessment of marital satisfaction. *Journal of Marriage and the Family, 41,* 813–823.

Snyder, D. K. (1981). *Marital Satisfaction Inventory (MSI) manual.* Los Angeles, CA: Western Psychological Services.

Snyder, D. K., Wills, R. M., & Keiser, T. W. (1981). Empirical validation of the martial satisfaction inventory: An actuarial approach. *Journal of Consulting and Clinical Psychology, 49,* 262–268.

Spanier, G. B. (1976). Measuring dyadic adjustment: New scales for assessing the quality of marriage and similar dyads. *Journal of Marriage and the Family, 38*(1), 15–30.

Spanier, G. B., & Thompson, L. (1982). A confirmatory analysis of the Dyadic Adjustment Scale. *Journal of Marriage and the Family, 44,* 731–738.

Stabenau, J. R., Tupin, J., Werner, M., & Pollin, W. (1965). A comparative study of families of schizophrenics, delinquents, and normals. *Psychiatry, 28,* 45–59.

Stein, S. J., Girodo, M., & Dotzenroth, S. (1982). The interrelationships and reliability of a multilevel behavior-based assessment package for distressed couples. *Journal of Behavioral Assessment, 4,* 343–360.

Steinbock, L. (1978). Nest-leaving: Family systems of runaway adolescents (Doctoral dissertation, California School of Professional Psychology). *Dissertation Abstracts International, 38,* 4544B.

Steinglass, P. (1976). *Family interaction coding instrument.* Unpublished manuscript.

Steinglass, P. (1978). The conceptualization of marriage from a systems theory perspective. In T. Paolino & B. McCrady (Eds.), *Marriage and marital therapy: Psychoanalytic, behavioral and systems theory perspectives.* New York: Brunner/Mazel.

Steinglass, P. (1979). The Home Observation Assessment Method (HOAM): Real-time naturalistic observation of families in their homes. *Family Process, 18,* 337–354.

Steinglass, P. (1980). Assessing families in their own homes. *American Journal of Psychiatry, 137,* 1523–1529.

Steinglass, P. (1981). The alcoholic family at home: Patterns of interaction in dry, wet, and transitional stages of alcoholism. *Archives of General Psychiatry, 38,* 578–584.

Steinglass, P. (1987). A systems view of family interaction and psychopathology. In T. Jacob (Ed.), *Family interaction and psychopathology: Theory, methods, and findings.* New York: Plenum Press.

Steinhauer, P. D. (1984). Clinical applications of the process model of family functioning. *Canadian Journal of Psychiatry, 29,* 98–111.

Steinhauer, P. D. (1987). The family as a small group: The process model of family functioning. In T. Jacob (Ed.), *Family interaction and psychopathology: Theories, methods, and findings.* New York: Plenum Press.

Steinhauer, P. D., & Tisdall, G. W. (1984). The integrated use of individual and family psychotherapy. *Canadian Journal of Psychiatry, 29,* 89–97.

Steinhauer, P. D., Santa-Barbara, J., & Skinner, H. (1984). The process model of family functioning. *Canadian Journal of Psychiatry, 29,* 77–88.

Stierlin, H. (1974). *Separating, parents and adolescents.* New York: Quadrangle.

Straus, M. A. (1969). *Family measurement techniques: Abstracts of published instruments, 1935–1965.* Minneapolis, MN: University of Minnesota Press.

Straus, M. A. (1979). Measuring intrafamily conflict and violence: The Conflict Tactics (CT) Scales. *Journal of Marriage and the Family, 41,* 75–88.

Straus, M. A., & Brown, B. W. (1978). *Family measurement techniques: Abstracts of published instruments, 1935–1974.* Minneapolis, MN: University of Minnesota Press.

Straus, M., Gelles, R., & Steinmetz, S. (1980). *Behind closed doors: Violence in the American family*. New York: Anchor.
Strodtbeck, F. L. (1951). Husband–wife interaction over revealed differences. *American Sociological Review, 16,* 468–473.
Strodtbeck, F. L. (1954). The family as a three-person group. *American Sociological Review, 19,* 23–29.
Sturgeon, D., Kuipers, L., Berkowitz, R., Turpin, G., & Leff, J. P. (1981). Psychophysiological responses of schizophrenic patients to high and low expressed emotion relatives. *British Journal of Psychiatry, 138,* 40–45.
Symonds, P. (1939). *The psychology of parent–child relationships*. New York: Appleton–Century–Crofts.
Tarrier, N., Vaughn, C. E., Lader, M. H., & Leff, J. P. (1979). Bodily reactions to people and events in schizophrenia. *Archives of General Psychiatry, 36,* 311–318.
Tarver–Behring, S., Barkley, R. A., & Karlsson, J. (1985). The mother–child interactions of hyperactive boys and their normal siblings. *American Journal of Orthopsychiatry, 55,* 202–209.
Teleki, J. K., Powell, J. A., & Dodder, R. (1982). Factor analysis of reports of parental behavior by children living in divorced and married families. *Journal of Psychology, 112,* 295–302.
Tennenbaum, D. L. (1980). *The effect of observer salience on family interaction in the home*. Unpublished master's thesis, University of Pittsburgh, Pittsburgh, PA.
Tennenbaum, D. L. (1984). *Spouse observation: An investigation of reactivity effects*. Unpublished doctoral dissertation, University of Pittsburgh, Pittsburgh, PA.
Tennenbaum, D. L., Jacob, T., Bargiel, K., & Rushe, R. (1984). *The Home Interaction Scoring System (HISS) manual*. Unpublished manuscript, University of Pittsburgh, Pittsburgh, PA.
Terman, L. M. (1938). *Psychological factors in marital happiness*. New York: McGraw–Hill.
Tharp, R. (1965). Marriage roles, child developmental and family treatment. *American Journal of Orthopsychiatry, 35,* 531–538.
Thibaut, J. W., & Kelley, H. H. (1959). *The social psychology of groups*. New York: Wiley.
Thomas, A., & Chess, S. (1977). *Temperament and development*. New York: Brunner/Mazel.
Thomas, E. J. (1977). *Marital communication and decision making: Analysis, assessment, and change*. New York: Free Press.
Thornton, C. C., & Gottheil, E. (1971). Social schemata in schizophrenic males. *Journal of Abnormal Psychology, 77*(22), 192–195.
Titchner, J. L., & Golden, M. (1963). Prediction of therapeutic themes from observation of family interaction evoked by the "Revealed Differences" technique (pp. 464–474).
Titchner, J. L., D'zmura, T., Golden, M., & Emerson, R. (1963). Family transaction and derivation of individuality. *Family Process, 2,* 95–120.
Tittler, B. I., Friedman, S., Blotcky, A. D., & Stedrak, J. (1982). The influence of

family variables on an ecologically based treatment program for emotionally disturbed children. *American Journal of Orthopsychiatry, 52*(1), 123–130.

Udry, J. R. (1981). Marital alternatives and marital disruption. *Journal of Marriage and the Family, 43,* 889–897.

Valone, K., Norton, J. P., Goldstein, M. J., & Doane, J. A. (1983). Parental expressed emotion and affective style in an adolescent sample at risk for schizophrenia spectrum disorder. *Journal of Abnormal Psychology, 92,* 399–407.

Van Hasselt, V., & Hersen, M. (1987). Family interaction with blind children. Manuscript submitted for publication.

Vaughn, C. E., & Leff, J. P. (1976a). The influence of family and social factors on the course of psychiatric patients. *British Journal of Psychiatry, 129,* 125–137.

Vaughn, C. E., & Leff, J. P. (1976b). The measurement of expressed emotion in the families of psychiatric patients. *British Journal of Social and Clinical Psychology, 15,* 157–165.

Vincent, J. (1980). The empirical-clinical study of families: Social learning theory as a point of departure. In J. Vincent (Ed.), *Advances in family intervention assessment and theory* (Vol. 1). Greenwich, CT: JAI Press.

Vincent, J. P., & Friedman, L. C. (1979). Demand characteristics in observations of marital interaction. *Journal of Consulting and Clinical Psychology, 47,* 557–566.

Vincent, J. P. Friedman, L. C., Nugent, J., & Messerly, L. (1979). Demand characteristics in observations of marital interaction. *Journal of Consulting and Clinical Psychology, 47,* 557–566.

Volkin, J. I., & Jacob, T. (1981). The impact of spouse monitoring on target behavior and recorder satisfaction. *Journal of Behavioral Assessment, 3,* 99–109.

Wahler, R. G. (1980). The insular mother: Her problem in parent–child treatment. *Journal of Applied Behavior Analysis, 13,* 207–219.

Wahler, R. G., & Dumas, J. E. (1987). Family factors in childhood psychopathology: Toward a coercion-neglect model. In T. Jacob (Ed.), *Family interaction and psychopathology: Theory, methods, and findings.* New York: Plenum Press.

Wahler, R. G., House, A. E., & Stambaugh, E. E. (1976). *Ecological assessment of child problem behavior: A clinical package for home, school and institutional settings.* New York: Pergamon.

Wald, H., Greenwald, M., & Jacob, T. (1984, August). *Perceived family environments among children of alcoholics, depressed and normal fathers.* Paper presented at the meeting of the American Psychological Association, Toronto, Ontario.

Waldron, H., & Routh, D. K. (1981). The effect of the first child on the marital relationship. *Journal of Marriage and the Family, 43,* 785–788.

Walters, L. H. (1982, November). Are families different from other groups? *Journal of Marriage and the Family.*

Watson, K. M. (1982a). An analysis of communication patterns: A method for discriminating leader and subordinate roles. *Academy of Management Journal, 25,* 107–120.

REFERENCES

Watson, K. M. (1982b). A methodology for the study of organizational behavior at the interpersonal level of analysis. *Academy of Management Review, 7,* 392–402.
Watzlawick, P., Beavin, J., & Jackson, B. D. (1967). *Pragmatics of human communication.* New York: Norton.
Webster–Stratton, C. (1984). Randomized trial of two parent-training programs for familie with conduct-disordered children. *Journal of Consulting and Clinical Psychology, 52*(4), 666–678.
Weinstein, L. (1967). Social experience and social schema. *Journal of Personality and Social Psychology, 6*(4), 429–434.
Weinstein, L. (1968). The mother–child schema, anxiety, and academic achievement in elementary school boys. *Child Development, 39,* 257–264.
Weiss, R. L. (1981). Strategic behavioral marital therapy: Toward a model for assessment and intervention. In J. P. Vincent (Ed.), *Advances in family intervention, assessment and theory* (Vol. 1). Greenwich, CT: JAI Press.
Weiss, R. L., & Cerreto, M. C. (1980). The marital status inventory: Development of a measure of dissolution potential. *American Journal of Family Therapy, 8,* 80–85.
Weiss, R. L. & Margolin, G. (1977). Marital conflict and accord: A second look. In A. R. Ciminero, K. S. Calhoun, & H. E. Adams (Eds.), *Handbook for behavioral assessment.* New York: Wiley.
Weiss, R. L., & Margolin, G. (1986). Assessment of conflict and accord: A second look. In A. Ciminero, K. S. Calhoun, & H. E. Adams (Eds.), *Handbook of behavioral assessment* (2nd ed.). New York: Wiley.
Weiss, R. L., & Perry, B. A. (1979). *Assessment and treatment of marital dysfunction.* Eugene, OR: Oregon Marital Studies Program.
Weiss, R. L., & Summers, K. J. (1983). Marital Interaction Coding System-III. In E. Filsinger (Ed.), *Marriage and family assessment.* Beverly Hills, CA: Sage.
Weiss, R. L., & Wieder, G. B. (1982). Marital and family distress. In A. Bellack, M. Hersen, & A. Kazdin (Eds.), *International handbook of behavior modification.* New York: Plenum Press.
Weiss, R. L., Hops, H., & Patterson, G. R. (1973). A framework for conceptualizing marital conflict: A technology for altering it, some data for evaluating it. In R. W. Clark & L. A. Hamerlynck (Eds.), *Critical issues in research and practice: Proceedings of the Fourth Banff International Conference Modification.* Champaign, IL: Research Press.
Wetzel, J., & Redmond, F. (1980). A person–environment study of depression. *Social Service Review, 54,* 363–375.
White, D. (1978). Schizophrenics' perceptions of family relationships (Doctoral dissertation, St. Louis University). *Dissertation Abstracts International, 39,* 1451A.
White, R. W. (1959). Motivation reconsidered: The concepts of competence. *Psychological Review, 66,* 297–333.
Wieder, G. B., & Weiss, R. L. (1980). Generalizability theory and the coding of marital interactions. *Journal of Consulting and Clinical Psychology, 48,* 469–477.
Wild, C., Shapiro, L., & Goldenberg, L. (1975). Transitional communication disturbances in families of male schizophrenics. *Family Process, 14,* 131–160.

Wills, T. A., Weiss, R. L., & Patterson, G. R. (1974). A behavioral analysis of the determinants of marital satisfaction. *Journal of Consulting and Clinical Psychology, 42*, 802–811.

Wolin, S. J., Bennett, L. A., & Noonan, D. L. (1979). Family rituals and the recurrence of alcoholism over generations. *American Journal of Psychiatry, 136*, 589–593.

Wolin, S., Bennett, L., Reiss, D., & Conners, C. K. (1979). *Alcoholic family environment: Consequences to children.* (NIAAA Grant Proposal).

Wolin, S. J., Bennett, L. A., Noonan, D. L., & Teitelbaum, M. A. (1980). Disrupted family rituals: A factor in the intergenerational transmission of alcoholism. *Journal of Studies on Alcohol, 41*(3), 199–214.

Wolpe, J. (1958). *Psychotherapy by reciprocal inhibition.* Stanford: Stanford University Press.

Wright, H. F. (1960). Observational child study. In P. Mussen (Ed.), *Handbook of research methods in child development.* New York: John Wiley.

Wynne, L. C. (1979). Five-minute speech sample and expressed emotion. *New developments in interventions with families of schizophrenics.*

Wynne, L. C., Ryckoff, II, Day, J., & Hirsch, S. (1958). Pseudomutuality in the family relations of schizophrenics. *Psychiatry, 21*, 205–220.

Wynne, L. C., Singer, M. T., Bartko, J., & Toohey, M. (1977). Schizophrenics and their families: Recent research on parental communication. In J. M. Tanner (Ed.), *Developments in psychiatric research.* London: Hodder & Stoughton.

Yelsma, P. (1984). Marital communication, adjustment and perceptual differences between "happy" and "counseling" couples. *American Journal of Family Therapy, 12*, 26–36.

Zuckerman, E., & Jacob, T. (1979). Task effects in family interaction. *Family Process, 18*, 47–53.

INDEX

ACQ. *See* Areas of Change Questionnaire (ACQ)
Adaptability, Family Adaptability and Cohesion Scales (FACES), 70, 74–78
Adolescent Individuation and Family Interaction, 134–135
Adolescent–parent relationship. *See* Parent–adolescent relationship assessment procedures
Affect, 30
   as family assessment construct, 17, 18
   Specific Affect Coding System (SPAFF), 121–125
Aggression, Family Interaction Coding System (FICS), 145–149
Alcoholism, Family Ritual Interview, 89–91
Alliance structure, 20
Areas of Change Questionnaire (ACQ), 31, 36–38
   Parent–Child (PC-ACQ), 63–66
Arousal, emotional, biochemical indicator, 171–172
Atrribution theory, 10
Audiotaping, of family interactions, 14–15

Bales, Robert, 2, 3
Bandura, Albert, 9
Bateson, G., 4
Behavioral reports, 14
Bell, D. C., 7
Boundary permeability, 20
Burgess, Ernest, 1–2

Camberwell Family Interview Schedule (CFIS), 86–87
Card Sort Procedure (CSP), 3, 101–105
   cross-method correspondence analysis, 166
Card Sort Task. *See* Card Sort Procedure
CD. *See* Communication deviance
CECS. *See* Constraining and Enabling Coding System (CECS)
CFIS. *See* Camberwell Family Interview Schedule (CFIS)
Child psychology, 6–8
Child-management models, 11
Child Report of Parental Behavior Inventory (CRPBI), 53, 57–60
Child–sibling relationships. *See* Sibling relationship assessment procedures
Children. *See also* Parent–child relationship assessment procedures
   aggression assessment, 145–149
Children's Relationship Questionnaire, 67
Circumplex model, of marital and family systems, 74–75
CISS. *See* Couples Interaction Scoring System (CISS)
Coding systems, 3, 10, 14, 114–138
   Adolescent Individuation and Family Interaction, 134–135
   Constraining and Enabling Coding System (CECS), 130–133
   Couples Interaction Scoring System (CISS), 122, 123, 135–136, 154
   Dyadic Parent–Child Interaction Coding System (DPICS), 138

201

Coding systems (cont.)
  Facial Action Coding System (FACS), 122
  Family Alliances Coding System (FACS), 115–116, 133–134
  Family Interaction Coding System (FICS), 115, 117, 144, 145–149
  Interaction Process Analysis (IPA), 115
  Marital Interaction Coding System (MICS), 116–121, 154
  parent–adolescent relationship, 114–116, 130–135
  parent–child relationship, 114, 116, 136–138
  Philadelphia Child Guidance Clinic Family Task and Scoring Procedure, 169
  Relational Communication Coding System (RELCOM), 126–129
  Response Class Matrix (RCM), 137, 138
  Specific Affect Coding System (SPAFF), 121–125
Coercion, 10
Cognitive theory, 9, 11
Cohesion, Family Adaptability and Cohesion Scales, 70, 74–78
Communication deviance (CD), 23, 26–30
  children's cognitive development and, 19–20
  double-bind, 19–20
  as family assessment construct, 17, 19–20
  schizophrenia and, 17
Communication Rapid Assessment Scale (CRAS), 138, 141–143
Communication theory, 4–5
Conflict Tactic Scales (CT), 49–51
Conjugal therapy. See Marital therapy
Constraining and Enabling Coding System (CECS), 130–133
Constructs, in family assessment, 16–21
Control, as family assessment construct, 17, 18–19
Cornell Parent Behavior Inventory (CPBI), 57–58
Couple Communication Program, 141, 143
Couples Interaction Scoring System (CISS), 122, 123, 135–136, 154
CPBI. See Cornell Parent Behavior Inventory (CPBI)

CRAS. See Communication Rapid Assessment Scale (CRAS)
CRPBI. See Child Report of Parental Behavior Inventory (CRPBI)
CSP. See Card Sort Procedure (CSP)
CT. See Conflict Tactic Scales (CT)

DA. See Dyadic Adjustment Scale (DA)
Developmental psychology, 6–8
Dominance, 18
Double ABCX model of family stress, 82
Double-bind transactional thought disorder, 19–20
DPICS. See Dyadic Parent–Child Interaction Coding System (DPICS)
Dyadic Adjustment Scale (DA), 33–36
  Parent–Child Areas of Change Questionnaire and, 66
Dyadic behavior units (DBU), 119–120
Dyadic Parent–Child Interaction Coding System (DPICS)

EE. See Expressed Emotion (EE)
Expressed Emotion (EE), 30, 85–89
  sibling relationship assessment applications, 168

FACCS. See Family Affect-Content Coding System (FACCS)
FACES. See Family Adaptability and Cohesion Scales (FACES)
Facial Action Coding System (FACS), 122
FACS. See Facial Action Coding System (FACS); Family Alliances Coding System (FACS)
FAM. See Family Assessment Measure (FAM)
Family Adaptability and Cohesion Scales (FACES), 70, 74, 75, 76, 77
  cross-method correspondence analysis, 166
Family Adaptability and Cohesion Scales (FACES) II, 75–78
Family Adaptability and Cohesion Scales (FACES) III, 76–77
Family Affect-Content Coding System (FACCS), 154
Family Alliances Coding System (FACS), 115–116, 133–134

INDEX

"Family as a Unity of Interacting Personality, The" (Burgess), 1–2
Family Assessment Measure (FAM), 70, 78–81
  construct validation paradigm, 175
  sibling relationship assessment applications, 168
  subscale interaction, 162
Family assessment procedures, 13–21, 23–158. *See also* names of individual family assessment procedures
  audiotaping, 14–15
  classification, 23, 24
  constructs assessed, 16–21
    affect, 17, 18
    communication, 17, 19–20
    control, 17, 18–19
    systems properties, 17, 20–21
  correspondence between methods, 165–167
  data source, 13–15
  family member response discrepancies, 163, 164, 165
  individual assessments, 25–30
  interrater agreement, 163
  laboratory observational procedures, 14–15, 100–143
    coding systems, 114–138
    outcome measures, 3, 100–114, 168
    rating scales, 138–143
  limitations, 159–161, 170
  naturalistic observational procedures, 144–158
  need for additional methods, 170–173
  observation procedure, 23–24
  relationship assessments, 30–100
    marital questionnaires, 30–52
    parent–child questionnaires, 52–66
    quasi-observational procedures, 92–100
    sibling questionnaires, 66–69
    structured interviews, 84–91
    whole family questionnaires, 70–84
  report procedures, 13–14, 23, 24, 159–161
  subscales, 162–163. *See also* Coding systems; Outcome measures; Rating scales
  substantial variables, 174–175
  theory/instrument development interplay, 173–176

Family assessment procedures (*cont.*)
  underdeveloped assessment targets and concepts, 167–170
  unit of assessment, 15–16
  videotaping, 14–15
  within-method assessment, 161–164
Family Categories Schema, 78
Family Crisis-Oriented Personal Evaluation Scales (F-COPES), 70, 82–84
Family Environment Scale (FES), 70–74
  cross-method correspondence analysis, 166
  factor analysis, 162
Family Hierarchy Test, 110–114
Family Interaction Coding System (FICS), 115, 117, 144, 145–149
Family paradigm, 102–105
Family Ritual Interview, 89–91
Family sociology, 1–4
Fatty acids, as emotional arousal indicators, 171–172
F-COPES. *See* Family Crisis-Oriented Personal Evaluation Scales (F-COPES)
Felt Figure Technique (FFT), 101. *See also* Family Hierarchy Test
FES. *See* Family Environment Scale (FES)
FFT. *See* Felt Figure Technique (FFT)
FICS. *See* Family Interaction Coding System (FICS)
Friendship Questionnaire Scale, 69

Group functioning, primary dimensions, 3
Group process, structural–functional model, 2–3

Haley, J., 4
Hall, G. Stanley, 6
High affective style, 30
HISS. *See* Home Interaction Scoring System (HISS)
HOAM. *See* Home Observation Assessment Measure (HOAM)
Home Interaction Scoring System (HISS), 145, 153–158
Home Observation Assessment Measure (HOAM), 144–145, 149–153, 169

Individual assessments, 25–30
  communication deviance, 23, 26–30
Influence, 18

INDEX

Marital relationship assessment procedures (*cont.*)
  marital questionnaires, 30–52
    Areas of Change Questionnaire (ACQ), 31, 36–38
    Conflict Tactic Scales (CT), 49–51
    Dyadic Adjustment Scale (DA), 33–36
    Marital Adjustment Test (MAT), 31–33
    Marital Alternatives Scale (MA), 52
    Marital Comparison Level Index (MCLI), 51–52
    Marital Satisfaction Inventory (MSI), 31, 39–41
    Marital Satisfaction Scale, 51
    Primary Communication Inventory (PCI), 41–43
    Relationship Belief Inventory (RBI), 46–48
    Sexual Interaction Inventory (SII), 43–46
    Relationship Enhancement Program, 143
    Specific Affect Coding System (SPAFF), 121–125
    Spouse Observation Checklist (SOC), 92, 95–98, 99, 100, 168
Marital Satisfaction Inventory (MSI), 31, 39–41
Marital Satisfaction Scale, 51
Marital therapy. *See also* Marital relationship assessment procedures
  behavioral, 11
  marital communication effects, 43
MAT. *See* Marital Adjustment Test (MAT)
MCLI. *See* Marital Comparison Level Index (MCLI)
MCRaS. *See* Marital Communication Rating Scale (MCRaS)
MFHT. *See* Madanes's Family Hierarchy Test (MFHT)
MICS. *See* Marital Interaction Coding System (MICS)
Minnesota Couples Communication Program, 143
MSI. *See* Marital Satisfaction Inventory (MSI)

Naturalistic observational procedures, 144–158

Naturalistic observational procedures (*cont.*)
  Family Affect-Content Coding System (FACCS), 154
  Family Interaction Coding System (FICS), 115, 117, 144, 145–149
  Home Interaction Scoring System (HISS), 145, 153–158
  Home Observation Assessment Measure (HOAM), 144–145, 149–153, 169

Object sorting test, 27
Objective tests, 14
Observational procedures. *See also* individual observational procedures
  advantages, 159–160
  dimensionality evaluation, 163
  laboratory observational procedures, 14–15, 100–143
    coding systems, 114–138
    outcome measures, 3, 100–114, 168
    rating scales, 138–143
  limitations, 160–161
  naturalistic, 144–158
  participant, 92
  quasi-, 92–100, 164, 170–171
Operant conditioning, clinical applications, 9
Operant learning theory, 9–10
Outcome measures, 100–114
  Card Sort Procedures (CSP), 3, 101–105, 168
  Family Hierarchy Test, 110–114
  family member response discrepancies, 163–164
  Felt Figure Technique (FFT), 101
  Revealed Difference Technique (RDT), 3, 101, 106–110
  Unrevealed Difference Technique (UDT), 106, 108

PAC. *See* Parent–Adolescent Communication Scale (PAC)
Palo Alto group, 4–5
Parent Daily Report (PDR), 92, 93–94
Parent Perception Inventory (PPI), 58
Parent Relationship Questionnaire, 69
Parent–Adolescent Communication Scale (PAC), 60–63

Parent–Adolescent Observation Schedule.
  See Parent–Child Observation
  Schedule
Parent–adolescent relationship assessment
  procedures
  Adolescent Individuation and Family
    Interaction, 134–135
  coding systems, 114–116, 130–135
  Constraining and Enabling Coding System (CECS), 130–133
Parental behavior, primary dimensions, 6
Parent–Child Areas of Change Questionnaire (PC-ACQ), 63–66
Parent–Child Observation Schedule
  (PCOS), 92, 93, 98–99, 100
Parent–Child relationship assessment procedures, 15
  affect and, 18
  coding systems, 114, 116, 136–138
  Dyadic Parent–Child Interaction coding
    System (DPICS), 138
  lack of assessment instruments, 168–169
  parent–child questionnaires, 52–66
  Response Class Matrix (RCM), 137, 138
  theories of, 6–8
    Child Report of Parental Behavior Inventory (CRPBI), 53, 57–60
    Cornell Parent Behavior Inventory
      (CPBI), 57–58
    Parent Perception Inventory (PPI), 58
    Parent Relationship Questionnaire, 69
    Parent–Adolescent Communication
      Scale (PAC), 60–63
    Parent–Child Areas of Change Questionnaire (PC-ACQ), 63–66
    Structural Analysis of Social Behavior
      (SASB), 53–57
Parent-training models, 11
Parsons, Talcott, 2–3
Participant observation, 92
Patterson, G. R., 174
PC-ACQ. See Parent–Child Areas of
  Change Questionnaire (PC-ACQ)
PCI. See Primary Communication Inventory (PCI)
PCOS. See Parent–Child Observation
  Schedule (PCOS)
Philadelphia Child Guidance Clinic Family
  Task and Scoring Procedure, 169

Physiological indicators, of emotional
  arousal, 171–172
Plasma-free fatty acids (FFA), as emotional arousal indicator, 171–172
PMFF. See Process Model of Family Functioning (PMFF)
Power, assessment procedures, 18
  cross-method correspondence, 165
Primary Communication Inventory (PCI),
  41–43
Process Model of Family Functioning
  (PMFF), 78–79
Projective tests, 14
Psychiatric patients, Expressed Emotion
  (EE) interview, 85–89
Psychopathology, familial
  family sociology and, 3–4
  interactional context, 5
  social learning theory and, 8–11
  systems/communications theory, 4–5

Quasi-observational procedures, 92–100,
  170–171
  family member response discrepancies,
    164
  Parent Daily Report (PDR), 92, 93–94
  Parent–Child Observation Schedule
    (PCOS), 92, 93, 98–99, 100
  Sibling Observation Schedule (SOS),
    92–93, 99–100
  Spouse Observation Checklist (SOC),
    92, 95–98, 99, 100
Questionnaires. See also names of individual questionnaires
  family member response discrepancies,
    164
  marital, 30–52
  parent–child, 52–66
  sibling, 66–69
  whole-family, 70–84

Raters, interrater agreement, 164
Rating scales, 138–143
  Communication Rapid Assessment
    Scale (CRAS), 138, 141–143
  Marital Communication Rating Scale
    (MCRaS), 138, 139–141
  Verbal Problem Checklist (VPC), 139
RBI. See Relationship Belief Inventory
  (RBI)

INDEX

RCM. *See* Response Class Matrix (RCM)
RDT. *See* Revealed Difference Technique (RDT)
Reciprocity, 10
"Reinterpretation of the Direction of Effects in Studies of Socialization, A" (Bell), 7
Reiss, David, 174
Reiss Card Sort Procedure, 3, 101–105, 168
Relational Communication Coding System (RELCOM), 126–129
Relationship Belief Inventory (RBI), 46–48
Relationship Enhancement Program, 143
RELCOM. *See* Relational Communication Coding System (RELCOM)
Report procedures, 13–14, 23, 24
  advantages, 159–160
  family member response discrepancies, 163
  limitations, 160–161
Response Class Matrix (RCM), 137, 138
Revealed Difference Technique (RDT), 3, 101, 106–110
Rituals, familial, 89–91
Role structure, 3, 4
Rorschach test, communication deviance applications, 27, 28

SASB. *See* Structural Analysis of Social Behavior (SASB)
Schizophrenia
  Card Sort procedure, 101
  communication deviance and, 17
  Expressed Emotion (EE) interview, 85, 88–89
  Family Hierarchy Test, 111, 113
  family theories of, 4
  family variables in, 174
Self-report procedures, 13, 14
Sequential analysis, 10
Sexual Interaction Inventory (SII), 43–46
Sibling Observation Schedule (SOS), 92–93, 99–100, 168
Sibling relationship assessment procedures
  lack of assessment instruments, 167–168
  questionnaires, 66–69
    Children's Relationship Questionnaire, 67

Sibling relationship assessment procedures (*cont.*)
  questionnaires (*cont.*)
    Friendship Questionnaire Scale, 69
    sibling Relationship Questionnaire (SRQ), 67–69, 167–168
  Sibling Observation Schedule (SOS), 92–93, 99–100, 168
SII. *See* Sexual Interaction Inventory (SII)
Skinner, Harvey, 174, 175
Small group theory, 3
SOC. *See* Spouse Observation Checklist (SOC)
Social exchange theory, 10
Social learning theory, 8–11
  Family Interaction Coding System (FICS), 145
Sociology, of the family, 1–4
SPAFF. *See* Specific Affect Coding System (SPAFF)
Specific Affect Coding System (SPAFF), 121–125
Spouse Observation Checklist (SOC), 92, 95–98, 99, 100, 168
Stress
  Double ABCX model, 82
  physiological response measurement, 171–172
Structural Analysis of Social Behavior (SASB), 53–57
Structured Family Theory, 169
Structured interviews. *See* Interviews, structured
Subscales, 162–163. *See also* Coding systems; Outcome measures; Rating scales
Subsystem relationships, 20
Systems properties, as family assessment construct, 17, 20–21
Systems theory, 10
Systems/communication theory, 4–5

Task accomplishment, 78, 80
Telephone interviews, 93–94
Tests. *See also* names of individual tests
  family member response discrepancies, 164
Thematic Apperception Test (TAT), 27, 28
Theory/instrument development interplay, 173–176
Time-series analysis, 10

UCLA Parent Interview, 86
UDT. *See* Unrevealed Difference Technique (UDT)
Unrevealed Difference Technique (UDT), 106, 108

Verbal Problem Checklist (VPC), 139
Videotaping, of family interactions, 14–15
Violence, Conflict Tactic Scales (CT). 49–51
VPC. *See* Verbal Problem Checklist (VPC)

Wahler, R. G., 174
Weiss, R. L., 174
Whole-family relationship assessments, 70–84
  Double ABCX model of family stress, 82

Whole-family relationship assessments (*cont.*)
  Family Adaptability and Cohesion Scales (FACES), 70, 74, 75, 76, 77
  Family Adaptability and Cohesion Scales (FACES) II, 75–78
  Family Adaptability and Cohesion Scales (FACES) III, 76–77
  Family Assessment Measure(FAM), 70, 78–81
  Family Categories Schema, 78
  Family Crisis-Oriented Personal Evaluation Scales (F-COPES), 70, 82–84
  Process Model of Family Functioning (PMFF), 78–79
Within-method assessment, 161–164
Witner, Lightner, 6
Wynne, L. C., 4